Theatre in the Expanded Field

Methuen Drama Engage offers original reflections about key practitioners, movements and genres in the fields of modern theatre and performance. Each volume in the series seeks to challenge mainstream critical thought through original and interdisciplinary perspectives on the body of work under examination. By questioning existing critical paradigms, it is hoped that each volume will open up fresh approaches and suggest avenues for further exploration.

Series Editors

Mark Taylor-Batty
Senior Lecturer in Theatre Studies, Workshop Theatre, University of Leeds, UK

Enoch Brater
Kenneth T. Rowe Collegiate Professor of Dramatic Literature & Professor of English and Theater, University of Michigan, USA

Forthcoming Titles

Replay: Classic Modern Drama Reimagined by Toby Zinman

Rethinking Brecht: Theatre, Theory and Performance by David Barnett

Howard Barker's Theatre: Wrestling with Catastrophe edited by James Reynolds and Andrew Smith

Rethinking the Theatre of the Absurd: Ecology, the Environment and the Greening of the Modern Stage edited by Carl Lavery and Clare Finburgh

Ibsen in Practice: Relational Readings of Performance, Cultural Encounters and Power by Frode Helland

Theatre in the Expanded Field

Seven Approaches to Performance

Alan Read

Line Drawings
Beryl Robinson

Series Editors
Enoch Brater and Mark Taylor-Batty

B L O O M S B U R Y
LONDON · NEW DELHI · NEW YORK · SYDNEY

Bloomsbury Methuen Drama

An imprint of Bloomsbury Publishing Plc

50 Bedford Square
London
WC1B 3DP
UK

1385 Broadway
New York
NY 10018
USA

www.bloomsbury.com

Bloomsbury is a registered trademark of Bloomsbury Publishing PLC

First published 2013

British Library Cataloguing-in-Publication Data
A catalogue record for this book is available from the British Library.

ISBN: HB: 978-1-4081-8548-3
PB: 978-1-4081-8495-0
ePub: 978-1-4081-8341-0
ePDF: 978-1-4081-8564-3

Library of Congress Cataloging-in-Publication Data
A catalog record for this book is available from the Library of Congress.

Typeset by Integra Software Services Pvt. Ltd.
Printed and bound in India

In memory of our mothers
Rosina Miriam Robinson, 1920–1978
Veronica Mary Read, 1926–2001

and

To the future of our daughters
Florence Ruby Read
Hermione Grace Read

Hell is the impossibility of expanding.

Peter Sloterdijk, *Neither Sun Nor Death*, 2011

Examine the sense in which 'Outlines,' 'Guides,' and so on are touchstones for the state of the discipline. Show that they are the most demanding of all, and how clearly even their phrasing betrays every half-measure.

Walter Benjamin, *We Ought to Re-examine the link between Teaching and Research*, fragment written in 1930 or 1931, unpublished in his lifetime

The code is more what you'd call 'guidelines' than actual rules.
Welcome aboard ...

Geoffrey Rush to Keira Knightley, *Pirates of the Caribbean: The Curse of the Black Pearl*, 2003

Contents

Acknowledgements

I am grateful to those colleagues who through their editing, curation and commissioning have created the circumstances within which this work has come about:

Freddie Rokem, Patrick ffrench, Carl Lavery, Bojana Kunst, Joe Kelleher, Nicholas Ridout, Una Bauer, Ric Allsopp, Richard Gough, Steve Bottoms, Adrian Kear, Claire MacDonald, Maria Delgado, Dominic Johnson, Dan Rebellato, Aoife Monks, Lara Shalson, Kélina Gotman, Theron Schmidt, Karen Quigley, Ioli Andreadi, John London, Mischa Twitchin, Laura Cull, Alice Lagaay, Peter Lichtenfells, Lynette Hunter, Steve Tompkins, Michael Morris, Teresa Critcher, David Williams, Adrian Heathfield, Tim Etchells, Jo McDonagh, Lois Keidan, Heike Roms, Romeo Castellucci, Lin Hixson and Matthew Goulish.

The Leverhulme Trust supported the research which gave rise to this book, as well as the development of the *Performance Foundation* (2010), the *Anatomy Theatre & Museum* (2011) and the *Inigo Rooms* (2012) at King's College London, where these ideas were first tried out in the public realm. I am indebted to Jan Fabre for permission to reproduce a cover image of *The Power of Theatrical Madness*, to the designer of this volume Louise Dugdale and to Hilary Brown who provided digital support. Georgina Guy catalogued the primary sources, formatted the manuscript and offered thoughtful bibliographic assistance.

Mark Dudgeon responded to the idea of a book to celebrate the fiftieth anniversary of Richard Southern's *The Seven Ages of the Theatre* with great generosity and editorial acumen, and Mark Taylor-Batty as co-editor of the *Engage* series and Enoch Brater, the series editor guided it towards its new home with critical care. Nicholas Ridout, Rebecca Schneider, Shelley Salamensky and Sara Jane Bailes improved the manuscript in measurable ways. The book's shortcomings are mine alone.

Beryl Robinson illuminated this book with line drawings and images, but also at the outset conceived the book's relation to Rosalind Krauss's essay 'Sculpture in the Expanded Field', and thus the shape of this work. We have dedicated this book to the memory of our mothers, Rosina and Veronica, and to the future of our daughters, Florence and Hermione.

Line Drawings

Beryl Robinson

To My Readers

This book marks an anniversary and it looks to the future. Fifty years ago Richard Southern wrote his formative work *The Seven Ages of the Theatre* (1962) and began with a modest note 'to his readers' that could not have predicted the seminal impact his thinking would have for a coming generation of designers, historians and producers. Richard Schechner was, at the same time, through his transformation of *The Drama Review* (*TDR*) in Tulane, adopting the term 'performance' to describe an expanded field within which theatre played a part. In the coming half-century the relations between these two terms and the practices they describe, theatre and performance, will shape not only the cultural and aesthetic forms to which they were once related but also a growing expanse of social terrains that are the ground for this book.

There are a number of introductions and primers, 'outlines and guides' as Walter Benjamin referred to them, of performance available that have begun to articulate this terrain since Southern and Schechner set out on this quest. These readily define the various relationships that exist between theatre, performance and their border disciplines: anthropology, psychology and sociology for instance. This book goes about this task in a somewhat different way, though perhaps with common cause. It does what theatre does, putting these things, ideas and feelings on their feet. Instead of telling you what archaeology might offer performance, for instance, it 'does it', or at least 'tries to do it'.

Theatre in the Expanded Field will hopefully add to the disciplinary discussions that are currently actively reshaping the performance arena, but not primarily through explanation. It rather seeks to put the promise of such diversity of approach into action. So instead of describing what a pre-historical approach to performance might be, an explanation that is as likely to inspire mimicry as much as imagination, the chapter titled 'Pre-Historical & Archaeological' works on the materials at hand, seeking to demonstrate what a pre-history of performance might *in practice* look and feel like.

It is only in this practised manner that the approaches to performance engaged with here can do more than promise. By treating archaeology in this way, for instance, without presuming what it is, or could be, there would be no response possible to the philosopher Edmund Husserl, who in the 1930s regretted that a 'positive science' had already appropriated an expression that truly captured the essence of philosophy.[1] That expression, 'archaeology', the study of the beginnings of knowledge 'as such', becomes in the context of this book a means to access something that I would like to call 'performance as such'. The following chapters, in different modes, manners and moods, play out that performance 'in' and 'through' the theatre.

There are *Seven Approaches to Performance* explored here, as the subtitle says. Richard Southern, and Shakespeare before him, identified 'Seven Ages' as a form worthy of a book, a soliloquy and a life. But unlike life, which at the time of writing has a chronological movement from youth to older age, performance complicates the relations between previously sundered disciplines. It is in recognition of the simple fact that 'All the world is not a stage' that these approaches have been tethered with an ampersand (&), on the one hand inviting us to think about the connectedness of fields of operation, on the other hand facing up to the way one approach might resist or blank another by turning its back on it. The ampersand between 'Psychological & Legal', say, does this very nicely, figuratively as well as semantically.

While there are undoubted risks inherent in binding apparently diverse disciplines in this way, not the least of which is a certain doubling up in the complexity of the chapters that follow, these are risks that are not just worth taking but they have to be taken. The names given to fields such as theology and history cannot, despite the best efforts of professional specialists, become an excuse for ignoring their complicated and complicating association with their own partial conditions of disciplinary emergence, never mind the everyday they were clearly, once, intended to describe. Surely this is the source of unease one might feel on picking up 'Theory for …' or 'Introduction to …' books that survey fields with comprehensive reports from their disciplinary base, but in their strictly demarcated chapter divisions struggle to account for the ragged realities one is dealing with in one's own life, one's own performances. While such boundaries are intellectually reinforced and protected, even one could say 'policed' by the Academy, for the sake of temporary lucidity, this, in my book, cannot become an excuse not to risk reacquainting old friends from what have now become foreign fields.

Although this book makes no claims to a chronological development of a discipline, it does indicate a date from which each 'Approach' might be said to come into appearance, to be counted as a means to examine experience. By approach I am thinking rather literally, not figuratively, that is the physical way humans in history have advanced towards things they wish to grasp, before retreating from those things realising what they have just approached has something uncanny, fearfully familiar about it. In that sense the book could have been subtitled 'Essays in the Prehistoric and Postdramatic' as that is its broad sweep. But the dates offered for each chapter are soon exposed to a pulling back and forth that indicates ways in which a history of performance is always a matter of returns, what Hal Foster once referred to as 'a complex relay of anticipated futures and reconstructed pasts'.[2] The chapter 'Theological & Historical', for instance, begins by dragging the postdramatic back 400 years to the Early Modern period, while finding its way forward to *Les Misérables* today.

The book closes with a reflection on the 'Tactical & Critical' to mark the peculiarly local, nevertheless challenging, nature of what has gone before. In each chapter you will notice that I am 'on my feet', approaching things, taking my bearings from what I know, and what I imagine about what I know, and coming to terms with the obvious pleasure that more will escape me in any such location, and awaits the look of someone who has read this book and wants to check out the place for themselves, for what I have made up, and how I have made do. This itinerary is not only written by way of a series of approaches to the field, excursions through performance you could call them, but also drawn by the artist Beryl Robinson in a series of images that outline performance and its contours. These 'line drawings', as Richard Southern called them in *The Seven Ages of the Theatre,* are there not to illustrate something said in words but to exercise a way of looking and reading that is yours.

If this is what the book 'does', what is the book 'about'? They are not quite the same thing. Inadvertently and surreptitiously this book has come to be about that most necessary of things, community. With the failure of those hard fought-for communisms, of which Victor Hugo's *Les Misérables* was the first literary example, with the obsessive individualism that characterises the early decades of the twenty-first century and its 'solo performances', the question of community is a preeminent problem of our time.

The chapters of this book will resist conceiving of community as a property, reducing it to an object, already there to be described and somehow ministered to. *Theatre in the Expanded Field* activates a resistance to any such presumption, and in such a distancing will reveal situations, events and engagements through which 'communities to come' might be glimpsed. I will have failed in this project if you, my reader, were to surmise that this is what I think community 'is', or perhaps even worse, what 'community theatre' might be. I will have succeeded if I can multiply the conditions consequent upon community to such a point that performance and its publics offer some possibilities in the theatre, but also importantly through and beyond the theatre in the expanded field, which might not have been apparent before I ordered experience in the way I have chosen to here.

In 1962, that same year marked by this book and its half-century anniversaries, the novelist William Styron sat down in front of an audience at Boston University and read the first chapter of Richard Yates's *Revolutionary Road*, published to widespread acclaim the year before. The chapter Styron read is one which sets the 1950s scene for what Richard Yates described as his abiding concern: 'that most human beings are inescapably alone, and therein lies their tragedy'. But at the outset of this chapter, there are high hopes for an opening night in the theatre, where more is at stake than performance. As the director says to the cast in the aftermath of a dress rehearsal that has gone better than expected: 'Remember this. We're not just putting on a play here. We're establishing a community theatre, and that's a pretty important thing to be doing'. And the omniscient narrator, somewhere in the auditorium but also somehow with an eye to the outside, concurs: 'the main thing was not the play itself but the company – the brave idea of it, the healthy, hopeful sound of it: the birth of a really good community theatre, right here, among themselves'.[3] That *The Petrified Forest*, as rendered by the Laurel Players, does not quite work as the cast had hoped is perhaps no surprise; its failure foreshadows the novel that lies ahead. A failure that ends with the defacement of a home: 'a stone path going halfway down the front lawn and ending in a mud puddle'. But Styron does not get to the path; he only chose to read that first chapter, and leaves his Boston audience in the lonely company of a shattered assembly, in the 'crunching gravel of the parking lot', beyond the theatre, 'where the black sky went up forever and there were hundreds of thousands of stars'.

Alan Read
Truinas & London
2012–2013

Preliminary

To say what theatre is would be to start an argument. To say what performance is? A fight. Or at the very least an intense disagreement. But fifty years ago, at the time of writing, there were brave hearts willing to stake their colours to the mast. Foremost among them was the theatre historian and architect Richard Southern, whose book *The Seven Ages of the Theatre* (1962) systematically peeled back the accumulated layers of theatricality, scenery, auditorium, stage, costume, mask and finally player and audience, to reduce (or raise) his subject to a state he called 'no theatre'.

In a chapter in that work called 'The Essence of Theatre', a title that might seem incomprehensible to relativists today unwilling to prescribe value judgements to artistic endeavours, Southern acknowledges: 'The story has complications. Instead of a simple development, there seems to be a succession of intrusions from outside upon what would otherwise appear as a self-contained, modest, and not unpopular human act; the act that is to say, of performing something before a group of other people'.[1]

In answer to his own question 'What is the essence of theatre?' Southern begins with a useful proposition, laid out in poetic form:

Any work of Art
is an address (in some form)
by an individual
to a number of people.[2]

In the realm of theatre this implies that something arises in the time span of the event from the manner of such an address and the meaning of theatre is embedded in its acting out. Southern goes on to qualify this definition:

An address through 'doing' however it is prepared, depends on a concentrated effort on one *particular occasion*; more-over your audience is limited to the group present on that occasion. A creation, then, you can perfect in solitude before the people see it; but an action is done before them once, and is finished – the only chance of perfecting it if it has failed lies in an opportunity of trying it all over again on another occasion.[3]

So, fully thirty years before the cultural theorist Peggy Phelan was finessing this 'ontology of performance' in her formative collection of essays *Unmarked* (1993), where she defined what it is that gives such a peculiarly live, un-repeatable character to performance as distinct to other acts, Southern was willing not only to characterise theatre's live-ness but to wager that the purpose of such an act was to achieve it in a way that accorded with a standard of some sort.[4] Again, half a century on, there would be few performance studies scholars who would invest in such qualifying standards of 'attainment', and the metaphysics of perfection has long since lost its virtuous lustre. 'Against being right', the epigraph to Phelan's book, has, in the meantime, become more of an epitaph to the virtuosity of performance's forebears and counterparts: theatre, ballet and opera.

But in *The Seven Ages of the Theatre*, Richard Southern seeks ways of thinking about space for the theatre of *his* contemporary moment, the 1960s, and there are more reasons than nostalgic, talismanic ones to dedicate part of this Preliminary to reflecting on that moment here as we mark its half-century passing. For it was not a parochial development. While Southern was reflecting on histories of theatre in this avowedly internationalist way in the UK, and William Styron was reading that first literary treatment in *Revolutionary Road* of theatre's failure to cohere community, Richard Schechner in Tulane in the US in 1962 began to mobilise the term 'performance' to distinguish a phase of 'anti-illusion' from this longer history of theatre. He did this principally, and in the first instance, by his taking up of an existent journal *Tulane Drama Review* and turning it into *The Drama Review* (*TDR*) which would have a wholly distinct orientation to what had gone before. Richard Schechner, as he himself has generously acknowledged, and others have been quick to point out fearful of forefathers for a field that claims no patronage, was here recycling a term that had already, during the 1950s, gained broad currency across a range of US thinkers and academics.[5]

Fifty further years of this history and the 'new' category of Performance, drawing its lineage from the gamut of live arts, Performance Art and, perhaps inevitably, Performance Studies, has usurped and replaced the previous position that Theatre held for a new audience embarking on the study of a very old subject. The canonisation of performance as all that is 'good', all that is efficacious in terms of the arts, that is challenging, transgressive, spontaneous, live, free, fluid, real, explicit, with the sexual energy of everything from the improvisation of the jazz era to burlesque, via the dynamics of a vast range of practised things from abstract expressionism to relational participation, was undoubtedly a necessary step to unsettle all that was normative in the orthodoxies of a dominant culture.

But, as Thomas B Hess said (or is said to have said) of a Barnet Newman exhibition in 1959: 'Aesthetics is for the artist as ornithology is for the birds'. From this enigmatic observation we can surmise that the integration of a form within any culture (for example, the history of 'Western Art') returns us to the inevitable problem of the normative, the dominant, the hegemonic and the canonical. By way of bearing this out, a gestalt shift occurred through the 1980s and 1990s when the universities of North America, Europe, Asia, Australia and New Zealand began to teach Performance Studies and the 'shock of the new' turned into the perhaps unintended but nevertheless omnipresent lionisation of anti-illusion. Here a ragged movement that had begun as an anti-paradigm found itself as paradigmatic as the next discipline, or so some of its most innovative chroniclers believed.[6]

The Performance Gene

This book is not about to escape any of these admittedly broadly drawn lineaments of accommodation to cultural continuity, nor bound free from power's continuous appropriation of its provocateurs. But starting with these Preliminary remarks I would like to contest the grounds on which such sparring takes place. To this end let's reconfigure performance, not as a noun but as a verb, not as a genre or a field, but rather as a stimulus to change, a medium of action and reaction. I would propose performance effects such change through a very precise mechanism that we all carry – you could call it a 'gene', which makes humans what they are. The Latin term I will give to that gene is *Genus Irritare*, the capacity to excite or provoke, or in plain English, irritate.

Francis Glisson, a physician who studied at Cambridge University in the early seventeenth century, declared that the tiniest particles of matter 'perceive, desire and have the spontaneous power to enter into motion, and thus to act and react'.[7] Glisson was the first scientist to identify this capacity for irritability in his work *De Rachitide* (1650), and while what he discovered has shaped everything about life sciences since, I want to demonstrate ways in which such a capacity has a much longer performance history than the genetic trail suggests. It is unlikely, for example, that without Glisson's early work on the substantive 'irritation', Denis Diderot, the author of the first secular treatise on the actor, could have written the following: 'man [...] is a theatre of action and reaction, even in fulfilling the higher faculties proper to his species'.[8]

On the basis that life in all its forms first demonstrates its sentience through an ability to be irritable, and given that life in *all* its forms from the orientation of lichen on a rock to the pirouette of a Capoeira dancer has now been demonstrated as having potential for performance, it would not appear too far-fetched at the outset to suggest that a capacity for performance is a capacity to irritate, and to be irritated. The useful work that such a concept does for us, literally the tool-like quality that lies at the heart of the Latin root of the word 'concept' and gives all concepts their force of leverage, is the suture this word allows between the most banal, quotidian perception of performance and the most sophisticated sense of its potential, a range from the base to the beautiful and back that this book welcomes.

On the one hand it is obvious that performance is irritating in its most common, pejorative sense. It irritates commentators otherwise known for their rational behaviour. Take John Humphrys for instance, well known to UK listeners as a doyen of morning radio at the BBC for thirty years, regularly heard by close on 7 million people. With an extended silence, or a quizzical inflection to the link, the nation's favourite political interrogator can consign a performance 'package' by a put-upon BBC arts commentator to the aesthetic margin beyond the serious attention reserved for the gravity of the 'news proper'. Performance invites otherwise rational beings to froth about something that never meant them any harm, and almost certainly has done no one any harm.

Of course in generalising in this way for the purposes of an introduction, it should not be forgotten that such apparent irrelevance, and it must be admitted performance (as a licensed cultural form at least) remains a seeming irrelevance to the vast majority of people, has not prevented those most irritated by performance from harming those who have the courage to deploy its provocations against regimes who consider themselves at its mercy. Rustom Bharucha has written with great insight on those for whom a 'right' to performance should never be taken for granted, and those practitioners whose lives have come under threat for the uncomfortable truths regimes of power perceive in their images.

Nevertheless performance irritates publics into responses that make them appear as though they have become audiences to something they never subscribed to, nor thought they had an attitude about. It irritates bureaucracies who perceive the cutting of a flag in a Croatian gallery in Rijeka, by the artist Emil Hrvatin working under the political pseudonym of Janez Jansa, to be a demonstration of something that means more than the cutting of a coloured cloth in an apparently neutral space. It irritates conservatives who believe there to be something faintly subversive about performance's strict disciplines, and socialists who perceive performance as lacking in the ideological critique that might undermine the enforcements of brute politics.

I would not wish anyone to proceed further with this book on the misunderstanding that I think performance *per se* exists beyond this genetic capacity for action and its appetite for reaction. In my view performance has only ever operated in tension with other things and does all its best work when operating in those relations. It could be said to act as a foreign body, as a third person, always at odds with those things upon which it does its work.

As I will hope to demonstrate through this book, where the 'I' and the 'you' of the first and second person imply each other, bound in the symmetry of an audience of some sort, the third person, over there somewhere, always escapes such circulations and in so doing maintains its potential to provoke by way of performance. These relations will become clear when we set out in exploration of the seven approaches to performance that provide the subtitle of this work. But it remains for me to clarify what I believe the characteristics of this capacity for performance to be, you might say how it becomes irritable, before detailing the combination of its relations.

To mark this genealogy of irritation, we could (as Beth Hoffman and Dominic Johnson have each done over the last decade) trace the relations, semantic, political and formal between those practices commonly circumscribed by the terminologies of theatre practice, and those subscribing to the vocabularies of live art and performance practice.[9] Each finesses this field of mutual operations that go a very long way to dispelling a phoney war between the two. In Hoffman's case the nuancing of the terms of engagement is very fine indeed and is well summarised by the following proposition:

> [...] in imagining a new 'theatre of the future', the question isn't: 'How can we incorporate live art into theatre history?' or 'Is live art the new theatre history?' but 'How can we reconfigure the rhetorical habits and practices of distinction that underwrote the aesthetic and historiographical split, creating a live art in contradistinction to theatre in the first place?'[10]

It is these arguments that have most urgently shaped and encouraged the approaches to performance laid out in this book. The always already shifting relations between performance and theatre will be played out within specific historical and culturally located frames. But, in order to get to that consensual arrangement between adult fields, there is perhaps, here at least, an opportunity to mark the more antagonistic contention with which this preliminary began: that to ask what performance was would be to start a fight. In the now unfashionable spirit of binary separation, and very much in the spirit of the rest of the book, we could perhaps start with dissensus rather than consensus here, to see what happens when we place one term in tension with the other. Theatre *versus* Performance one might say. We could begin in the simplest possible way by differentiating theatre to the left and performance to the right:

Theatre   Performance

We could then start to list some qualities that distinguish each:

linearity	simultaneity
character	autobiography
acting	authenticity
invention	revelation
potency	impotency

Laying them out in this presumptuous way immediately raises some questions that we might otherwise mistakenly think have been answered as to their relations, or indeed their formal properties, or further and more troublingly their infinite mutability as terms of reference, their ability to be anything to anyone despite the generations of classificatory work conducted upon them by Richard Schechner, Richard Southern, Richard Gough and those who followed not called Richard. At the very least it is impossible to imagine 'we' agree as to which identity should remain in which column.

My pleasure in 'theatre in the expanded field' as I have coined it for this book would be the precise way in which the order and history of the left is irritated and disturbed by the electricity of the right. The diagrammatic aspect of this work, rendered by the artist Beryl Robinson, and paying regard to Richard Southern's line drawings in *The Seven Ages of the Theatre*, maintains this simple classificatory system throughout and outlines where in each scene performance is operating at this level of itinerant irritant. It is not quite that this irritant carries 'the shock of the new', as the art critic Robert Hughes coined the phrase, but rather in the spirit of the philosopher – Alain Badiou's simple exhortation in his 'Theses on Theatre' for us to consider how it is we become 'struck' by something on the stage through performance, how that striking quality of performance occurs to us as a charge.[11] Picturing this metaphysical charge might appear somewhat foolhardy, but it does at least interrupt the chameleon prose that can be coined to cover all theatrical conditions without committing to any.

Jon McKenzie wrote about this charge, somewhat parodically, in the final pages of his work *Perform Or Else* (2001) in which his anti-hero, Jane Challenger, becomes more and more agitated at her lectern towards the end of her interplanetary keynote speech: 'From somewhere near the back of the hall a deep blue light engulfs the space, while waves of feedback spew out from the lecture machine. There's a slight pause – then a brilliant explosion, a blinding yet muted jolt, a chilling blast of the outside'.[12] It is perhaps no surprise in our material, and studiedly materialist, world that in the comprehensive literature dedicated to Jon McKenzie's formative work for the field, there is a complete absence of commentary on a passage such as this that so engagingly captures the metaphysical quality of performance and its expanded field.

Where theatre might be perceived as an anachronistic form that is more or less mechanical in its means of production, performance, in the manner in which it has so far been configured in this Preliminary at least, is thus charged with a drive towards modernity, a 'deep blue light' engulfing the space as Jon McKenzie put it. Performance continues to insist on the event in the here and now, whereas theatre may be seen, to all intents and purposes (we might as well admit it, given the rhetorical and disciplinary force of the soothsayers from Richard Schechner onwards), as an abandoned practice, one which relies upon rehabilitation to bring it into the current, the circuit, the field of operations which we ascribe as of this contemporary moment. Directing is one relatively recent, century-and-a-half long manifestation of this requirement that theatre finds itself again anew in each epoch with which it has such complicated and sometimes antiquated relations. Adaptation is another, while the very word 'revival', rarely used to describe performance, but commonly used to signal the return of a familiar text or production in the theatre, is a mark of such continuous recovery of that which is otherwise abandoned. No wonder there is so much discussion as to the merit of archives in the theatre field. I will return to the rather contentious idea that theatre might be perceived as an abandoned practice, not least of all given its recent, in the West End at least, soaring box office takings, after outlining some of the implications of the enforced separation in the columns above within a specific performance setting. Suffice to say here that 'abandonment' does not imply for a moment a lack of care, on the part of this book at least; this work is precisely titled as it is in honour of theatre's Lazarus-like resistance to extinction.

Such a columned separation for the purposes of convenience, or clarity, could, as with the willingness to offer diagrammatic representations of the ethereal and the enigmatic throughout this work, be construed as unduly simplistic or, worse in a field that has so celebrated diversity, the re-instigation of conservative and conserving binaries. But the point here would be to emphasise, in the spirit of Beth Hoffman and others from a very different perspective, the complicating effect of the one on the other through processes of action and reaction, rather than the sources from whence they might arise. Origins, contrary to Richard

Southern's impulse, and despite the title of Chapter 1, which might suggest otherwise, will not be the ordering principle here.

The theatre stage must, to even the most sympathetic eye in the twenty-first century, appear something of an anachronism, if not the 'string quartet' that Richard Schechner compared it to when looking for a way to signify its abandonment by contemporary sensibility. Performance on the other hand, and it is on another hand as columned above, does despite its institutional establishment appear to continue to aggravate all those people who would prefer their culture re-heated. It seems to confuse, celebrate and chastise in its variety and persistence.

It is that persistence I would like to characterise here by way of suggesting that a genetic make-up that is composed partly of performance is a 'make up' with definable characteristics, which like other DNA elements can be identified both diagrammatically in theory and also in practice as witnessed over the last decades since Richard Southern offered us his seven ages of the theatre. News at the time of writing that scientists from the European Bioinformatics Institute (EBI) in Cambridge have chosen Shakespeare's 154 sonnets to test the storage capacity of DNA as a means to archive the bard's work for tens of thousands of years recommends to me the urgency of a project such as this one, where the genome is treated less as a vast mainframe computing device for the past, and more for the irritant it offers to any such official view of reality or presumptions as to a canon worth keeping.[13] If when written in DNA one of Shakespeare's sonnets weighs 0.3 millionths of a millionth of a gram, as it does, I suspect when the scientists at the EBI locate the performance gene, it will be a good deal lighter on its feet and less predictable in its effects.

Live Culture

The performance gene is not everywhere; it only operates within a *live culture*. Tate Modern, in its London monument to power generation, Gilbert Scott's Bankside Power Station, has just revealed two spectacular spaces dedicated to fostering such a culture, something that would have been quite inconceivable just a decade ago, let alone when Richard Schechner started to mobilise the term 'performance' against the theatre. The *Tanks*, the crucible for this culture, have a long structural history with their own electric charge but also are not without a past when it comes to the shock of the new. It took an act of faith to bring this development about. As a first leap in this process, a space of vision, an institution dedicated to the fine art of 'looking on', became temporarily, early in the twenty-first century, a place for performance. The name given to this gathering by its curators, Adrian Heathfield, Lois Keidan and Daniel Brine, was *Live Culture* (2003), a strategic attempt to shift attention from the theatrical traditions as exemplified by all those identifiers in the left-hand column of words above, but more specifically a subtle swerve from the recent ascendancy of the visual arts themselves in the popular imagination that had seen visitor numbers at Tate exceed all expectations by a factor of ten.

The terms of this transition from visual to live art required negotiation by an unprecedentedly well-informed assembly of mediators whose task was to articulate the conditions through which live culture could be accommodated within a visual art history with which it had complex but difficult relations. To speak up for performance as a live art, while insisting on its distinction from live arts 'as such', was a wholly appropriate mission in this generational setting. Where power had always been produced the generation of heat for light had long been taken for granted. The background hum from the electric substation imbedded in the Bankside walls was a persistent reminder that the flow of power past was only, ever, temporarily to be short circuited by this 'temporary installation'. The 'return to normal service' that followed the series of power cuts discussed here was perhaps just that bit livelier for having been conducted at all, and after a decade's commitment has now led to the establishment of the *Tanks* at Tate Modern as a dedicated site for live art exploration.

The figures of visual and performance art, theatre and theatricality put into play by this international gathering were mirrored elsewhere across a curatorial domain from the Guggenheim in New York with *theanyspacewhatever* (2008–2009) show curated by Nancy Spector, *Double Agent* (2008) curated by Claire Bishop and Mark Sladen at the Institute of Contemporary Arts in London, to the Tate itself with *The World as a Stage* (2008).[14] Each of these complicating occasions took place alongside the sweep of 'relational' art projects, many of which were forerunners of these exhibitions, documented by Nicolas Bourriaud, and the participatory and social dynamics narrated by Shannon Jackson in her volume *Social Works* (2012) and Claire Bishop in her recent work *Artificial Hells* (2012).[15] I am not suggesting for a moment that these many and varied projects owed their existence to *Live Culture*, but the prescience of that project at the threshold of a decade of such intense interest in relations between the performative, the theatrical, the socially engaged, the collaborative and the visual does lend the event a certain distinction worth examining briefly.

What *Live Culture* as an event was supremely sensitive to was the simple fact that the irritant gene I have identified is always already everywhere, but simultaneously is so elusive to documentation and to sustenance. You could say in this respect that live art is 'barely live' and 'barely art'. When I say barely I do not mean in contrary distinction to Richard Southern that performance is somehow naked where theatre is costumed, though he would insist on costume as critical to theatre's genealogy, but rather that live art and performance exist in a continuously *exposed* state. It is in their DNA, if not in our DNA, to operate at odds with any official view of reality, any assumed order of power, any inherited deference to circumstance. In this exposed state live art is absolutely exceptional, for on the one hand it is everywhere apparent, in all of us one might say, as the genetic capacity for irritability is in us all, but in the event it appears as the exception to this rule of commonality. Simply put, performance takes others to remind us it is ours. It is at once eminently elitist while being consummately democratic. This accounts, perhaps, for the irritability humans feel in its presence. This book maintains that this irritability is not just a 'good thing'; it is the 'only thing'. It is what distinguishes us from the inanimate.

So, what sort of irritation does performance bring about, what kinds of *acts* does it initiate, what *can* it do, is there anything it *cannot* do? Let us focus on the opening night of *Live Culture*, and the reception which took place in the cavernous chamber of the Tate Turbine Hall, for a decade now dedicated to the outstanding Unilever Series of installations (2002–2012) and the site on that night for the work of the Russian performance maker Oleg Kulik, in *Armadillo for Your Show* (2003). Taking the columned distinctions between performance and theatre ventured above, how might one look at, and listen to, such a piece and begin to understand its *simultaneous* as distinct to its linear characteristics, its *impotential* as much as its potential, its *revelatory* rather than its inventive character? (Figure 0.1)

The set-up was simple if vertiginous. A figure, suddenly and without visible assistance, appeared in searing light high above us. He (and it was apparent 'it' was a he from below) was covered in hundreds of stamp-sized mirrors, adorning his body, was turning, or being turned, on a trapeze-prismed light like a human 'glitter ball' over those being illuminated below. This rotation was orchestrated to a resounding, bass-heavy beat that throbbed through the Turbine Hall and pulsed the assembled party-goers who were now, inadvertently, moving if not dancing beneath someone, or was it some*thing*?

What more to say, why not just dance? For it would seem that this prop was there to support something more than itself; it was there to instigate a good

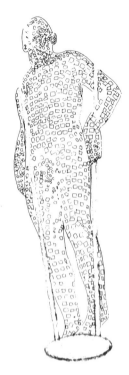

Figure 0.1 Oleg Kulik, *Armadillo for Your Show*, London, 2003

time, less a 'Good Night Out', as David Edgar and John McGrath once referred
to theatre in search of an audience, as a 'Good Night In'. Well, for a start,
taking hold of the genetic thread initiated earlier, Oleg Kulik encourages those
experiencing his work to move beyond an antiquated ideal of human being as
either *Homo Simplex*, as one-directional human being seemed to the Vitalists of
the eighteenth century, or *Homo Duplex,* as human nature was described by the
French natural historian Buffon. In this condition Buffon identified the contrast
between a 'spiritual principle' and an 'animal principle' in the human, extending
and developing an Aristotelian-Thomist tradition that acknowledged a large
share of animal life in man. Rather Kulik in turn, and turning, is evoking a state
that I would like to characterise (with an opportunistic eye on the inherent
relationship between the live and the already-archaic mediatised of the edge-
strip cinema chain) as *Homo Multiplex*. Here, in Oleg Kulik's work, showings are
happening continuously, without intermission, and with constant awareness of
selling out. Performance would appear to have borne out the hopes expressed
for it during war-time Britain when it was theatre that proclaimed its durability,

continuity and simultaneity by advertising itself on hoardings, walls and in neon, as in a state of 'Continuous Performance'.

Kulik's work has emerged over the very period being considered by this introduction as an exemplary sequence of continuous performances, identity defying and affirming projects in which he has, as he puts it, 'fallen out of human nature', sacrificing his vertical status as a human for the horizontal elevation of a dog.[16] He has not quite been playing 'as a dog', more 'being one', or if the French philosopher Gilles Deleuze is to be taken literally, 'becoming animal'. In his best-known work, for the Interpol group in Stockholm in 1996, he exhibited alongside a sign marked DANGEROUS, and, given the express intention of this sign, he was resolutely unapologetic for the attacks he unleashed upon passers-by who ignored the warning, and on other artists whose work he destroyed in his canine persona.

Watching Oleg Kulik spinning above me, high in the Tate roof, it is neither the ability to say something *more* about the state of humanity and animality in his work that is interesting to me. Indeed I don't get much from the work in this utilitarian sense, and would take as much analytic interest in my pet dog as Jacques Derrida did in his pet cat for his work *The Animal That Therefore I Am* (2008), if I did. Nor am I quite so interested in the way the action works hard to show something *less* in the sense of a variety of means (suspended spinning mirrored figure, with soundtrack, begins and ends after an interval). Rather I am fascinated by the *simultaneity* with which the propositions and effects are offered; it is these coeval qualities that are striking. The formality of this apparently simple gesture does not seem to worry anyone, and shouldn't, for it is the strict formal means that does not 'say' anything about the 'limits of contemporary art conventions', as Kulik describes the scene he is researching (his word), but simply *is* the disco ball for the night. The question to ask underneath this artefact was once, at the Hammersmith Palais say, 'would you like to dance?' Now the imperative shines out: 'look at me and look at yourselves', perhaps not surprisingly in this context at Tate Modern, 'not dancing', or at least 'not quite dancing'.

But what does this act have to do with theatre? How does *this* performance irritate my sense of what theatre can do? Its relations are contrary ones, but critical ones also. Kulik would not appear to be interested in the dramatic 'as if', an alleged elsewhere in space extending beyond topology or geography that makes for so much drama, memorable nights in the theatre, good nights out. An 'as if' made up of *character* acting, say of scenic or illusory escapism, or you might use the phrase 'suspension of disbelief' to take on some of the implications of the terms in that left-hand column of theatre identifiers laid out above. On the contrary he is 'without alibi' to borrow a phrase from the writing of the philosopher Jacques Derrida in another context.[17] Kulik would appear to have collapsed his alibi, the ubiquity of the theatrical alibi, 'honest I have another day job and it's more serious than the thing you have caught me doing', into himself, his self.[18] There are no curtain calls here.

So far so much in keeping with all those who, since the French proto-Surrealist and 'Pata-physician, Alfred Jarry, in 1898, have written themselves into the performance scene, from the biography in the wings to the autobiography in the public eye. The presentation of self here (albeit on a trapeze and excessively mirrored) now offers its peculiar everyday banality, as a corollary to the 'there', the 'then' and the 'extra-daily' of the stage – an excess of a different kind in which the apparently mundane is magnified at a distance to appear exceptional. Above me, this self that is spinning on a high bar, if I am understanding the principles of Kulik's project *Zoophrenia* of which this act might be considered a part, is a divided self of 'species relations' rather than the artificially isolated and unified human subject beloved of the life sciences and exemplified by the romanticism of Jarry and Co.'s exaggerated humanism. The event of Kulik's spinning mirror is the simultaneous *rupturing* and *redoubling* of what on earth he is up to. He reflects light upon us, apparently beyond our collective gaze covered as he is by a carapace of mirrored camouflage, while ensuring that we cannot take our eyes off him. He is exposed as he exposes. He is 'in the third person' and as such has become a thing, an 'it', beyond you and me below, who, in our first and second personalities, 'I' and 'you', begin by our exception from this third-person rule to understand something more about each other.

This simultaneous, directness of form and content as exemplified here in Kulik's work reminds me in its economical elegance of the American philosopher J.L. Austin's symmetry of word and intention in what he called 'performatives'.[19] The concrete examples of performatives, wedding vows, boat launches and namings, drawn from Austin's seminal work have always seemed to me relatively thin and uninteresting compared with the discussions of everything, from hate-speech to pornography, that has surrounded them. Of course 'I do' said at an altar in a marriage ceremony carries a certain practical as well as symbolic freight for as long as it takes to perjure oneself. But I would go along with Jacques Derrida when he alerts us to an inherent contradiction that lies within the performative: 'It is too often said that the performative produces the event of which it speaks. To be sure. One must also realize that, inversely, where there is the performative, an event worthy of the name cannot arrive'.[20]

The simultaneity of each of Kulik's actions over the last decade, from *Deep into Russia* in 1993 via *Armadillo* in 2003 and back to his most recent work shown at the Regina Gallery in London in 2012, initiates an event worthy of the name by precisely complicating this economy of words in which some kind of saying brings about some kind of effects in the world. Here there is no performative *per se*, but a performance in which, what the linguist Émil Benveniste called the 'third person', is revealed to us as that 'thing' upon which 'you' and 'I' below have somehow become dependent. We will explore quite how we have become dependent on this 'other' through performance as this book proceeds through its various approaches. We will also explore by the end of this book the measures we have taken to immunise ourselves from its uncanny embrace.

Abandoned Practices and Endangered Uses

For the purpose of these Preliminary arguments I have chosen to engage with just one of those things that the irritable gene works its work upon, but one that provides the very best culture within which performance can be at its most irritating. That thing is its more established, less fashionable other, theatre. Don't worry, as the book opens out, each 'approach to performance' will range far and wide across a more inclusive and expansive field of relations with more purchase on the world than the twin pair performance and theatre. But that said, it does occur to me that performance has done its best work as a constant irritant to its closest cousin. If, as Peter Sloterdijk suggests, all arts practice is simply a form of exaggeration, then theatre's long history of exaggeration is one that has been irritated from the outset by performance.[21] If the list laid out above, between simultaneity and impotentiality, are for me at least the five senses of performance, then I wonder what the vital signs are of a theatre that I have had the temerity to describe as an abandoned practice?

Performance research can, among those disciplines that constitute the humanities and social sciences, claim a rigorous, historicised approach to the study of 'practices'. In recognition of this facility, fields as diverse as legal studies, material sciences and medicine have joined the established academic disciplines of anthropology, sociology and psychology in their deployment of performance research paradigms. It is the nuanced vocabulary of making, doing and showing, drawing on critical theory and continental philosophy, that has established performance study at the centre of twenty-first-century intellectual engagement, from political theory to historical re-staging, from the metaphoric representations of nano-physics to forensic reconstructions of crime scenes.[22]

What has been heralded from within the emerging discipline of performance research as the 'performative turn' has, on closer scrutiny, always been definitional to each of these border fields and their means of operation. Defence theories, practices and technologies were always 'demonstrated' (a term popularised by Carl von Clausewitz in the early 1800s) in 'theatres of operation' and 'theatres of war', laboratory sciences always had to 'test' their outcomes within 'control groups', criminal legal cases were always determined by 'advocacy' and 'defence' and medical case notes always narrated symptoms and cures within ward 'rounds' and 'operating theatres'.

The ubiquity of performance measures within a diverse range of disciplines and fields is no longer contested, if it ever was. Certainly, since Jon McKenzie's definitive work *Perform or Else* there can be few in the field who are not familiar with the larger claims being made for performance now. But the precise definition of the role of 'practices' in these operations remains vague and largely unaccounted for. This is partly because most research into practices, such as that conducted in theatre itself, but also much more widely across the material and social sciences, has been disproportionately interested in those practices which have 'survived', continued or been successful in impacting upon contemporary operational modes. This is understandable given that one of the principal interests of historical recovery is the better understanding of how such pasts shape our presents. Such enquiry informs the vast majority of current research across disciplines, especially in areas of 'practice as research' (such as theatre studies), for whom the re-invigoration of art forms now is a declared intention of many of the best and most relevant researchers in the field.

But it is the view of this book that such shock treatment is tantamount to the resuscitation of the rogue Riderhood, in Charles Dickens's last great novel of the Thames, *Our Mutual Friend* (1864–1865). There, in an episode widely written about in recent continental philosophy but largely ignored by the theatre, an apparently drowned man is brought to a tavern table adjacent to the river, where an audience of onlookers witness his 'fight' for life. The criminal life that once made up the persona of Riderhood has given way to the survival of 'life itself', 'a life' as Gilles Deleuze insists on calling it, and one that the onlookers, previously impervious to the fate of someone they had no feelings but antipathy for, now invest their will within. Their 'will' has to be directed towards this apparent corpse as what is at stake here is life itself, the same life that breathes into them and one day will leave them too. Riderhood, abandoned to his fate when living his 'worthless' life, is now somehow separated from a life that no longer carries the stigma of his character. It might seem rather far-fetched, but it strikes me that theatre is the Riderhood of our age – for all its criminal misjudgement of its times, its insistence that it is waving when it is drowning, its very persistence as an anachronism is theatre's most enduring feature. An affect machine that will just not run down and idle away its later age, it is theatre among the arts that is constantly being separated out from the bourgeois character of its misspent past and reinvested with hope by audiences who *will* it to be of relevance again, who wish to give it 'a life' of this sort.

This idea of theatre as a once abandoned practice, now invested with revitalised hope, is perhaps unusual, but not new. It simply pushes to a somewhat extreme limit the very well-known phrase that Richard Schechner offered some years ago and was noted earlier – that theatre constitutes something akin to the string quartet of the twenty-first century.[23] The critical difference between our positions is that while Schechner heralds theatre's demise in the interests of a newly enfranchised performance studies, I celebrate and articulate its necessary returns. But beyond performance's irritation with its forebears, the idea of theatre in its abandonment is furthermore and more tellingly located at the convergence of two strands of European thought and practice, indeed thought about practice with which the sweep of this introduction has been chronologically contiguous: histories of 'eliminated practices' and philosophies of 'endangered uses'. While a diversity of theorists and cultural practitioners from a variety of fields across the arts and sciences have explored and foregrounded these problems recently, two contributions in this arena could be taken as paradigmatic: the work of the historian of science Isabelle Stengers and the philosopher of play Giorgio Agamben.[24]

On the one hand, Isabelle Stengers (Free University of Brussels), as a historian of science, and particularly of chemistry within the context of what she calls 'the invention of modern science', has drawn our attention to the elimination of practices in the name of scientific 'progress'. Stengers, along with a number of historians and philosophers, including Bruno Latour and Lorraine Daston (whose work comes to the fore in Chapter 2), has redrawn the map of what matters about the material, how 'things' operate within a laboratory setting and the politics that inscribe any scientific procedure in its claim to become Science (with an upper case S). The 'eliminativist' principle, as Stengers puts it rather more polemically than my own term, is one that has fuelled the establishment of Science over competing claims to knowledge through five centuries. Stengers is concerned about the terms on which these operations have been conducted and with what effects for practices that are eliminated in the wake of the 'advances' of scientific rationality. An unforeseen irony for Stengers's own historical field of enquiry is the simple yet harrowing example for the contemporary University in the UK: the accelerating loss of Chemistry departments and the laboratory practices that were common to them.

For Stengers the landscape is one 'ghosted by the spirit of past practices'. As she puts it, 'We live in a cemetery of already destroyed practices'.[25] To locate theatre in a 'graveyard of abandoned practices', a warehouse of waste, would be serious enough but would leave unattended the pressing, civic question that arises in such a place. The historical and philosophical merit of such an exercise would be unquestionable, but a performance gene introduces another imperative to this project. The question which arises then engages with practice itself. That is the means to recover and retool *theatre* practices whose relevance to pressing contemporary dilemmas demands attention. While the first explorations of each chapter that follow will identify losses of practice, the second will examine the potential for the reactivation of previously excluded theatre practices through the genetic irritations of performance.

If on the one hand theatre can be conceived as an 'Abandoned Practice', as this book attests is the perhaps unintended yet belligerent opportunism of performance study, then it should not go without saying in this age of affects and audience responsiveness that there will, with abandonment, be a parallel set of practices to consider: that of 'endangered uses'. I would propose that it is precisely here that community is brought into question. Once again, and against the vague prognoses of successive theoretical frames from postmodernity to cosmopolitanism (including the rampant individualism of much performance theory and practice), this book attests that the diversity in those cultures being described here is threatened by conformity not plurality. For Giorgio Agamben, in a corollary to Stengers's identification of the political impulse to abandoned practices, this dynamic works in a peculiarly theological frame. There is a religious dimension to the manner in which things, practices and subjects get moved away from, and out of, use that is worth addressing.

What might this religious domain imply for such a performance-oriented book? We will catch up with the theological roots of history and politics in Chapter 3, but for now Giorgio Agamben gives us a way forward. In his writing on the concept of 'profanation' Agamben talks of the way in which a sacralised object that has been made separate can be profaned back into use through 'play'. Taking the root Latinate term of *sacrare* literally, he proposes that those things that are sacred are distinguished by being made separate. From one point of view, this is the obverse of the abandonment of practice as it implies a lack of investment, not a surplus of critical interest. In Stengers' view, though, the forces and imperatives of capital (and by implication the economies characterised by their investment in the market forces associated with Capitalism) are the equivalent of just such a religious belief system that Agamben is describing. Such systems, for Stengers at least, share the eliminativist tendencies of all other religions.

Those things that are removed from common use are effectively 'consecrated'; they are taken from the operations of human law (economy, education, the public realm) and placed beyond reach. It is in this shared dynamics of exclusion that disciplinary diversity is threatened in the interests of a less conflictual orthodoxy – one that can be 'believed in' for the purposes of economic and social stability. Such an eliminativist ideology does not, as the late twentieth-century abandonment of financial practices of 'regulation' attests, necessarily, always afford the best protection to those it was meant to represent in the interests of the 'free' market.

But to profane such separated objects of interest, according to Giorgio Agamben, is to return those things to 'the free use of men'.[26] For Agamben, 'use' is not something natural; use value is never to be presumed, but always to be worked upon – a proposition that performance, with its repetitive regime of restored behaviours and theatre with its no less repetitive paradigms of rehearsal, would have no quarrel with. The theoretical arena that Agamben is drawing upon here is that of the twentieth-century anthropologists of sacrifice, such as Marcel Mauss and Georges Bataille. In their work sacrifice was once the thing that removed things from the sphere of the profane to the sacred, from human to divine. Usefully for performance, theatricality and its interest in liminal processes and shifts, Agamben notes that the threshold is what is important in this anthropological context. The threshold across which the practice, the object (or, in religious terms, the victim), must cross is one which is often only discernable through the performances that occur there. For instance, the simplest form of profanation is that of the gesture of touch, in ethnographic terms a contagion, which returns something from one sphere to another across a strictly marked threshold. Touching here disenchants and alleviates the petrification of the thing in its sacred passage back to human use. There are few mechanisms as gesturally sensitive available for the interpretation of such tactility, such haptic concerns, as performance study and research.

While this ethnographic emphasis announces a common cause with much recent performance thinking, Agamben shifts attention from the anthropological sphere and redirects his analysis in a further, helpful performative direction, when he announces: 'The passage from the sacred to the profane can, in fact, also come about by means of an entirely inappropriate use (or, rather, reuse) of the sacred: namely, play'.[27] For Agamben *play*, somewhat problematically but enthusiastically for those of us engaged with performance questions that circulate around such discredited objects, becomes the privileged figure of reactivation. This is how I have begun to think of performance genetically rather than aesthetically, irritably rather than ideologically.

In a short series of epithets in his book *Profanations* Agamben situates his astonishing faith in the possibilities of play, leaving no doubt as to either the seriousness of the subject at hand or the consequences of ignoring its continued trivialisation: '[…] play frees and distracts humanity from the sphere of the sacred, without simply abolishing it […] the powers of economics, law, and politics, deactivated in play, can become the gateways to a new happiness […]'.[28] Meanwhile Agamben, to further accentuate the seriousness of the stakes, heralds the threat to this realm of meta-practice: 'Play as an organ of profanation is in decline everywhere […] To return to play its purely political vocation is a political task'. Thus Agamben in legitimising the often-infantilised realm of 'play' provides a hinge between the previously tense realms of performance research and theatre studies, where play can operate as a mediating mechanism between two sundered entities, a genre and a gene, as well as a rigorously theorised frame of practical exploration. It will be this playful suturing of approaches, as the book proceeds, that insists on the coeval qualities of theatre and (&) performance: one an abandoned practice for ever to be recited, resuscitated and reviewed; the other a gene, ubiquitous, endemic and constantly evolving its immunity to the theatrical medium through which it is most readily staged and made apparent.

Theatre in the Expanded Field

In order to explain why I prefer something so modest as irritation and playfulness as signifiers for performance's weak powers, in the face of heightening claims for its socially engaged excitements, efficacy and ethics, let me turn now to the fourth part of these Preliminary remarks to the title of this book. For, while 'Seven Approaches to Performance' operates as a subtitle in direct echo and recognition of Richard Southern's work, the title *Theatre in the Expanded Field* is a direct cull from the art critic Rosalind Krauss and her influential essay of 1979, 'Sculpture in the Expanded Field'.[29]

Rosalind Krauss's essay radically opened the possibility of redefining sculpture in the late twentieth century, knocking it off its pedestal of monumentalism, and engaging us in anti-establishment delight in the hole, the grid, the environment, the soft, the absent, the female and the performative. Taking as its starting point the experience of an earthwork in Long Island, New York, by Mary Miss, *Perimeters/Pavilions/Decoys* (1978), this essay encounters what Krauss describes as the decade of 'rather surprising things that have come to be called sculpture', none of which would particularly surprise us today with visitor figures to Tate Modern in London and the Museum of Modern Art in New York booming among aficionados and amateur aestheticians alike. The work in question is a pit, with a ladder appearing clear of the ground providing access to the excavation. Krauss describes the work as 'entirely below grade' with the hybrid identity of an atrium, tunnel and boundary where the mutability of outside and inside become the point (Figure 0.2).

This excavation work takes its place among a panorama of other interventions that have also been given the name 'sculpture', ranging from screenings on TV monitors in corridors to transient lines etched into a desert floor. This 'motley of effort' would have no purchase on the word 'sculpture', Krauss believes, unless the category sculpture can be made to be infinitely malleable, which of course is what has happened in the decade in question between 1969 and 1979 at the time of Krauss's writing. Krauss sees the critical work of aestheticians and others in the US as having serviced this manipulation, a process in which not only

Figure 0.2 Mary Miss, *Perimeters/Pavilions/Decoys*, Long Island, 1978

the categories of sculpture but also painting have been elasticated and breached. But the potency of this influential essay does not so much rest with this insight. Rather, Krauss's point is one of temporality and category. Where Krauss perceives the general view to be one in which such mobilising is being conducted in the name of the new, as she says: 'its covert message is that of historicism'.[30]

Krauss's work is significant here because it describes, and helps us to articulate, Richard Southern's historicist view of the development of theatre. Where Rosalind Krauss sees the new as being made more comfortable for us by being made familiar, having gradually evolved from a secure past, so Richard Southern's work, despite its better efforts to internationalise and problematise theatre, perhaps inevitably smoothes the complications he believes there to have been in the developmental processes he describes, by the simple chronology of their lay out and their successive, summative relations. Here Krauss believes historicism will always have the habit of finessing the 'new', diminishing difference in the process, and in so doing explain away differences that are hard to reconcile with conservative and conserving continuities. So at work here is an essentially evolutionary theory that is indeed essentialising as it secures essences in the place of dissonances and disturbances to the system. We are relieved to discover in this process that despite the apparent challenges of Mary Miss's 'hole in the ground', we need not fear anything, as that void is just the next, perhaps predictable stage of a sculptural process that was always likely to proceed in just this fashion.

As Rosalind Krauss was deftly able to point out, through such minimal actions and interventions, even those of the 1960s in the period we are remarking on here were quickly appropriated by a paternal criticism to a lineage that, surprise-surprise, appeared to recognise the work of a genealogy of constructivist father figures that would legitimise the strangeness of these interventions. This all, despite the obvious fact that the work of those fathers bore little or no relation to the works in question.

Where contingency was obvious to Krauss, cultural confidence was apparent to these (predominantly male) critics. As the 1960s gave way to the 1970s for Krauss, it is not that the word 'Sculpture' is not retained; it is just that it becomes harder to pronounce. The word 'Theatre' has been going through its own mutations recently which suggest it might be susceptible to just such interlocutionary scrambling in the process of its abandonment. While one might forgive the peculiar Atlantic divide between two Anglo-Saxon words, 'Theatre' and 'Theater', there can be no mistaking the, dare I say it, pompously particular, rounded vowel-led French quality of the European term, while delighting in the flinty if rather more aggressive North American rendition of the equivalent word.

The deployment of 'Approaches' to performance in this work takes account of Krauss's pertinent critical address of this historicising process, and without wishing or remotely able to 'correct' Southern in any way seeks not the seven 'ages' of the theatre but rather seven approaches to performance's relations *with* theatre.

The seven approaches this work will lay out in the following pages are these:

> The first approach is pre-historical & archaeological 38,550 BCE
> The second approach is pastoral & anthropological 429 BCE
> The third approach is theological & historical 1613
> The fourth approach is digital & technological 1720
> The fifth approach is psychological & legal 1889
> The sixth approach is social & sensible 1964
> The seventh approach is tactical & critical 2012

Although there is a nominally chronological order to these approaches, pre-historical and archaeological come before theological and historical, which in turn come before psychological and legal, it is stressed that these approaches are considered as coeval. All this means is that rather than one following the other, in the way that Richard Southern's various stages follow each other, they all pre-exist each other and emerge and diverge at various moments at which performance and theatre are most interestingly related and relatable. The reversal of the common ordering of the technological and the digital might further point to these kinds of reversals and chronological complications. What is more, these approaches do not exist alone, like disciplines that have somehow been etched out of the fabric of the everyday, never to return to their points of reference, but rather exist in a continuous tension with each other. Hence the manner of braiding two figures side by side as an 'Approach', suggesting the tension that continuously exists between fields & disciplines.

For instance, an Approach that is described as Pre-Historical & Archaeological is one that takes seriously prehistories and the depth of the field being explored, but does not eschew the complications of space and time that these two categories invite us to consider. In a non-binary, Trinitarian world, these combinations will not suit those who believe that any thinking that operates from the apparent stability of a table with four legs (2×2) is one that necessarily misses the delightfully unbalanced surprises of the rickety table with three. But this book, while respecting and celebrating those who have been propping these tables up for a while now (including Jon McKenzie in his book *Perform Or Else*), will diagram these processes in the spirit of Rosalind Krauss's formative essay. And it has to be said that Krauss was not fearful of binaries if they served her purpose of dislodging the manner in which patriarchal continuities of historicist incorporation levelled off and diluted all that was invigorating and disturbing about contemporary artistic making (most often by those women whose work appeared rarely to appear in such histories).

Theatre in the Expanded Field continues a similar line of enquiry to those described by Krauss and Southern, both concerning themselves with the 'spatial' as a mode of understanding an old discipline extended into a multi-faceted modern world. The motive of finding an equivalent 'expanded field' for theatre is to expose the establishment and architecture of theatre to a process whereby, as Karl Marx said of modernity's force, 'all that is solid melts into air', and the proscenium arch and red curtains (much like the pedestal in sculpture and the frame in painting) are seen for what they are, a fanfare around the illusion of (and disillusionment with) the classical form. There is nothing new in this process of course when it comes to other genres. Since the endeavours of the London Film Makers' Cooperative in the 1970s, film has always had its own history of a sustaining and unsettling 'Expanded Cinema', a history that was very well represented in the Tate *Tanks* in 2012 for its opening series of installations.

The seven approaches to performance proposed in this work address the subject area through many shifting perceptions and ways of viewing the world as detailed above, but it should also importantly be recognised that this process has occurred through a time of financial austerity following a heightened period of capitalist excess and fiscal chaos. Marcel Duchamp's 'ready-mades' and the *Arte Povera* movement of the 1960s–1980s taught us variously in the twentieth century that the objects we have abandoned are able to be re-used re-invigorated or re-habilitated to form new relationships and meanings. The image of the world's children who scavenge from heaps of twenty-first-century garbage where this 'recycling' can become a meagre currency tells us we are living in a world of Marie Antoinette ethics where abandonment does not only describe the neglect of disciplines. We may, in such an economic climate, increasingly feel that the intervention of theatre as 'event' in the real world surpasses the importance of a hallowed event on a sacred stage. Perhaps, fifty years after Richard Southern wrote *The Seven Ages of the Theatre*, we no longer need new buildings for the production and appreciation of new ideas, but can find ways of recycling or intervening in other realms and disciplines in an expanded field of performance.

We should step outside the performance studies frame to view ''Theatre' (in its base theatricality, abandonment and all) and 'Performance', its irritating and irritable other, as braided like a Moebius strip in twentieth and twenty-first century's cultural production. To do so would be to edge closer to the sort of ground encouraged by Beth Hoffman in her essay 'Radicalism and the Theatre in Genealogies of Live Art' referred to earlier.[31] But beyond this encouragement, two rather different objects of cultural interest invite us to think not just *in* the theatre but also *through* the theatre.

The first is the century-long ascendancy of the quotidian now reaching into all forms of media production that has been roundly documented by the simultaneously proliferating discipline of Cultural Studies. Early in that process my own work, *Theatre & Everyday Life: An Ethics of Performance,* written in the 1990s concerned itself with popular culture as well as what is generally termed 'Theatre'. But since that moment the voyeuristic eye of television's *The Family, Big Brother* or celebrities in the jungle represent this change much more broadly in public taste, way beyond the rather limited and niche domains of artistic processes.

At the time of writing, the 2012 genre of British reality television includes the confusingly hybrid form of *The Only Way Is Essex* (aka TOWIE) and *Made in Chelsea*, where the storyline is taken from the 'known form' (be it Soap Opera, Sophocles or Shakespeare) but is acted out in a 'spontaneous' manner by 'real' people. The need to suspend disbelief has returned. Where the cameras were technologically remote or hidden in *The Jungle, The Family* or the *Big Brother* house, we can no longer pretend that the whole sound and camera team is not present in the Bluebird Café in Chelsea or The Sugar Hut in Essex. At the start of each episode of Channel 4's TOWIE we are told by voice-over: 'These people are real, but some of what they do has been set up purely for your entertainment' (2012). The strict rules of engagement have been broken, the 'but' in that sentence has become all-important.

How then are we to engage with such a form of cultural production as the popular context for this book? The image of a known carrier, be it the shape of a soap opera or an opera stage, is electrified by the live action of unscripted players or the confrontation of physicality of those who perform. Imagine finding (as Richard Southern and Rosalind Krauss have done in their texts) drawings, diagrams and spatial or physical forms, other than words, to convey just such a constellation of forces. We have chosen not to frame these figures as the book proceeds, to suggest ways in which the actions inscribed are ones which bleed beyond the border of the page into the gutter and beyond.

The second invitation to consider these relations between Performance and Theatre comes from our own experience, yours as a reader and mine as a writer (for the moment), of their relations over the same period of half a century under discussion in this introduction. For me a pivotal moment of rule-breaking for theatre came a good deal earlier than these cultural manifestations of the quotidian, in 1983, with the production of Jan Fabre's *The Power of Theatrical Madness* set in an opera house, acting out episodes of grandiose theatricality punctured by performance banalities. A scene from this work, costumed figures offset against a 'field', illustrates the front cover of this book. The pomp and ceremony, the red velvet and gold ornament, high 'culture' and the smoke and mirrors of theatrical illusion were here operating alongside the physical means of theatre image production. In all this glory, characters appear naked and members of the cast are thrown back from the front of the stage into the orchestra pit over and over again.

Thirty years ago I sat transfixed by this performance. I was attending the *Theatre of Nations* festival in Nancy in North East France looking for an antidote to the British parochialisms of the National Theatre and Royal Shakespeare Company, in those days before the foundation of the London International Festival of Theatre and the internationalisation of British theatre, which still largely lay in the future. I had walked from the energetic discussions that were being hosted on the fringes of the festival to the Opera House to see the work of a young director. I had heard of an earlier piece that Jan Fabre had made with a portentous title: *This Is Theatre as It Was to Be Expected and Foreseen* (1981). The successor to this piece, in Nancy, appeared to have settled like a virus upon the opulent opera house, turning its lush interiors inside out as it got to grips with the occupation of its stage by something which appeared to be of its dinner-jacketed species, but threatened to overturn its demure protocols.

At one point in the action a brutal sequence which seemed to have been going on for eternity (this was after all a four-hour show without interval) came to some sort of denouement with the young women, who had formerly been on the stage, being kept from it, hurled back from it by the equally young men. While everyone seemed to be playing to the traditions of the surroundings, taking note both of the history of where they were and the expectations one might bring to such a place, this did not stop them from turning this tradition upon its head and revealing it for what it was, a long history of exclusion and abandonment (Figure 0.3).

I was not only drawn to the exquisite soaring soundtrack, combining Mahler and heightened lyrical works over the most mundane actions, but was riveted by the gestures, movements and technical dexterity of the performers, who though they looked like theatre people had something of the dancer, the salon habituée and the sporting prodigy about them. They were, it appeared to me, from another

Figure 0.3 Jan Fabre, *The Power of Theatrical Madness*, Nancy, 1983

place. They occupied both the stage on which they strutted and simultaneously another world of performance that they insisted on injecting into the longeurs of the action as it unfolded in stately operatic time. They appeared to be playing out some sort of autobiographical narrative while covering themselves throughout in the panoply of theatrical deceit, the paraphernalia of past events on this and other stages which appeared in the scenes like some freight from another era of theatricality and spectacle. Here revelation after revelation flowed in a sequence as moving as it was momentous, while there was apparently nothing they could do to escape their circumstances. This was everything they could be getting on with in the meantime, from smoking cigarettes to smashing dinner plates, and they showed it.

But more than all this, what became apparent in the performance, as much as by subterfuge as through sense, was a profound melancholic meditation on the long history of theatre's resistance to community. I cannot discount that such a 'reading' of what I saw was disproportionately shaped by my imminent departure, in 1983, to London, to take responsibility for a neighbourhood theatre, for which the term 'community', let alone dare I say it, community theatre, would have been the pre-eminent markers of the cultural moment. But I also, sitting there, had to account for why I suspected what I was watching in this Opera House, in this opulent setting, was touching the very nerve that would irritate me throughout the coming decade's work, in such a different setting, in the derelict, dilapidated and sometime delinquent margins of Docklands London at a time of political crisis and upheaval.

What was obvious here was that community, as it was being played out by this troupe of performers, could not be conceived as simply a wider subjectivity, simply a multiplication of selves, joining those individuals at odds with each other, on the stage, to those of us in the audience whose expansion was a measure of a 'loss' up there, as one after another who could not survive on the stage were hurled amongst us. It was not that this property that made us cohere as a community, an audience, was a matter of adding those who fell back into our own number to save themselves from the brutal blows being reigned on them by the male sovereigns of the stage. We were already a 'Full House' after all; we had long 'sold out' and in the fashion peculiar to the French amongst all theatre goers, individuals had prostrated themselves at the opera house steps, bearing begging notes to be allowed to join those who were privileged to be admitted, a 'paying public' derived from a people whom they yearned to be counted amongst.

As these actresses 'joined us', bruised, but being Fabre's company, Belgian and beatific, it was not that their presence enhanced our own; there was nothing 'proper' to us in this instance. And it was in this sequence of 'lacks' that I learnt something on that night about the elusive quality of community that might once have been presumed, or pre-figured, or predicted for just such a gathering, just such an assembly for theatrical show. As those performers who had become actresses now became women, joined us in the stalls, their distance from us was palpable, and our distance from each other, more so. In this falling between heightened stage and lowly auditorium a 'rend' opened up between one surface of faces looking up and another looking down. And it was in this rend, rather than anything more akin to a substance, object or property, that one could sense that something was at stake for any condition of community here, any community to come.

The thirtieth anniversary revival of *The Power of Theatrical Madness* took place in Antwerp just the other day for more sold-out houses, on the eve of my completing this book. It has not been uncommon for works that once might have been defined by their precariousness at a certain historical moment to have been recovered against the performance grain, to be restaged for another audience, many of whom who would have little idea of the significance of this work's first outing on a European tour at which it blazed across the opera house schedules, laying waste the conventional repertoire. The return of *The Power of Theatrical Madness* to European stages is perhaps, if only in title, a pressing reminder of the longevity of an apparently abandoned theatre, the persistence of the irritant that is performance, in the expanded field.

First Approach
Pre-Historical & Archaeological

The room that you are reading this in almost certainly has walls. I would like you to look up for a moment from the page and look at them. They could be the walls of a café, a library or a waiting room, but you will know they are *your* walls if you have taken them for granted, maybe for a long time. Take a minute to re-acquaint yourself with these walls. You might have decorated them, papered them, adorned them, mirrored them or mounted things upon them, but these things that you have done to these walls will themselves have become, more or less, taken for granted.

It was Vilém Flusser, the philosopher and historian of media, who first suggested that putting things on walls is what makes humans *cultural* animals.[1] Living between walls, as humans tend to do, appears to encourage most humans to strive to make the best of them. But now I want you to move beyond the contained room that Flusser imagined you in. Just think now how things would differ should one of these walls be removed and the room you are in becomes exposed to the world outside. The space that was once a room, with mediating walls, would now resemble the stage of a theatre upon which your moves, your feelings and your words would become the stuff of comedy or tragedy, a performance for those beyond this fourth wall that has disappeared – for those whom we might call here, for want of a better word, an audience.

If you make lots of tea and constantly discuss moving to a nearby city, the name for what you are doing is *The Three Sisters*; if you are an older man and have had an argument with your daughters, an onlooker might call you *King Lear*. I won't go into details about the social conditions that might pass in this room for *Antigone*, given what happened after she was walled up, but you can guess. You do not have to step outside to imagine what the walls of your home look like, even when one has disappeared. The reason you can conjure this up is that you have an idea of what a wall looks like, you could call this an *ideal* kind of wall, and when you have this idea it does not have to subscribe to the look, scale or elevation of the walls you are looking at now.

In this sense we are all, still, cavemen of sorts, cave-persons at least, troglodytes, whose relationship with the walls within which *they* lived, the walls *they* decorated with handprints in their caves in Peche Merle, was part of a continual effort to not take quite as much for granted about what protected them from the elements and the animals outside; that is, the elements and animals that they knew existed beyond the gaping aperture, at the end of the cave, where there was no wall. And we are still cavemen of sorts, or cave people, to the degree that our understanding of what constitutes a community beyond these walls that announce the end of our privacy remains limited by a failure of imagination that shapes everything performance can reasonably do.

It would be premature to presume that our understanding of what lies beyond that fourth wall is any more sophisticated than our ancestor in the cave, and indeed given the rich pictorial record we have at our disposal of the relations that were pursued between those beings inside and outside the cave, it would be plain wrong. But it is undeniable that in manifesting this relation between one community of sorts and another, between humans reliant upon proximate animals for their survival as well as their spiritual and emotional well-being, it is hard to say otherwise why so much effort would have been expended on the aesthetic rather than the utilitarian; it is undeniable that something about performance became possible at this moment that would not have been possible in quite the same way before. And I am not talking about Ritual here, whatever that slippery word stands for. There is no need for something so complicated and demanding of ethnographers' expertise, no reason on earth to deploy appeals to the sacrificial, if what we seek is the generating principles of performance among humans, the performance gene.

When humans first blew earth-red pigment from their mouths towards their hand placed upon the cave wall, *they* were doing what *we* have been doing to the walls around us ever since. But 40,000 years ago, in those caves of Peche Merle and Chauvet, humans stepped back, and away from that wall, removing their hand, and in that moment witnessed themselves *at a distance* for the first time, now an onlooker to what was their own handprint, but now part of a larger composition.

Is it fanciful, the writer Marie-José Mondzain asks, to consider this very action the 'invention of the spectator'?[2] I would like to take Mondzain's imaginative proposition seriously for a moment, but progress it to a place for which she cannot be held responsible, so far out as it is from the boundaries deemed sensible by philosophical restraint. Is this the moment when *Homo Faber*, the one who works, or *Homo Ludens*, the one who plays, becomes *Homo Spectator*, the one who watches? It is all very well for everyone to work and everyone to play; Karl Marx and Johan Huizinga would have appreciated the equality in such an arrangement, but such continuous equality of action does not account for the commensurate degree of *reaction* upon which a performance economy could be built. If this is the case and the kind of economy a book of this kind might wish to build its propositions upon, then I want to ask: Who is the watcher *watching with*? What might *Homo Spectator* be *looking at*?

It took just 37,000 years for someone to write an answer down to that question, an answer that would survive the travails of climate, the vicissitudes of war and the precariousness of what had to remain pre-history because there was, as yet, no retrievable record. Don't worry, we will be returning to the more interesting pre-history of performance in a moment, but perhaps inevitably we have to briefly take a detour via an extant text to shore up the strain on the imagination that such pre-historic speculation demands.

It was Plato, the Greek philosopher, who wrote a story about this spectator that for two millennia has captured the popular imagination, which is surprising, given it took place in a dank cave. It is a myth, a narrative, a legend that played a small part, in a big work, on the form of the ideal Republic, and follows several lively passages of dialogue between his teacher and brother, Socrates and Glaucon, as to the nature of justice and education.

For some, this story will be about as familiar as the walls you have taken for granted. But for others, the story, as Plato conceived it, goes like this:

Picture men dwelling in a sort of subterranean cavern with a long entrance open to the light on its entire width. Conceive them as having their legs and necks fettered from childhood, so that they remain in the same spot, able to look forward only, and prevented by the fetters from turning their heads. Picture further the light from a fire burning higher up, and at a distance behind them, and between the fire and the prisoners, and above them, a road along which a low wall has been built, as the exhibition of puppet shows have partitions before the men themselves, above which they show the puppets.

'All that I see' replies Glaucon, [and Socrates continues describing something that, years later, surely influenced the producers of the UK TV series *The Generation Game*]:

'See also, then, men carrying past the wall implements of all kinds that rise above the wall, and human images and shapes of animals as well, wrought in stone and wood and every material, some of these bearers presumably speaking and others silent.'

'A strange image you speak of' Glaucon said 'and strange prisoners.'

Like to us says Socrates. For to begin with, tell me, do you think that these men would have seen anything of themselves or of one another except the shadows cast from the fire of the wall of the cave that fronted them?

How could they Glaucon said if they were compelled to hold their heads unmoved through life.[3]

The dialogue continues, raising the spectre that the shadows seen on the wall, of the humans, animals and objects, the sounds echoing from the wall from their cries, would be perceived by the prisoners as a reality. This *illusion*, as Plato wants to encourage his reader to think of it, would only be dispelled should the prisoners be released from their chains, to see for the first time their own situation, and to emerge from the cave into the sunlight that would illuminate things *as they are.*

Those 'forced' to be brave enough to make that upward journey, and Plato suggests living under the spell of illusion might be more comfortable than such freedom, despite the seating arrangements, would first experience shadows above. But they would gradually adjust to the light and, in an act that young people should not try at home, see the Truth, the Good, by staring at the sun itself. Having experienced enlightenment, Plato then expected them to give up on their new life and return below to educate those still wasting their time at the spectacle in the cavern.

Despite some other benefits that Plato brought to the table, it has to be admitted at this point that performance in general and theatre in particular are not getting the best of starts here in the philosophical record. But Plato's antagonism to the mimetic practices to which we have given names such as performance and theatre, his preference was for terms in Greek with the translations poetry and dance, is contrarily perhaps the best possible start to defending performance from its detractors – a remorseless and continuous detraction that was described by Jonas Barish as 'anti-theatrical prejudice'. And as this book takes seriously the idea of a long history of performance as being somehow endemic or constitutive of human being, it makes sense to acknowledge from the outset precisely this ideological commitment to performance as something that improves that human life rather than inhibits it.

Given Plato's professional instinct for clarifying these matters, it would be as well to be clear where we differ on this from the outset in case we assume that those who have been rewarded in history by the endurance of their oeuvre, and their archive (Plato would be a prime case of someone who got very lucky in this respect), somehow intrinsically have more to say about the things we are interested in through performance than those who were not so fortunate – those whose work remains anonymous, lost or extinct. In this chapter, for instance, we will see how two manifestations of imagery over writing, the cave wall and the ceramic tile, are both at least as rich and as abundant as Plato's texts, but have had very little attention from precisely those whose interest one would have thought would be in keeping with the physical, image-rich rhetorics of performance, rather than the two-dimensional page with its alphabetic digital code.

So, before we leave the cave for this *supposed* enlightenment we should dwell on this scene in the cave, which like the walls around us, we have, perhaps, taken for granted.

It is a most peculiar scene, and especially so when coming to it, as I do, as someone who works in and through performance, who cherishes what is special about performance's irritation of theatre and theatricality, beyond the privacy of our walls. For if this caved-in life is the stuff of dreams, illusions, where does that leave performance, not just in Plato's ideal Republic, but for us, wherever we are, now?

The Cave that Plato has Socrates describe is a particular *kind* of theatre, or, as the writer and philosopher Samuel Weber would prefer, a particular *interpretation* of a theatre.[4] It is unmistakeably a theatre nonetheless. And there are two things that mark it out as such for Weber that have nothing to do with the upsetting fact that Plato mentions *puppets*, strange figures we are all understandably dubious about from childhood.

First we are invited to picture a defined, limited place, a positioning of the people and things that are constitutive of what is taking place there. This is the first characteristic of a theatre for Weber: the events it depicts are *not indifferent* to their placement. Performance as distinct to theatre might, as the Preliminary laid out, give the impression it can be more *laissez faire* about such arrangements, but by the nature of performance all is conscious from the outset of a framing that gives that something the title 'performance'. It must be admitted, however, that in this myth the cavern has been *fabricated*; it is a theatre in which the prisoners see a highly organised, staged spectacle. This is more West End or Broadway than PS122 or the Institute of Contemporary Arts (ICA). Shadows are apprehended as reality because a fire, which is natural, has been set up precisely to create this artifice. It has been placed behind them in such a way as to be unavailable to them, yet to deliver its special effects.

The second theatrical trait for Weber in this famous scene is the no-less constitutive role of *spectators*. A theatrical scene after all is one that plays to others, called variously spectators, with a subtle difference to those Mondzain identified in the cave, or given sound is involved here too, perhaps *audience* might be more accurate a description. But what is unsettling here is that Plato's protagonists are spectators of a very peculiar kind; they are *riveted* to their places. They are prisoners unaware of their imprisonment; they have been there since childhood. So it is not quite as riveting as *The Mousetrap* in London, or *Perfect Crime* in New York, which seems to have been going on for an eternity, but almost.

It should be noted that not *all* the inhabitants of the cave are fixed to the ground, or their seats, or however they are riveted. There are also, importantly for Samuel Weber and for me, if less so for Plato, a shadowy group of stagehands who carry things past this wall, artists or roadies. It is hard to know quite how Plato conceives of these on the one hand technically 'free', but nevertheless 'labouring' others who are contracted to work in support of the illusion. How do *these* people relate to the spellbound audience of spectator prisoners? How do they relate to the organisation of the spectacle itself? Plato is resistant to such questions of theatre, and theatrical labour, as his metaphysical pursuit of Truth would be seriously derailed if he had to admit that this whole scene is one dependent on an external economy of market forces; like all the best cultural acts, this one cannot be free of an *outside* however *inside* it would appear.

And this provides us with a second serious problem in taking Plato, for performance at least, too prescriptively. Despite the fact that this Myth forms part of a work painstakingly detailing the ideal Republic, it does seem very sketchy indeed on what passes for the conditions of cultural production that would prevail in any such State. Performance has been figured from the outset here as something free-floating of economic determinants. Those acting are literally shadowy figures who are unlikely to have the benefit of a trade union such as Equity to support them should an extra show be added at the last minute to cater for an upswing in prisoners. And the audience would appear to be here free to remain as long as they have to, at show after show, despite the obvious fact that they are imprisoned and do not appear to have bought tickets. If there was ever a more derogatory founding myth for drama in cultures beyond the Greco-Roman European, it would be hard to imagine it. So we do need to attend to its pervasive power here in a book that seeks to unsettle some of the premises of performance.

Indeed, from this moment on, the necessarily image-led world of performance was to be condemned by successive generations of educated commentators operating in the name of Plato's Truth against the veneer of spectacle, an anti-theatrical prejudice that performance is an unruly ornament to human life, rather than what it is – the irritable gene – the thing that makes *living human life* possible in the first place, as I want to rather outlandishly suggest. The theatre like the cave has historically been denied any exteriority, any significant meaning in the more real world, beyond artifice and aesthetics. This prejudice started here in the Cave, and it has finished up in the room that you are in now, the one with the walls.

But contrary to our popular presumption as to what makes for a decent cave, this is *not* a self-contained space; it has a long entrance open to the light 'on its entire width'. Plato says it, not me, and in doing so he gives away his reluctance to bury bad news for the Republic quite as securely as he would appear to suggest. This is very surprising indeed and is hardly ever mentioned in commentaries on this episode. It does not perhaps quite suit our stereotype of a cave – that *this* cave, Plato's cave, should be so explicitly *open* to its outside. If it has such an entrance it sounds not that different to the room I am now imagining you in as I am writing these words. It is certainly, at the very least, a very 'open prison'.

Plato's 'opening' allows me to ignore his intemperate insistence on cutting this cavernous theatre off from its world, his attempt to figure the shadowy theatre in stark contrast to immutable Truth in the glare of the sun. It compels me to evoke a less metaphysical, more material alternative to this tale on behalf of performance and in distinction to Plato's theatre. It demands a pre-history of performance that takes more seriously the cave itself, or at least 'a cave' if we are not going to essentialise cavernous openings and their theatres in quite the way Plato has so unhelpfully done. So, not quite The Cave as evoked by Plato, but caves in the plural, perhaps livelier and more detailed in their dimensions, more materialist than mythic, more performative than proscenium.

I am well equipped to draw a distinction between Plato's Cave-like theatre and an alternative pre-history of performance given that I am, as I have said, a theatre lover, who enjoys sitting in dark spaces looking forward, rarely turning to the side, concentrating on shadowy spectacles of illusory love. The 'prisoners', despite what some performance studies specialists who have swallowed their anti-theatrical prejudice from Plato might wish, are, from where I am sitting at least, not really prisoners at all; their way of seeing marks them out as a typical theatre audience. *They are us*. Socrates was right. We are there of our own accord and insist, in a Screen Age for which theatre should have absolutely no attraction, that we retain a peculiar appetite for doing something that despite all faux revolutions to the contrary has remained remarkably consistent since Plato's first description of it. And, if Audiences 'R Us, to coin an inclusive phrase, then I would like to know more about what brought us to such a state of celebration in the security of theatrical spectacle, as well as submission to its sly, stagey civility in performance.

Stone Age

Following Plato, if all writing about theatre would appear to be between a rock and a hard place, between an imprisoning Cave and an ideal Republic which cannot tolerate poetic mimicry, then we might remember that performance has a pre-history that is not only as material as it is conceptual and mental but also as imaginative as it is indicative. Myth might be mobilised in a somewhat different direction to that followed by Plato should we pay heed to the echoes of that subterranean chamber now, echoes that are felt reverberating through performance's recent history as well as its pasts. To this point we have been drawing upon the philosophical imagination of Plato and Marie-José Mondzain. To pursue the question of how Mondzain's singular spectator, *homo spectator*, was *already and always* part of a congregation, a collective or a community of watching well before Plato's prisoners, will require not more philosophical imagination in the absence of history but an imaginative philosophy from a more recent past.

The cavernous elevations of a public housing project might appear a peculiar location within which to start this search for the crowd that precedes the individual, but an act of falling, about as primeval an act as one could imagine, provides us with a connection to the near present. In a founding narrative of Mathieu Kassovitz's film *La Haine*, the coruscating 1990s film of *les banlieues* on the outskirts of Paris, the protagonist of the film tells of two youngsters who have just thrown themselves off a high building. In an ironic inversion of Plato's Cave, here enlightenment proceeds by way of descent. Half way down one turns to the other and says: 'So far so good'. Remaining in the recent past, and in London rather than Paris, in a founding narrative, *The World in Pictures (2006)* by UK-based performance collective Forced Entertainment, Jerry Killick shares an interminable, well twenty-minute, tall tale about an individual taking the same route to the ground. The sudden suspension of this tale for the sake of a show, the retelling of the founding myth of humanity, from Stone Age to digital age, suggests there is more to be said in the time between one man falling and another following.

Both narratives would appear to recognise the futility of presuming the efficaciousness or indeed existence of community, yet both the film and performance seek a collective means to express the affirmation of community as an act of defiance. The mordant humour of the falling men in their collective expression of optimism in *La Haine* plays off against the split personality of the lonely figure in Forced Entertainment's 'play', appealing to a company of colleagues as to how he might improve his theatrical rendition of suicidal flight, his extinction.[5] Both of course are insufficient means of representing the fate of such precarious subjects in this world, but both in their recognition of the impedimenta to any theatrical fidelity to such an event draw us closer to the side effects of performance that generate laughter and poignancy simultaneously. We don't laugh at their suffering, but we laugh with them as sufferers of a different order. Our degree of distance within an order of suffering, itself a form of collective for which the word 'audience' might apply, allows us to judge ourselves fit to continue beyond the venue of witness and become responsible once again for others' plights.

Both men – one cinematic, the other present – would appear to be telling us something about suffering, while suffering. This is interesting in the context of Plato's fear about the power of theatre that we have been considering so far in this chapter, for Plato was specifically concerned about the moral threat that might accompany an act of imitation in which suffering was rendered by a third party, a performer of poetry. If we wish to progress Plato's thought here towards performance rather than away from it, perhaps in a homeopathic act of recruitment against his better judgement, then we could do worse than to adopt an ally in one of his philosophical colleagues, and one who while working in the contemporary continental tradition takes the power of images and their unsettling association with suffering just as seriously.

'The end of representation is not in sight', the French philosopher Jean-Luc Nancy says at the outset of his work *The Birth to Presence*, by which I take it he means there is no presumed terminus to image making despite the fact that it is as 'old as the West', as he puts the concurrency of humanity and humanity's figuring of itself.[6] Nancy would appear to contest Plato's fear of such secondary orders of representation when he not only equates the epoch of the specifically *Western* human with such representation but also insists that there is no such thing as humanity without its constituent representations. Extending Nancy, therefore, beyond where he might be willing to go but is necessary for our argument here, representations effected through performance are not a consequence, an after-effect of our sense of being culturally formed beings, but a *founding*

Figure 1.1 Forced Entertainment, *The World in Pictures*, London, 2006

constituent of humanity and animality and their relation to each other prior to cultural capacity and its communications. Representation-forming systems are ontological to *all* species rather than the preserve of 'people like us', zoological rather than homological. They are the measure of our irritability more than they are the source of our signs (Figure 1.1).

If Jean-Luc Nancy had been to Riverside Studios to see that Forced Entertainment performance, he might have recognised in Jerry Killick's undoing of himself the peculiar manner in which representations only become visible at those moments where they are at risk of their own collapse. Nancy puts this process like this in *The Birth to Presence*: 'Representation is what determines itself by its own limit'.[7] A limitless virtuosity would render performance invisible amidst a technique so total as to proscribe human affect. The continuous essaying of representation, the repeated attempts in the theatre by the forced entertainer Jerry Killick to 'get his story right', or at least 'get his story half-decent', designates the dynamic *inoperativeness* of theatre of course, but also the inoperativeness of any community to whom we appeal when we suffer. Not one of this theatre collective, a theatre cooperative apparently made up of friends if not family, appears to be able to offer anything like the coherent summative advice that might be able to move him on. The interruptive processes that go to form this collective's modus operandi as performers are exactly this re-presenting, that is presenting again and again, of the most pressing questions, the most serious matters of concern. When audiences leaving *The World in Pictures* commented on it being 'like torture', and I heard that phrase used on more than one occasion at Riverside Studios in London, I took that to be something of a definition of a good night out, a definition indeed of human irritability. It was after all only *like* torture, which meant it was not torture but performance, which unlike torture will end. So it is to this tortuous, yet not tortured repetition, this capacity for irritation, that I want to give the name 'performance' once again.

Performance in the last human venue, the one we are currently inhabiting before our inevitable ecological demise, thus becomes not that different to the spectatorial process of adjustment described by Marie-José Mondzain in the first human venue, the constant recalling and testing of the *faithfulness of the representations*, the fidelity of the theatrical event and of course listening for the signs of animals and others there-out. In this sense we perceive echoes of a cave and a spectator as imagined by Mondzain, checking their hand against its representation on a wall. It is no longer a question of whether Jerry's story is true or not, but rather the degree of faithfulness his telling has to the fidelity of the event he describes. In its dreadful inadequacy, a collective of care is inaugurated, not just for those who operate under the name Forced Entertainment, between that performer, this audience and those other cast members, but for someone who might otherwise leave us quite cold in the smug sense of his own self-attraction. This is the critical contrariness of cultural creation, and performance in particular, that we can empathise with the inadequate, a delight in disappointment that Plato seems to have understood but overestimated.

This contrariness of performance, its power to disappoint rather than exceed expectations, might provide us with neat, anti-Platonic conceit, but in the spirit of working with, rather than against Plato, I would appeal here for a more nuanced sense of what such an audience is that might feel such disappointment. We might here begin to extend Mondzain's imagination of a singular spectator towards the multiplication of such spectators through the constitution of a collective, a collective we might reasonably presume to be somehow essential to the theatre act. To this end, there is another way to look at this question of assembly in a cave that performance seeking something more than the condescension of an imprisoned audience might do well to consider. And this will require me to reverse the excision of the political from theatre that I have recommended elsewhere, an attempt to prompt performance back to its truer politics well away from the dogmatic instrumentalism of political imperatives.[8] In so doing one might follow our same philosopher, Jean-Luc Nancy, in proposing that 'the political is the place where community as such is brought into play'.[9] If politics are brought *into play*, in other words performatively by the coming together of the collective, then the means by which performance mediates a shift from a singular spectator to some kind of community of awareness would seem to be moot.

Inverting the common direction of thought and argument when it comes to 'audience studies' from the singular eye to the many, from an originary individual to a secondary group, from the solo self to the collective, it is for Jean-Luc Nancy at least, and I would say equally for the residents of the caves we have been considering, the situation of 'being in common' that gives rise to the experience of being self. It is obvious that 'being plural' (in the cave then, in country and city now) comes before being singular, in that there was never a situation into which a 'one' was born outside company; there was always someone else, and often many others, there, before you. There is, and always was, someone there to receive you however quickly they might abandon you. It is only *through* such community that one is posed within the context of an exterior sensibility, and that one experiences an outside to one's self and you. In Nancy's provocative term, you become 'exposed' in such a condition. The photographic metaphor is not wholly inappropriate in Plato's Cave, though never used by Nancy, for the singular being only becomes present *in their exposure* as they leave the dark-boxed aperture for the light of the sun and the Truth. Indeed, for Plato identity is subject to such an exposure in the sun's light to the Truth and what passes for life below is not worthy of that name. You could, taking a pre-digital photographic logic to its end, thus call life in the cave, for Plato at least, undeveloped.

But this linking of community of the Republic with departure from the immunity of Plato's Cave is not quite right either. There is 'nothing out there' when it comes down to it (or goes up to it); the highest endeavour for Plato's newly enlightened citizens, despite all the attractions of the new Republic, is in fact to *return* to the Cave to educate those who remain imprisoned below in the shadowy world of theatrical illusion. But if we think of caves in the 37,000 years prior to Plato, in all their populated diversity, rather than Plato's Cave in its peculiar philosophical isolation, we can imagine a rather more responsive relationship between that exterior and interior, that community and its essaying of representations; for those other caves would appear to have something of the character of the performance space about them, and a rather more relational space than Plato allows for with his riveted customers. Such caves would appear to subscribe to the origin of the word *venue* in its French ancestry: the recognition of something 'coming to' (from *venir*) the community of the cave in this more material, less mythic sense. The cave was, after all, presumably the primordial venue for such human 'coming to' and together, not as Plato suggested in serried ranks, in forced entertainment, but in three-dimensional disordered depth and amongst, not against or contra to, animality. The geological and palaeontology record suggests a variety of ways this would have been the case, not least of all in the form of collective cooking and ceremony, but also in the remarkable number of child handprints that indicate such places were wholly cognisant of the imaginative intensity of the 'yet-to-be adult' and gave due regard and prominence of position to these playful expressions.

The presupposition I would then like to contest here is that communities of this, or any kind, are necessarily *human*, and that it is through community that humans register something of that which is essential to their humanness. Reversing this egoistic, hyper-humanistic, goal-oriented ambition, Jean-Luc Nancy suggests a far more enigmatic but useful velocity for performance and proposes the opposite of the dynamic from self to collective that we might have expected: 'the individual is merely the residue of the experience of the dissolution of community'.[10] Or in our own terms, Marie-José Mondzain's imagined spectator working solo against the wall is not the origin of anything but the retreating *remains* of a collective who once watched together. The artist followed their audience in this respect.

Like the ruins and fragments of Rome that Freud so loved and pictured on his consulting room-walls (see Chapter 5), like the stone pediments scattered to the side of the stage at the Theatre Antique in Arles, the parts of the whole only become singularly visible on the dissolution of the entity they once were. This is what we see when we see the bones and the stones in the caves. It is in this historical reverse of their later arrangement that they become apparent, and they really have no identity prior to that forming. The collective or the assembly in this sense only understands itself on its dissolution into the 'singular identity' of what we have called *Homo Spectator*. It is only when we perceive the lonely spectator stepping away from the wall that we understand the group from which they undoubtedly depart to make such an act readable as singularly artistic in its motives.

If a certain resistance to representation and repetition has left performance studies increasingly concerned with questions of mourning the loss of its materiality, its ephemeral status, then the 'loss of community' has surely pervaded theatre studies with its elegiac air. The point being made here, rather, is that despite the obituaries for its loss, community *cannot be lost* because it has not taken place, yet. We have been waiting for community since our time in the caves, and it cannot come yet, for an apparently simple reason. Jean-Luc Nancy makes this reason clear when he says: 'community, far from being what society has crushed or lost, is what happens to us.'[11] Community is in this sense neither a work to be produced, unlike the collective in the process of expansion, nor is it the figure of a lost communion beloved of the nostalgia for neighbourhood, but it is the experience of an outside to the self as a space, a proportion or even a measure. And I would suggest it would have been the caves, as we understand their diversity here, that would have provided just that space of an early, if not 'first', measurement for the performance gene of the *homo sapiens*. It is this experience of the community that makes us able to be irritated in the first place, and paradoxically given we are talking about something that often implies loss of subjectivity, makes us be singular, sovereign subjects. It is in this sense that the spectator who registers themselves *as spectator* is also the participant of a community who have nothing in common but the faculty to be aware of themselves as a distinct watcher among the watching. Audiences are by this measure invisible to us as we are by definition lost amongst them, and this of course is their elusive strength.

The representations of falling men in performance and film discussed at the beginning of this part of the chapter are just that, representations in narrative. Each is set off and materially distinguished from other deaths of a different nature, more palpable, more material elsewhere. In *La Haine* the comparisons to material mortality are obvious; kids die in these conditions of poverty and racist hate. In the case of the representation of *The World in Pictures*, the primal scene is represented by a return to the cave and to the origins of aesthetic man and woman distinguishing themselves from mere animality (see Figure 1.1). But this founding moment of 'man', birth, that which is essential to man, his ability to fail to represent other animals with fidelity, is also the birth of man's ability to consciously conceal the inherent inhumanity that accompanies all acts of failed representation, when that act of representation is one which concerns fidelity to another species and its distinction to human being. These dark workings, or work in the dark of the caves, provide the location of not only the first human venue but also the last human venue.

The caves I have been talking about have names, unlike Plato's idealised subterranean world, and they can be found, and were, are and will be. And they have histories as they, at least at a late point in their development, became humanised by those who occupied them. It is in Chauvet and Lascaux in continental Europe that (pre-French) human-animals first made representations of their own strangeness in the melée of another collective of figures with something in common. The self-knowledge of humans here was of their inherent *strangeness* to those others depicted there on the walls – bison, horses and stags. Their hands were different when they looked back at them. The human, Jean-Luc Nancy says in this context, is the stranger, but 'monstrously similar'. The human is already associated with its prey. Thus, in a performative inversion: 'The similar came before the self and that is what it, the self, was'.[12] Nancy identifies the pleasure 'man' takes in mimetic acts as this troubling strangeness. Performance plays out and plays back this estrangement in the caves to allow for the pursuit of the prey.

The history of human animals and their strange relations with other animals, their community of being in common in the caves, is a happening and an event that took its first performative place in chambers such as Lascaux and Chauvet. And according to Georges Bataille, from whom Nancy drew significant aspects of his work in this pre-historic sense, this site was a privileged site of 'pre-history'. For Bataille, the very images that Nancy refers to announce a generational moment for human being not just for spectation and performance but for the ontological category marked as the social animal, the human assembled: 'The passage from animal to man announces the birth of the subject, the birth of the human community, the we' (Figure 1.2).[13]

But if one looks more closely at the evidence, at Lascaux for instance, these earliest depictions of 'man', this 'we', were significant not for their humanist

Figure 1.2 Lascaux, Laughing Man, Montignac, 15,000 BCE

centring of the subject but for the way that humanity is *remaindered*, at the edge of everything else which is actively occurring. Bataille figured this edging out in the following way: 'Far from seeking to affirm humanity against nature, man, born of nature, here voluntarily appears as a kind of waste'.[14] Here humans are already seen apologising for their status, at the edge of this collective, having not yet prevailed in the order of things. They marginalise themselves in these first pictorial significations and, tellingly, they are always alone, unlike the other animals in their herds, flocks and prides. They are literally *wasted*, their tusk and horn likenesses smashed in a genocide of self-representation, littering cave floors from one end of Europe to the other. Of course this is just another, rather illustrative, act of performance, a 'feigned apology' Bataille calls it, so that the human predator can continue to do what he has to do, kill other animals, without remorse. These are not tragic figures like the sufferers of *La Haine*: quite the opposite, they are rather like the pre-tragic figures of *The World in Pictures* who are in the process of working these things out amongst their own company.

The human community is one figured in its oldest representations as self-reflexively *mocking* itself in its disgracefulness. The 'laughing figure' in the earliest extant painting of a human, in Lascaux, is not therefore an aberration but the recognition that the earliest relations between humans and other animals were *comic theatrical* ones. Some 10,000 years later, between 31,000 and 27,000 BCE in Dolni Vestonice, Moravia, the first known human sculpture carved from a mammoth tusk has slits where 'eyes should be'. But it is obvious when looking at this fine object, brilliantly detailed in other respects, on display at the British Museum that the maker has not 'fallen short' of verisimilitude, as the caption on the vitrine suggests, but rather has represented quite perfectly what they sought to represent: the neolothic equivalent of a 'gimp mask'. It would appear from this evidence (there are even indentations to the top of the head that 'might have held decorative stones') that leather hide was fashioned for playful purposes as well as protective uses. A mammoth tusk puppet from the same place and the same period, finely articulated in its joints, suggests that by the time Plato got around to figuring the illusions of the puppeteer in the Cave there was already at least a 40,000-year puppet repertory to draw upon. If, for Bataille, art is 'wealth expanded without utility', then the lack of instrumentalism in these first images and physical forms suggests that the economy of pre-historic art lacks the instrumentalism we might once have presumed to be symptomatic of art's more recent responsibilities. Forced Entertainment caught this tone beautifully in their Stone Age rendition of *The World in Pictures*, a characteristically energetic but ambivalent endeavour in confounding the chronology of historical construction.

If, as Bataille said, 'every animal is in the world like water in water',[15] the cave-wall images and sculptures that we are considering here suggest there is something unfathomable for man about the depths of that sense of *continuity* between humans and other animals. Man, and, again after Oleg Kulik earlier, given what is standing between his legs it is man, is figured across these walls as the *interruptive* animal, the irritable one, not just because he does not eat his own kind but because he alone is lacerated by the *end* of his kind; it is only then he stops laughing. The human animal is 'the discontinuous one' and therefore contrary to René Descartes in his *Discourse* of 1637 much the more machinic for signifying the break in the flow, the streaming, that is immanent to animality at home within its various habitats. This interruptive dimension to the human animal is another way of marking the human's propensity for performance, a faculty that fractures the human animal into identity and rôle which makes humans what they are.

The discovery of the subterranean images in Lascaux in the South of France in the 1940s can be used to deliver a pleasingly elegant thesis on the mimetic rupture of the earliest pictorial representation of the human animal in their creature discomforts. But the chance discovery of those very images in the first human venue, as Georges Bataille recognised, was happening at precisely the moment of another not un-associated cave-like discovery, of man's inhumanity to man in the last human venue, the Nazi death camps. The birth of the subject through cave-painting is here being exposed at the moment of the exposure of the fullest sense of human death in Europe. In the former a necessary evil, the eating of another for survival, is set off by the coincidence of history against a superfluous evil, the absolutely unnecessary killing of another who cannot be allowed to survive. The beginnings of community are, perhaps inevitably, bound in this historical coincidence by the discovery of their end, an end we will return to by way of closing this book in the final chapter, an end that represented in the West, and for Jean-Luc Nancy, the 'limit to representation' that might not yet have been in sight but represented the cruellest insight of our age.

Ceramic Age

Having proposed a 2,500-year leap to Plato and the Classical Age, then a 40,000-year jump to the first Stone Age, I want now in the third and last part of this chapter to come back towards today via what I would like to call the Ceramic Age and make some simple observations about a theatrical stage that has, despite all performance claims to the contrary, somehow remained impervious to attempts to puncture its solid state, to loosen or disrupt its originary relationship to Plato's Cave. I hope that's clear as a timeline. When I was interviewed for my first proper academic job in the 1990s, I was asked by an eminent theatre historian, with a raised eyebrow, whether my approach to historical study in my monograph *Theatre & Everyday Life* was not more on the side of piracy than custom in our field deems responsible behaviour. I am afraid that as Johnny Depp mimics his Captain in *Pirates of the Caribbean: Dead Man's Chest*, I see the necessary caution with plundering and pillaging time frames less as a rule and more of a *guideline* to inform a critical performance practice now.

So where *was* I 'yesterday'? Back at the ICA in London for the first time since directing the talks programme there in the 1990s. Hermione, my younger daughter, eight years old at the time, was booked into what was described as a *drawing workshop*. I took this to be a salve to the local Westminster council that the ICA did serious outreach work and grabbed the chance to sign up, along with other middle-class parents, to some cheap crayons and paper subsidised by the central-London dispossessed. I also knew there would be a copy of Nicolas Bourriaud's celebrated work *Relational Aesthetics* (1998) in the bookshop (there were several), and having heard it referenced over the last half-decade at almost every performance and visual arts event I had participated in, I decided it was my chance to read it and quote it to ensure the systematic topicality of this contribution to the performance field.

When we arrived, and had been briefed by the ICA staff, it became apparent that this community workshop was not quite what it appeared. Hermione was with her friends Iona and Isabel, and alongside twenty other children aged between seven and nine they were asked by a staff member convening the workshop an apparently straightforward question: 'What is this place?' A bright spark said, 'a museum', to which the staff member replied: 'yes, an art gallery'. I almost interjected that this might be something of moot distinction, but saw Hermione giving me the warning eye, so I didn't. 'And do you make art?' a staff member asked. 'Yes', said the children unanimously. 'And are you artists?' 'No', said most of the children forgetting the permission granted them some years before by Joseph Beuys. 'Would you like to be artists?' asked the grown-up. 'Yes', the children cried (and our inner parenting-artist-selves concurred from the sidelines).

'Right', they said. 'Before you can get on with your drawing workshop we would like you to split into two groups. One group will be asked to go downstairs to the gallery space and there, without objects of any kind, you will be asked to play. Who would like to say something?' So Hermione put up her hand. 'Where's the toilet?' Hermione asked. 'No', said the staff member, 'I mean say something in the gallery?' 'Well if I can go to the toilet first, I am happy to say something later', said Hermione. 'Right', said the grown-up, 'you will step out of whatever game you are playing at the time, and go up to and say the following line to anyone who comes into the gallery during today: "Hello, my name is, whatever your name is, and I would like to call the work, *This Success*". Or you could say if you feel otherwise: "Hello, my name is, whatever your name is, and I would like to call the work *This Failure*". "My name's Hermione"', said Hermione, with an economy of language that I mentally jotted down as being inherited from her mother's side.

Despite the fact that this drawing workshop had never been named, it quickly became apparent to me, from this instruction, as an insider now masquerading as an outsider to the workings of this institution, that my daughter was being briefed to become part, a speaking part no less, of a Tino Sehgal work, *Tino Sehgal 2007*, the third in his trilogy for the ICA over three years, described in this way rather enigmatically in the ICA programme: 'Whether dancing museum guards, two people locked in a kiss, someone writing on the floor of an empty gallery, or a conversation with a child, Tino Sehgal's situation based pieces can be as enchanting as they are disorientating.'

As parents who, according to the staff, would inhibit everything that was about to happen, we were shown the back door onto Carlton House Terrace while the shrieks and cries of our independents echoed through the building. We were allowed back in between 6.00 pm and 7.00 pm, six hours later, that evening to see how things ended up. This, after five weeks of continuous success and failure, was the end of the work in its ICA form, and we could participate in that ending as we wished.

I will leave it to others more expert in the reticence of Tino Sehgal's marvellous work to mine the performance dimensions at work here; indeed, the secondary literature on Sehgal's oeuvre has exponentially grown over the last half decade as evidenced by Claire Bishop in her recent work *Artificial Hells* (2012), but I was struck by something precisely material about the success and failure of this work. And it is that materialism, a form of generational shift, that I hope to get to somewhere between the 'Pre-Historical' and the 'Archaeological' of my chapter title.

The event was being conducted in an absolutely 'neutral' room, albeit obviously an architecturally formed exhibition space, with a white door covering the normally cherished escape route via the front desk. There was an intense display of play at work when we parents returned, with various degrees of faux theatricality and apparently innocent goodwill-brushing of girls' hair (still no objects) and clapping games. But amidst all this to-ing and fro-ing, what was inescapable was the floor, which was way too hard for its own good, or indeed for the children playing on it. At one point a boy fell and hit his head quite hard in that slightly sickening thud-like way that adults just don't do. It was pure stone, laid by the great modernist architect Jane Drew in 1967, shiny and reflective of the action but unforgiving, the most utterly trapdoor-less floor that you could imagine. It was a quarried-out screen surface, but one so dense as not to appear to have any light of its own, nor offering any means nor hope to broach its impermeability. In this respect it was the solid inversion of Plato's theatrical volume with its side-long excision opening it out to the world and sun above.

And this struck me in the context of thinking about relations between the stage, theatre and performance, alluded to so far as an interesting inversion of my theatrical expectation. The rhetoric of staging I realised presumes that a certain *hollowness* is what precisely supports the stage action. This would certainly be the overriding phenomenology of the Cave as figured by Plato, despite its rock-hard exterior. This is the kind of hollow volume that the Norwegian performance ensemble Baktruppen have used to great effect, and made apparent in productions such as *Homo Egg Egg* (2002), constantly disappearing beneath the audience bleachers in their work across Europe in the last two decades of the twentieth century. But there, in the hollowed out, reverse figure to this ICA floor, is an eminent tradition of exploration that links the inner-stage to the potential for revolutionary acts, a potential that would appear to reside in the hollowness itself.

In Lindsay Anderson's 'anatomy of a public school film' from the 1960s, *If* …, this hollow sub-stage volume is the very seat of resistance for the schoolboy antiheroes. Beneath the school stage is a hidden world within which this kind of recovery of imagination and history, not to mention the relics of the formaldehyded anthropological machine, vitrines of preserved human parts and foetuses stored from some infernal biology class, can be brought to light and examined. And it is from here that the revolution against the school authorities is staged in the final part of the film: *Crusaders*. The liberal headmaster, whose school chaplain Malcolm McDowell has just shot with a rifle on combat exercises, is meting out his own idea of discipline to McDowell and his comrades. The startling, memorable, sub-stage scene that follows, a sweeping smoke-filled auditorium followed by a roof-top Kalashnikov assault on the fleeing parents and dignitaries, highlights what performative labour can give rise to by way of resistance. Off-stage is one thing, sub-stage is another, and perhaps worthy of more work where there is a volume of performance to be explored. In the case of the ICA it was the precise quarried density that threw up the resistances on offer that day.

Well, they announced the end of the Tino Sehgal piece, and I was glad that I had taken the chance to read *Relational Aesthetics* in the café during the afternoon, above the action of my own child who I was not able to witness in case I inhibited her pre-Lapsarian play. For in that work by Nicolas Bourriaud I was able to establish that what Tino Sehgal is up to, alongside his contemporaries – Philippe Pareno, Vanessa Beecroft, Maurizio Cattelan and Carsten Holler – is to do with what Bourriaud calls 'interactive, user-friendly and relational concepts'.[16] In exploring this work he asks a question that is of critical relevance to what is being discussed here: 'Is it still possible to generate relationships with the world?'. His ideas of conviviality and encounter sound very much like the kind of soft performative inherent to community engagements at the fringes of theatre practice since Sergei Eisenstein occupied a factory in Moscow for an event in the 1920s, and Jean Jacques Rousseau asked some years before what the public might be doing when they grouped at the village Maypole.

So my materialist model reminds me to take more notice of the ground on which performance occurs, not necessarily to dig into it in a hermeneutic enterprise, the kind of archaeological model so convincingly conducted by Mike Pearson in his recent works *Theatre/Archaeology* and *In Comes I*, but to account for it in my study of performances. If I am not initially interested in things hidden in the ground I am perhaps more interested in the way in which a certain concealing is already underway in the tools that I use to encounter performance as governed by these rhetorical arrangements. So I will shift the focus to a method of 'grounding concepts' now on the promise that I will return to the materiality of another theatre floor by way of conclusion to this chapter.

To suggest that there have been things hidden since the foundation of performance studies is to suggest that performance studies have been 'founded', in the first place, and that performance studies are somehow able to conceal things. This might be too close to an anthropomorphism of performance studies for your comfort, but all facts have a social life, and the fact of life is that disciplines have peculiarly active ones. When Randy Newman sang in his song *The Beehive State*: 'What is Kansas Thinking? What is Kansas for?' he was not asking whether Kansas had any *use*. I'm sure B.B. King, Dorothy from the *Wizard of Oz* and that wonderful song in the musical *Oklahoma* about buildings 'seven stories high' being about as far as a 'building ought to go' tell us what

Kansas is *for*: it is a place to be striven for. Rather what might it *stand* for, what would it wish to put its name to? My question in the third part of this chapter is not dissimilar: 'What is theatre thinking? What is performance for?' To what things might performance studies wish to put its name, in our name?

The history of paradigm, disciplinary or knowledge formation, is, as any *Archaeology of Knowledge* shows, one of concealments as much as revelations; an archaeology itself is a process of disinterring those things about epistemology that have become hidden in time. But it has been the common currency of all such strategies to conceal *things*, for objects have always had a recalcitrance about them, from the chemistry laboratory to the physics chamber, that resist our humanist expectations. Things *object* to our subjecting them to experiment. The sound of the ICA floor resisting the child's head is just such a physical measure of the limits to such experiment.

The root of the word 'laboratory', a word first used in English in 1608 around the time that Shakespeare was completing *The Tempest*, the 'labour of oratory', forcing things to speak, is a reminder of the violence inherent to all demonstrations of discoveries. So in its concealing of *things* performance studies is in good company. It is no slight to a discipline to admit its propensity to hide things, if only in order to reveal them dramatically with the magician's exclamation: 'lo and behold'. Look and behold. In this sense Richard Schechner's *Performance Studies: An Introduction* (2002) is a 'book of revelations'.

But looking is not the half of it I feel.

Evoking the 'father' of the field, or at least an avuncular figure to accompany Richard Southern with whom we opened this book, invites us to consider more carefully the generational reach of the field. When *was* performance studies founded? Certainly not in 1962, the date I selected in the opening note to 'my readers' as one worth marking, half a century on, despite the manner in which the *TDR* journal generated a refiguring towards performance, and the leap this represented for its cultural moment.

There are no records of the earliest performances that would have been studied; they are literally pre-historic. But it is logical to assume that once the two-dimensional readings of 'media studies' had developed, the *three dimensions* of 'live performance' would have been recognised, commented on and critically addressed for their contrasting depth and presence. To fancifully extend Philip Auslander's logic in his book *Liveness* (1999) that it was only at the inception of recorded television that the 'live' became identifiable as a discreet and distinct activity, it was in my view only at the inception of the first media-screen that performance could be separated out and examined for *its* difference.

The screen I am talking about here, contrary to Auslander and Bourriaud, who both presume the screen to have something to do with either televisions or computer terminals, was not the relatively recent invention of the television. But nor was it as old as the Stone Age milieu discussed in the first part of this chapter, the Upper-Palaeolithic cave interior at Lascaux, that Georges Bataille described as 'the cradle of humanity'. As we saw, that chalked-on wall provided an early if under-illuminated prototype of the ability of human animals to picture their animal quarry, and then to figure themselves as laughing at them.

But this was a bespoke artistry, unique on each extraordinary occasion from Altamira to Peche Merle. The tactility of this pigment work, the intimate relationship between hand and surface, shared more with the performance of each hunting sortie than was able to throw that performative action, restored behaviour, from one kill to the next, into any relief. We have no writing of that relationship as we have seen, and can only speculate with Bataille that this pre-history is our history because it announces the subject, the I, *it announces us*. Bataille figures this entrance of the human in reassuringly theatrical terms: 'What we now conceive clearly is that the coming of humanity into the world was a drama in two acts. Better still: that the second act, in which the essential matters were decided, was preceded by a much vaguer and much longer act, which is comparable in its slowness and indecisive appearance to a period of incubation'.[17]

In distinction to this Stone Age surface, the screen I am interested in here, one that was, unlike the cave wall, documented and largely survived, indeed survived in enormous numbers and diversity, can be discussed sensibly and with recourse to the evidence of history. This screen surface was the more modern invention of suspended narratives in mineral colour and glaze produced in the 15,000-year-old new technology of the ceramic tile. It was *this* invention, a mass-produced media technology with the limit of a prototype glass screen, that allowed commentators to distinguish between the repetitious, the mimetic and the bespoke for the first time.

If performance found its audience in the collective of the cave, as I have been suggesting before Mondzain's invention of the first spectator, then the foundation of *performance studies*, if you follow my reverse logic and timeline, occurred in Egypt in the fourth millennium BCE. The Near East, with its tradition of baked or sun-dried brick, was the geographical cradle of architectural ceramics and, therefore, logically of performance thought. From the year 4000 BCE onwards Egyptians were producing tiles of a siliceous, sandy composition whose surface glaze was stained turquoise-blue with copper. These tiles were used to decorate the jambs of inner doorways in the Step Pyramid at Saqqara, south of Cairo. This blue, of course, was not arbitrary nor remotely abstract, for everyone who saw it the mineral would have been instantly recognisable as concerned with contemporary conceptions of divine power and eternal life. It was readable. It signified. These tiles were written about and commented upon by contemporaries for the first time, marking them out as the first 'media' to be studied. The earlier glazed tiles used by the Assyrians and Babylonians in Mesopotamia between the thirteenth and the fifth centuries BC seem to have passed without record or notice.

Within 2000 years, by 1180 BCE in the Nile Delta at the Temple of *Medinet Habu*, the tiles are picturing captured slaves of different races, fabulous beasts, real animals and symbolic signs and ornaments. The age of narrative realism begins here, the veracity of the ceramic surface and its pictorial truth-to-life from now on set off against those things that happened in front of it, in true scale, in proximity to the spectator not abbreviated in size as demanded by the manufactured reduction of the mass-produced ceramic form.

The ceramic tile had the added dimension, critical for my argument here, of a porous surface to its rear-side that promised some sort of permeability with the outside world. It was this porosity that allowed Roman vessels later to absorb moisture from below to keep wine cooled in the earliest versions of a hostelry. At least it was a porosity that allowed the tile to breath with the surface to which it was attached, which in turn would commonly be a wall with an exterior aspect and therefore prey to the vicissitudes of changing levels of damp and drought. So in the ceramic tile we have the classic bonding of a surface of impermeable aesthetics founded on a promise of interactivity with the environment within which the work takes its place.

In my view we are still operating within the Ceramic Age, and not just in the operating theatres from de Waag in Amsterdam, Padua and Uppsala, for whom anatomy theatres have become tiled icons of another era of spectatorial medicine. Indeed, as though invented to demonstrate this dynamic, the Young Vic Theatre in London recently re-opened (2006), under the direction of the celebrated anthropologist David Lan, enveloped in an architectural remainder of the Ceramic Age (Figure 1.3).

It could not have escaped David Lan's anthropological eye that the only part of his theatre's wholly rebuilt interior left untouched by the site-sensitive architects Haworth Tompkins were the ceramic tiles that formed the wall of an Edwardian butcher's shop integrated into the building when originally built in the 1970s. The tiles of the butcher's shop, like those earlier in the century,

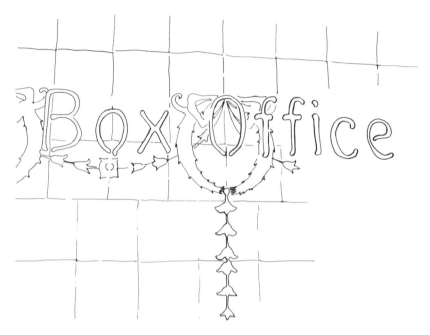

Figure 1.3 *Young Vic Theatre*, Haworth Tompkins Architects, London, 2006

in more ominous surroundings across Eastern Europe that we were reflecting upon earlier and will close this book, were of course well suited to the historical delusion that the bloody transition from the life of the live to the death of the dead could be wiped clean, a *tabula rasa* for slaughtered animals at the end of each busy day in the aptly named street in Waterloo where this butcher's shop stood, called *The Cut*.

There is little fundamental difference between the Nintendo DS Console my daughters used to game with in the late twentieth century and the ceramic tile. They weigh about the same and their dimensions and opaque, milky hue are familiar. The light now emanates from *within* the screen of the iPad, but the narratives are similarly suspended close to the near-side of that screen. And of course their easy violences can be wiped clean with a single modest gesture across the surface. There is the tease of interactivity, but this, like almost all gaming, is fantastically limited. It is a remedial activity rather like basket-weaving would have been in a nineteenth-century home for the insane. And the porosity to the world of the tile has been traded for a specious *WiFi* link to other gaming slabs but little outside engagement. The technology at work here in the Nintendo and the tablet, the *techné* or mechanics of revealing, has barely advanced on William de Morgan's Victorian tiles in my local pub *The Tabard* in west London, where narratives are continued across tiles in fluid temporal dynamics. And it falls well short of the heights of soaring, tile-clad, Moroccan Mosques.

It would be the holy grail of interactivity to be in a position, through the liberatory power of performance, to announce this moment as the *end* of the Ceramic Age. Interactivity would provide us with the much-desired figure to consign the ceramic model to history. But there is little about theatre and its study from the Greek site on, at least as documented in these seven approaches, that disturbs this essentially two-dimensional model with a lustrous yet impenetrable surface and a porous back. This volume will continue to insist that theatre is as much to do with the registration of degrees of immunity as the wilful celebration of community. The theatre volume could be figured as leaky to the world, as indeed Plato insists on figuring it, but only from one side, or aperture, at a time. The proscenium arch reinforced the screen war in its face off with a front-seated audience, surfaces at work rather than volumes to be entered.

A century of theatrical experiment from Sergei Eisenstein's immersive factory pieces in the early twentieth century through Jerzy Grotowski's para-theatricals to the current hegemony of site-specific performance (see Chapters 6 and 7) has done little to alter the essential face-to-face encounter of the theatrical. 'Looking on' and wondering is the common theatrical mode of spectation irrespective of cultural origin. It is my contention that it is this *impermeability*, like the glazed tile, that has necessitated what René Girard would have described, in *Things Hidden Since the Foundation of the World* (1987), as a certain scapegoating of the theatrical by performance studies as it chases the desire of all desires, involvement in a world that it seeks to cover while hiding the resistances it encounters to occupation.

I would figure this as the *recalcitrance* of the domain of theatre, the abandoned practice I described earlier, which the apparently newer, but primordial, deeply irritable discipline, performance, wishes to enter, a recalcitrance that one rarely sees quantified in the expansionist phase of disciplines. The recalcitrance of psychology to phrenology, the resistance of astronomy to astrology and the scepticism of political materialists to phenomenology are warning signs for us here in a long-established field that would appear to have welcoming subjects when it is in fact dealing, sometimes summarily, with precarious objects.

But as *Theatre in the Expanded Field* is beginning to illuminate, performance has a much longer pre-history than Plato's Cave would suggest for theatricality and its relation to humanity. Perhaps in response to this resistance to this economy of production and audience affects, performance studies always, from its earliest days in 4000 BCE, figured events as privileged at the point at which they confounded the apparent distancing of audience and illusionist that Plato's theatre myth enforced. More recently, in the late age of Performance Studies, the attraction of anthropology (Chapter 2) and psychoanalytic theory (Chapter 5), two modes of understanding that value embeddedness, participation and the allegorical interpretation of the hidden or repressed, is indicative of this urge for proximity. At least these hermeneutics announce an engagement with the 'less fake' if not the real.

Performance Studies' interest in processes as contrasting as legal practices and ritual ceremonial shares an investment in their volumetric quality, the rounded quality that can appear to be entered into, the promise of interactivity fulfilled. There is a sense in which performance studies have always wanted to *join in*, not to look on. Hence the recalcitrant, bloody-headed, if not bloody-minded, obduracy of Tino Sehgal's ICA floor piece to performance thought. Performance Studies via ethnography and relational aesthetics as conceived by Victor Turner and Nicholas Bourriaud has used the terminology of participant observation and therapeutic dialogue to imply the interactive quality of this practice at odds with the shackled audience of Plato's first theatre model.

This emphasis on interactivity is fine as long as it is not mistaken for a meaningful politics of performance. It is simply the participatory rhetorical ambience of a discipline that developed over several thousand years in tension with the dominant mode of distanced aesthetic seeing and reading that preceded it at the outset of the Ceramic Age. And while it has a welcome affirmative aspect, a collaborative social feel, it requires a synthetic conflict theory to act upon to do its work, to give its project a sense of dramatic tension beyond the obvious observation that with a floor that dense there is already enough resistance to go around.

My contention through this chapter is that Performance Studies, if it wishes to take the chance to reconfigure itself through a generational perspective of approaches rather than origins, might concern itself more actively with the longer historical material conditions, a set of 'ineffable conditions' that determine the distribution of the sensible within which we perceive performances now. It is in this respect that the permeability of Plato's Cave, the density of the ICA floor, the image-saturated cavernous Lascaux and the Young Vic foyer might be brought into a curious alignment seeking parallels in the world of the theatre and performance itself, to do what Richard Southern did in his work *The Seven Ages of the Theatre*, to intervene in the making of theatres (and with respect to this book, performance) 'now'.

Second Approach
Pastoral & Anthropological

I will begin at the beginning of Western dramatic literature, with *Oedipus Rex* (429 BCE), in the hills outside Athens, and mark a half-way stage in this chapter with the apotheosis of Western lyric verse, the work of Barry, Robin and Maurice Gibb, who gave us the classic hits *Staying Alive* and *Night Fever* (1977), and so from Sophocles to the Bee Gees, via a mountain. In the second part of this chapter I will come down from the mountain and try, in the spirit of other writing in this book, to propose some practical consequences of what I am saying for performance closer to home (presuming that the majority of the readership of this volume are currently occupying lowlands rather than highlands, a presumption that of course should not go unremarked in the age of rising tides).[1]

Oedipus asks in the opening verse of Sophocles' *Oedipus Rex*: 'My children.../ What purpose brings you here, a multitude...?' The Priest replies: 'the city is storm tossed.../The herds upon our pastures...barren'.[2] There is a lot of talk about this pollution in the first half of *Oedipus Rex*, but frankly not much action until two shepherds turn up. The first shepherd, the Corinthian, is described by Oedipus as 'wandering for hire' and the second shepherd, the Theban, when asked by Oedipus where he works, says: 'Now it was Cithaeron, now the country round'. The Corinthian knows the Theban and tells Oedipus, who years before had passed between them: 'He with a double flock, and I with one/We spent together three whole summer seasons, from Spring until the rising of Arcturus./ Then with the coming on of winter, I/Drove my flocks home, he his, to Laius' folds'.[3]

This is the first extant literature of an agrarian practice called transhumance, now virtually extinct in Western Europe in anything but a recovered performance form. As I explored briefly in the Preliminary introduction, with reference to the work of Jean Starobinski regarding the terms 'action and reaction', transhumance describes the movement of animals by shepherds, commonly sheep, but also goats, from low pastures to high pastures in the early summer months as a means to escape the arid heat of the Mediterranean. The relationship between human and animal, in this instance between sheep and shepherd, was what first interested me in transhumance for a book I was writing about the 'lesser animal', the human (Figure 2.1).[4]

The words 'transhuman' and 'transhumance' are neighbours in the *Oxford English Dictionary*. If transhuman is beyond the human, the superhuman, it is a word that describes a historical project, recently stalled, that since the Greeks has compared man, in turn, to gods and animals. As Mario Perniola has said in his small but potent book, *The Sex Appeal of the Inorganic* (2004), this game of differences and distinctions, affinities and correspondences has now ended in a tie; humans are now almost gods and almost animals, while gods and animals are almost human. Having completed the book on the lesser animal, *Theatre, Intimacy & Engagement* (2008), which is partly about how these relations are brokered through performance, I am now, here, keen to move on to the adjacent

Figure 2.1 *Transhumance*, Drôme, France, 1928

but different ground, slightly raised, if not elevated. And hence my title for the second part of the chapter: 'The obtuse angle'. 'The obtuse angle' deals with those things through performance that might on first appearance appear to be less acute in their significance than one might have hoped for, and yet, more than acute in their consequences. This then is one of a number of such anthropological studies I have been working on in which the reticent, the gentle, the meek and the patient are figured in the stead of theatre's more common conflictual dramas.

Critique acknowledges something's existence, but in order to confine it within limits. So I recognise the existence of transhumance in the literary/dramatic scene of Sophocles, but I would propose here that I can only critically address its performative nature by drastically limiting it, to a region, as an example (Figure 2.2). If I was a man of the theatre or film, a method actor, Robert de Niro perhaps, whose film *The Good Shepherd* is a standard of Mafia 'branding', I might seek the example of the transhumance in its act, follow it as a shepherd

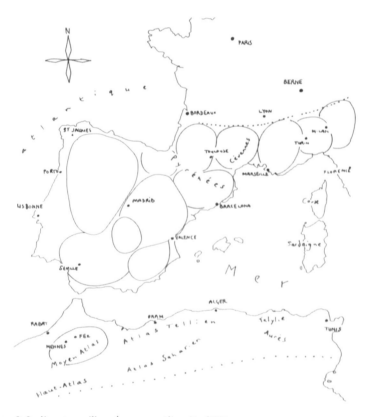

Figure 2.2 *European Transhumance Circuits, 2006*

might follow it, for what it might reveal to me about the affects of an occasion, to fill out the emotional through-line or sub-text of my character. I will return to this method later in this chapter for those of you interested in reading about that left-hand column in my Preliminary remarks, those things that we consider the purview of the theatre and the stage.

More likely, given my background, and the paradigmatic interests of this book, perhaps from a performance studies perspective as represented by that right-hand column at the outset, I could play off the political implications of the movement of sheep in the transhumance. The mapping of these multitudinous, global movements would provide us with a transnational, animal–human circum-navigation that makes the brilliant humanist bias of other geographically oriented works such as *The Black Atlantic* (1993) by Paul Gilroy, or *Cities of the Dead* (1996) by Joseph Roach, look positively pre-ecological.

Alternatively I could do what I have done in my previous work such as *Theatre, Intimacy & Engagement* and take something of a 'parallax approach' to the affective and the political and align myself with the Italian philosopher, Norberto Bobbio, when he says, 'One cannot cultivate political philosophy without trying to understand what is *beyond* politics, without venturing into the non-political sphere, and attempting to establish the boundaries between the political and the non-political. Politics is not everything. The idea that everything is politics is simply outrageous'. Being Norberto Bobbio, he follows this quite dry conundrum with a fantastically unambitious proposition: 'I can say that I discovered meekness during my extended journey of exploration beyond politics'.[5] I like Bobbio's idea of meekness, which from Leeds to Ljubljana (*Krotec*) has its own local register, especially in this sheepish context. But if meekness is quite different to patience, what might it offer an anthropology of performance, that is the continual negotiation between the human animal and other animals, that shapes the politics of personhood?

Unlike the literary fox and the lion, the meek lamb is not a political animal. It is the inevitable victim sacrificed by the powerful to appease the demons of history. A maxim of popular wisdom states: 'Those who behave like sheep will be eaten by the wolf'. The literary wolf is always a political animal – there seems little else left for it but politics. Thomas Hobbes's *homo homini lupus* (man a wolf to man) in the state of nature is the starting point for all politics. The wolfish political writer Christopher Hitchens, launching his book *God Is Not Great* in London in late 2008, looked appalled when asked by a quiet enquirer about the biblical prospect that the meek might ever be allowed to inherit the earth. The meek and the meek sheep somehow escape politics. But if we are meek in respect of others, and never ourselves, this can have nothing to do with modesty, which, as Uriah Heep showed in Charles Dickens's *David Copperfield* (1850), was always deeply selfish. Meekness is a historical choice when considered in relation to the violent society within which we live. Meekness is indeed the antithesis of politics, or I might suggest here the inauguration of another politics beyond the political, 'weak politics' (after the philosopher Gianni Vattimo) perhaps?

So if we are seeking another politics, as I propose we are destined to do given the disappointment that is the inevitable fate of binding theatre to the political, let's start again with the shepherd in mind. And let us consider that shepherd in their avowedly *pastoral* setting. Plato in his work *The Laws* evokes an almighty flood after which the only survivors are some well-meaning shepherds and their sheep on high ground. In Part 4 of *The Laws*, 'Lessons of History: Life After the Flood', the Athenian, commonly thought to be Plato in a dramatic guise, says: 'those who escaped the disaster must have been pretty nearly all hill-shepherds – a few embers of mankind preserved, I imagine, on the tops of mountains'.[6] Typically for the philosopher, they just happen to be 'unskilled and unsophisticated', which is OK because Plato through the voice of the Athenian wants them to be 'innocent of the crafty devices that city dwellers use in the rat race to do each other down'; they are blissfully unaware of the dirty tricks common to previous republics before the flood. It is upon this good-willed *tabula rasa* that Plato can propose first the shepherd's descent from the hill side and then the testing of models of government that are available to them: autocracy, monarchy and democracy.

Any idea of democratic politics begins from this possibility of an assembly of some kind, though *what kind* seems peculiarly attenuated and framed by the conservative theatrical model of gathering *in front* of something. This is perhaps why so many books on politics feature theatre audiences on their covers. The multitude of Paolo Virno is precisely figured in his book *A Grammar of the Multitude* (2004), in its Semiotext(e) edition at least, as a seated assembly apparently waiting for something to begin; the people of Ernesto Laclau's *On Populist Reason* (2005) are illustrated on the Verso cover like a scene from the end of the stage version of *Les Misérables* waiting for the applause of the serried ranks, us, for being so poor. Paraphrasing a line from the UK performance company Forced Entertainment in a piece called *Showtime*: 'Plato had a name for people like you, and that name was *theatrocracy*'. You, dear reader, are the audience *and* the mob, or demos, whose racket is authorised by the spectacle.

But some interesting questions arise here that the term 'public' cannot begin to address for human animals: what *shape* might such an assembly take if not seated, what *models* of conduct might performance of the collective offer, what *modes* of community might arise from such arrangements, what *movement* might theatrical expertise identify in such community, what *modalities* of action might ensue from this mass, what *modulations* of voices might arise from within its swarming liquidity and, lastly, what might the *modesty* of the meek have to do with each of these weak arrangements? I suggest those in care of the sheep might know. You could call these, after William Empson's work of the 1970s, *Seven Versions of Pastoral*.

The transhumance offers us specific arrangements of each of these seven questions if we choose to look beyond Plato's insistence that the shepherd must be killed. And, as the French philosopher Jacques Rancière points out, it is curious that Plato suggests the shepherd has to be killed not once but twice. This double expulsion seems somewhat disproportionate and deserves brief reflection if only to establish why such an apparently pastoral figure should be so threatening to right government. It is this abandoned figure of the shepherd that Rancière notices in his little book *Hatred of Democracy* (2006). Here he says: 'it is quite true that politics is defined in *contradistinction* to the model of the shepherd feeding his flock'.[7]

Why does the shepherd have to be killed twice? First, as Rancière makes clear, and Peter Hallward emphasises in his essay on Platonic 'theatrocracy', the vague threat of the divine shepherd, common long before the gospels standardised its purposes, had to be consigned by Plato to the era of *fables*, establishing political earthly order.[8] Second, the human shepherd whose solicitude like that of the doctor can be adapted to any particular case in their care had to be thwarted, stopped, for an obvious reason. The laws of democracy as Plato lays them out in *The Republic* are quite contrary to the model of the doctor and the shepherd and have to be applicable to *all cases*. In Plato's model, Hallward proposes, the ideal doctor would be the doctor who on leaving for an extended holiday left a single, generally applicable prescription for each and all of his patients who might present themselves with illness during his absence.

The problem, for Plato, and I suppose our pleasure as performance makers and critics, is that 'universal law' will always be sabotaged by the egotistical individual. While the collective might well precede the individual as we proposed in Chapter 1, there is no guarantee that the will of the assembly will survive the singularly intentioned. Under the *appearance* of political democracy will always be concealed, or lie, an inverse reality where private man, and it is commonly man, governs. The removal of the electoral apparatus from the public realm of a 'show of hands' (as revived by Occupy and discussed in Chapter 3) to the discrete and protected, private domain of the voting booth is merely the most obvious surface arrangement of these deeper forces of retreat from the collective sphere.

This inevitable and insistent return of individuality does not explain Plato's reason for hating democracy, but his avowed fear of theatrical doubling does evoke the topsy-turvy world of the rule of the untameable democratic ass(embly), amongst whom the threat from 'theatrocracy' was perhaps Plato's greatest fear. As we saw in the last chapter, it is well known that Plato took so seriously the extraordinary power of theatre that he condemned mimetic practices. But he was especially fearful of the way in which poetic performance dissembled the self-contained single identity, the idea that each citizen should take on one job, and one job alone. There was to be no moonlighting in the Republic. The doubling of theatre with its assumption of character was always going to be a role-play too far. But that was the point for Plato, all attempts to escape self-identity, to free oneself from self-enclosure, were to be vigilantly policed, if not condemned outright. Theatre for Plato was of course one preeminent example of precisely one such departure into a potentially chaotic world of deregulated crowds, what we have now in our strictly licensed auditoria called 'audiences', and was to be vigilantly policed, if not condemned outright. The prohibition on the apparently innocuous act of sitting in theatre aisles has a long Platonic pre-history. This is the theatrical evidence of the scandal of the presumed superiority of a minority based on nothing other than the *absence* of their superiority.

As Rancière points out, democracy is thus not for Plato a 'type of constitution', nor a 'form of society'. The power of the people is not that of people gathered together, of the majority as figured on those book covers, the proletariat as Marx called it. Democracy is simply the power peculiar to those who have 'no more entitlements to govern than to submit to being governed', as Peter Hallward puts it; they have neither the wealth nor the inheritance of birth that would make governing a foregone conclusion. Superior people, as Oedipus makes only too clear in a later scene in front of the Thebans, are always haunted by the equality that bedevils their best efforts to maintain distinction between one (them, often in a distinctive costume) and another (you, often in no costume, or at least a cheaper one).

This is the only 'natural law' of the transhumance: in-egalitarian society can only function thanks to a multitude of *egalitarian* relations. The brightness of equality thus shines from within the obvious inequality of shepherd (with transit van, mobile technology and whip in the twenty-first-century iteration) and their sheep. It is this natural equality, what I will call here *natural law* against every other use of this term, that allows the smaller inequalities to flow however powerful they may seem. Despite our better nature, should we be fortunate enough to find a surviving example of the transhumance, faced with the ovine event itself, this sheepish spectacle, we might now point our camera at these humanist instances of shepherding force and find it difficult to maintain our wider concentration on the myriad beauty and variety of the multitude, far from our desire for their conflict, our conflicted feelings for any conflict.

Democracy, if the shape of such events can be taken seriously, is thus not about those being governed, nor those governing, it is the *ungovernable* nature on which the government of this multitude has to discover eventually it is based. In their apparent subjection it is therefore all the more remarkable that sheep would appear to have evolved a range of sophisticated strategies which protect their individuality among an apparent mass while maintaining a curious economy of subjection to that mass. This would be the political lesson that the aristocrat Oedipus might have derived from the proletarian flock had he not been blind to his truer origins. His life *was* saved by two shepherds (even if Thebes had to pay the price) and yet the Chorus who confront him with the truth of their egalitarian relations remain a mystery among many – a mystery to which we have given the name Tragedy.

At this point of paradoxical inertia, we have had enough perhaps of these literatures of transhumance, or transhumanced literatures (reading texts for the lost shepherds and sub-textual sheep), and we should move on, by foot now, to some *practised* versions of Pastoral.

The Obtuse Angle

While my essayistic exercise in this chapter began dramaturgically, initially, tracing the genealogy of shepherds and flocks between the founding texts of Western drama and philosophy, this cultural enquiry perpetuates a certain metaphorisation of an animal that has already acted as a vehicle for too many myths and materials. So, through the second part of this passage, as with caves in the last, we will attempt to deal more fairly with those matted materials, the materiality of an event that happens to happen at the outset of Western drama, but chronologically had established itself long before pen was put to paper. In the event of *saying* the word 'transhumance', out loud, saying it now with more volume, as distinct to reading it to myself, I get another feeling, if not quite a political one, of peaks and troughs, of experiencing the plastic landscape, the more gentle gradient that lies in between these dramatic imposters to our attention.

The word's two parts, trans/humance, literally mean across ground, but it commonly describes the seasonal movement of livestock to regions of a different climate first dramatised by Sophocles. 'Livestock' is a nice word to describe the economy of this circulation of animals between Marseille and the Alps, but also between low and high in Germany, Asia and Latin America, that is the quintessential movement of early, wooly capitalism. 'Capital' after all derives from the Latin term *caputa*, meaning head, or the head count of the proprietor's fattening goods, and this is very much the economic, or at least circulating, realm I wish to retain your interest within during this part of the chapter. Yes, the 'good shepherd' of John's gospel in the Bible implies the paragon of care, but the fate of the lamb is a predetermined one and has always been an economic necessity as well as a higher-order sacrifice. There is no romance here, but it is not without its passions.

Transhumance invites us not only to think of this ceaseless vertical movement, up and down mountain sides, rising towards the divine or descending towards the animal, but rather to follow a horizontal movement towards something beyond the organic, *the thing*. It was Walter Benjamin, well before Mario Perniola, who first invited us in his reflections on the poet Charles Baudelaire to consider the 'sex appeal of the inorganic', and here, in the midst of an eminently romantic, pastoral, verdant, organicist plot, I would wish to encourage such lateral inclusivity of the material object, whose dynamics trace certain biographies of action. Indeed, in all their throbbing vitality it is only the *thing* that makes it possible to grasp the complimentarity that holds god and animal in circulation with human movement. Why else would watching characters in a Chekhov play reveal so little about their actual relations, while following the movement of the samovar and the unravelling bonds of familiarity and kinship around its silver form reveal so much, in the yawning spaces between another eternal afternoon tea?

Here, in a single scene, by way of a limbering exercise, away from the progressive summative nature of written texts to the dispersed tension between visual signs and sounds, are some of the things that compete for our humanist attention within the passage of the transhumance. They are mute on the page but could be restored to full volume through some judicious shaking and sound effects (Figure 2.3).

I welcome any exercise of this faculty to expand the collective, from shepherd to sheep to things, not because I hold any particular faith in political ecology, but rather because performance would appear to me, and many others now, to be much more than a matter of humans doing essentially human business.

Figure 2.3 *Transhumance*, Die, Drôme, June 2006

I welcome this exercise *because it is exercise*; it is more physically demanding than writing whose imagination is infinite but whose objects are impoverished. The stigmata of a writer, repetitive wrist strain or the scarring of the pen-indented middle finger are a measure of the uniformity of the scriptural. On the contrary, in this event the involvement amidst shepherds, sheep and their instruments keeps the circulation in order and is conducive to the heightened excitement that comes when one operates with multiple accessories and fetish objects. This in my view does not make what I do here labour. That is something else entirely, nor is it unduly libidinal; privations of the hillside do not lend themselves to undue familiarity with individuals in a flock. Rather what we have here is more a workout, a thinking *en route*, keeping the wolf from the door.

So, I went on a journey with some sheep up a hill, a modest gradient, from Die to Col de Rousset in the Drôme region in the south of France. I took with me a neighbour from the Drômoise valley nearby (Truinas, where I live for part of each year), Jonas Horning, who brought his camera along. We were both interested in a literal project – literally putting into practice some things that Sophocles, Plato and Rancière seemed to be implying about shepherds and their sheep. That the French word for flock was *la troupeau* was a slight theatrical bonus that passed us by at the time.

I had already been working for some time on the configuration of European events with unpredictable shape, whose fluidity of form practises something closer to a politics of performance than 'political theatre' has managed in its two millennia of staged revolutions. These events include following the peloton, the selfless group of bicycle riders in the Tour de France supporting their drugged-up stars in yellow jerseys, destined never to break the democratic will of the chasing pack and on another occasion running after the sackcloth-covered village dragons that enter Barcelona on festive anniversaries for the *corre foc*, the fire run through the streets of the city. Like the *corre foc*, which is a performative resuscitation of an ancient and long-submerged rural Catalan tradition, the transhumance is an event, which occurs to me to be an example of what I called theatre earlier, after Isabelle Stengers, an 'abandoned practice'. Like the *corre foc* the event sits uneasily between folklore and *fakelore* and is all the more interesting for that ambiguity. My contention here in linking *Oedipus Rex* to the performance of transhumance via a gentle gradient is to insist that there are always, at least, two ends to a journey and to forget the power of a theatrical origin is in all likelihood to experience it the second time as farce.

The transhumance is, in Europe at least, largely abandoned, due to the invention of the combustion engine, the development of tarmacadam to secure mountain roads, the globalisation of the meat market and the mobilisation of slaughter. But no sooner are a number of these practices abandoned, by which I mean they in this instance are not simply forgotten, considered surplus to requirement, but are literally banned by an authority, a sovereign power, or the European Community, their *repressed remainder* in the form of ceremony and spectacle would appear to appear. Here, in the case of the transhumance, it is literally brought to the gates of the town, a cathedral town called Die in the foothills of the Vercors in South East France, and dumped at the feet of the residents on a busy market day on the last weekend of June each year.

The event is three days long. Day one starts at sunrise at the gates of the town. Day two progresses through the town. Day three ascends the mountain to the high pastures. These days have been compressed here into a few paragraphs and a single image for the purposes of this chapter and of course true to the spirit of this visual and sensual disappointment are concerned with performing a particular kind of *patience*. The writing of the patience that this event performs includes those texts of neighbours of mine in this region; a poet of the local landscape and its weathers, such as André du Bouchet, beloved by Giacometti, and translated now by Paul Auster; and the writing of John Giorno, a devotee with the photographer Robert Doisneau of the transhumance and its histories in Europe, Asia and the Americas.

But the texts that this event performs are also those of degrees of 'lacking patience', impatience, of the protestor with their placards, protesting the EC's mandate from their headquarters in city-centre Brussels that *les loups*, the wild dogs and wolves, should be reintroduced to the Alpine pastures where their flocks roam; of the brander who marks up each of these bodies with organs that will soon be *haggis*; of the sign writer of the town for whom scriptural economy means a typography of the swimming pool; or of the supermarché selling the standardised cuts that are channelling by in a sea of teaming diversity.

As we moved from the foothills to the vertiginous slopes of the mountain, we, unlike the shepherds and their sheep, were only able to make progress by taking to a ski lift. As we ascended, a familiar lyric, *I Started a Joke*, sung by Katherine Williams, wafted across the landscape from a tinny speaker at the ski lodge. The Bee Gees' peculiarly tragic song, 'I started a joke that set the whole world crying, but I didn't know, that the joke was on me…', accompanied our view of a shepherd far below who we spent some time with later. He had, like the other shepherds in the transhumance, arrived after three days of walking at the top of this mountain. But his large, black, cross-breed dog, somewhere between a Rotweiller and German Shepherd, was profoundly deaf. The *berger* was quite unlike many of the other functionary and perfunctory shepherds that peopled this gradual ascent. He also had a big stick, but it was one that he waved in the air to signal to his dog his intentions, signing out his sense of the sheep and the ground they are traversing in a lucid canine semaphore. Later that evening we discovered he had a farm full of other disabled animals, or animals with disabilities, other deaf and blind dogs, dumb horses and a confused pig, abandoned by local farmers as surplus to need, with whom he works through a variety of more or less performative techniques, rebuilding their confidence to work with other animals – to trust the instincts of their heightened senses that have amply replaced the limitations of their reduced ones. We thought this was a wondrous joke worthy of the lyric offered by the brothers Gibb, because it made us cry with laughter, the kind of transcendent amazement that went out of fashion in literary studies a few years ago about the same time as beauty hit the dust.

We finished our film in the sky because the clouds on that hot day spelt out the words we were looking for, the title of our film perhaps: *How to Live Together*.

I wonder how we might 'use' or put into operation our own responses to this itinerary, this excursion? I would like to draw some broad conclusions from this example for the second of my *Seven Approaches to Performance* and then, as in Chapter 1, moving beyond the common assumption that once hermeneutic work is done we can close the book satisfied that we have drilled sufficiently for meaning, I would like to propose a shared *project* by way of a practical conclusion.

Following the logic of a number of writers, including Joe Kelleher and Alain Badiou, the apparent subject of my images does not *constitute* their appearance but suffers it, or participates in it without recourse.[9] It is obvious that these animals *suffer* appearance in a different economy to those who *consent* to suffer for their art. But that admission does not, should not, exclude the sheep from consideration on the same stage of political reflection, otherwise we are ecologically finished. To what extent can my work, on their appearance, not so much change them, they seem fine already (well at least until they are added to mint sauce at the end of this extended journey to market), but *how they appear*? I have always felt while reading theatre writers like Bojana Kunst and David Williams that my pleasure in what they do is that their research gives *all the chances to the performance*. In keeping with this spirit, and the evocation of Bruno Latour on behalf of the expansion of the collective, I want to give *all the chances to the sheep*.[10] Everything I do, just as with the primatologists whose business is their business, should allow them to be *more* not less interesting (for obvious reasons to do with radical inclusion, expanding the collective, never mind the ecological imperative of survival, which I lay out in my book with a portentious subtitle: *The Last Human Venue*).

My epistemological position to my subject here, and in that book, is, as Vinciane Despret and the primatologist Shirley Strum would put it, one of *politeness*, trying wherever possible not to construct knowledge about those subjects of my attention, behind their backs, beyond those I am studying. So following the example of the sheep watchers, sleeping with them in the fields for three days does not authorise my interpretation of what I imagine of their imaginings and wanderings, but it does *complicate* it. The useful thing about performance studies is the way it has tackled the 'hierarchical scandal', as Thelma Rowell has called it, that some things have had all the chances (in ethology the equivalent would be primates, in theatre Shakespeare) while other things have had none, or few. In animal studies, as Vinciane Despret has pointed out in a brilliant essay on Thelma Rowell's observation of ovine organisation, sheep have not been big; if they are studied at all, then they tend to be studied for what they eat.[11]

Like some forms of performance which we tend to privilege in performance studies we are apparently drawn to things because they have a certain *intensity of appearance*, or to put it another way are interesting to watch, if not fun to watch. This is the equivalent of examining sheep for what food they eat; it suits the researcher. What is much more difficult, as Thelma Rowell has pointed out often, is to watch the animals for the point at which they weaken, they *become food*, they are eaten. In performance terms, the moment at which theatre itself 'strikes' its captive audience, the fleeting second a spectator in Alain Badiou's term becomes 'stage struck'. It is that elusive impression of force that becomes the slippery signifier here. Predation, whether in performance or sheep, is just much more difficult to see than ingestion. By involving an unpredictable outside agent, either wolf or audience member, the internal economy of the grazing sheep or emoting actor is destabilised in useful and intriguing ways.

Predation, the killing of sheep, happens by day in abattoirs not far from the hills on the outskirts of Marseille for the sheep imaged above, but while they are in the mountains killing also happens at night. Curiously, this killing is authorised and indeed brought about and sanctioned by a European Community legal edict. Sheep are eaten by wolves and wild dogs. The wolves have been reintroduced to the Alps and the Vercors (where the sheep followed here are heading) by the European Community in Brussels in pursuit of sustaining biodiversity.[12] The protestors with placards in Figure 2.3 are shepherds whose livelihood is under threat from these wolves.

With the arrival of the wolves in the mountains, it happens that something happens. And something happens not just to these animals but also to these human animals, to these people. There is a fundamentally anthropological dynamic at work amidst this pastoral scene, and one as always in which the anthropological machine activates a range of distancings and proximities between humans and other animals. Gravelle and Mauz call it the *wolf crisis*.[13] It is not a question of the presence of wolves being a good or bad thing, but rather the point is to consider from a performance perspective the things that happen when wolves make *an appearance*. Here it is not just breeders, administrators and tourists but also wolves, dogs and hooved animals that are being called upon to make choices and decisions.

The protest we encountered on our way up the hill was a *political* one; we know that because it had people waving placards in it. But the political message might not be just told on these boards as much as in the actions of the sheep themselves. In our political metaphors since Plato, sheep-like behaviour has been equated with stupid behaviour. But this stupidity is of course sheep's *founding intelligence* and their greatest defence as Thelma Rowell's research on sheep conduct has made clear: an idiotic strategy of coordination and cohesion protects sheep from their predators – the closer and more attentive the animals remain to one another's movements, the sooner will the enemy be detected. Despite what George Orwell did to them in *Animal Farm,* unlike most other farm animals they are quite like us (before we got guns); they cannot really effectively protest. A horse, bull or cow will be treated with more respect for its scale, but a sheep rarely makes any obvious protests; they just seem to get miserable. To protest means above all to testify and, until Rowell began her work, and Vinciane Despret re-interpreted Rowell's research practices, it would appear that of all animals sheep have never really been asked what interests them, unlike apes, dolphins, elephants or even the tick, the flea, incarcerated in a box for eighteen years that Giorgio Agamben writes about and lavishly orchestrates as a kind of anti-hero in his work *The Open* (2004). I am of course being signed up, co-opted, *enrolled* by the sheep in this project as well, for as the researcher and filmmaker my presence in this flock with Jonas Horning makes predation, killing by other middle-scale animals, *less*, not more likely.

Explaining the work needed to 'construct a testimony' from among this flock and this panoramic, pastoral performance has three advantages that Vinciane Despret brings our attention to:

1. It is *relativistic* because it forces one to multiply the conditions that the entire device of appearing in this way will articulate. In this chapter so far I have been attempting to follow Despret's example by insisting at each turn of the sheep that their itinerary multiplies relations rather than reduces them. By opening with a figure of reduction, of geographical location, to allow for the interpretation from a scene of dramatic literature to get underway I have done everything I can, co-opting Despret, Rowell and Latour along the way, to complicate the associations between each of the agents, including the objects at work within the scene. How each of these operations relates constitutes the degree of relativism at work in the analysis, and my contention here is that the introduction of an embodied journey to the process (and I do mean journey here, not that enfeebled psychological concept of 'journey' adopted by actors on rehearsal floors at the behest of directors to imagine their character's life as anything but restrained by the limits of the cramped stage they are so obviously bound to) accelerates the degree of inclusion available to co-operative consideration, the purpose of radical inclusion as I practise it and the purpose of a politics worth its salt.

2. Second, this way of reporting invites us to give up transparency for
    visibility (or here appearance theory). The denigration of the visible
    in performance studies, thanks to an extreme and wanton outbreak of
    Lacanian neuro-scopic pathologisation of anything witnessed, has done
    much to harm an act that after all does, for those who can see at some level
    of luminosity, appear to have something to do with appearances. What
    allows certain things to become visible will, at the same time of course,
    and we do not need psychoanalysis to tell us this, exclude others and create
    new ones. This should not be a cause for infantilised wailing but surely
    adds to our sense of the incompleteness of the collective and the need to
    continue performative politics at every turn in the road of a true journey,
    one that really does go from A to B, even if only at an obtuse angle up a
    gentle gradient to come back down again to the sound of the Bee Gees.

3. Third, this way of working is *not* relativistic according to Despret, which
    is curious given that the first condition of this work was that it was. But
    as Despret makes clear, interesting research is research *on the conditions
    that make something interesting*. Of interest is he or she (or what) that
    makes someone or something else capable of *becoming interesting*.[14] I have
    commonly exasperated those leaving theatres who have been interested
    in my opinion about this or that show that (despite the fears in our field)
    I have 'seen'. I am after all paid to have opinions about performances, a
    rôle which is commonly finessed in job titles such as critic, theoretician or
    academic. I take each of these tasks seriously and am paid from the public
    purse to be serious, but none of these terms explains why I should have
    any opinion whatsoever about what I have just seen. What I have seen is of
    course as perfect as it can be given what was available to it at any one time
    or place. The conditions that make this interesting (by which I mean the
    passing of a baby between shepherds doing a certain kind of job) are only
    accessible to me by my embodied understanding of those conditions that
    gave rise to such a curious thing, and my limited ability to find a way to
    express what those precise conditions were, and, funnily enough, still are,
    if somewhat theatrically enhanced, 2500 years later.

Taking each of these points prompted by Despret further, one might extrapolate
from these reflections on the movements of a flock that form part of the
transhumance in the Drôme some questions for a general theory of *performance*
that does not eschew the political but hints at how politics are already a distribution
of sensibilities within this pastoral scene. For instance, how does the regulation

of distance make bonds legible and how does the troupe organise coordinated movement? As I said earlier, the French for flock is *troupeau*, so reading across to the theatrical example and how the patience of sheep is interesting might not be so far-fetched. Paradoxically the less 'sheepish sheep' make *less good* witnesses. Hierarchy, Thelma Rowell believes, allows us to think about the conditions and politics of brute leadership but not these more sophisticated social behaviours that we have been witnessing within the transhumance. Hierarchy leaves little room for the flexibility that this flock of sheep show. There is no coercion in the self-organisation of ewes according to Rowell's observations of the same evidence that led other conflicted ethologists to the opposite conclusion. Among males at their most appearance-driven-dramatic, there is only an imperceptible nod of the head. This muzzling to a certain direction is also barely hierarchy. Without hierarchy these animals appear, at least to Thelma Rowell and Vinciane Despret who study them closely, more inventive, freer and sophisticated than otherwise thought possible. Having spent a short time with them, the sheep that is, I would tend to agree. These sheep have, after all, spent months resting in fields with their heads on each others' backs. It would seem strange if they suddenly needed to 'make apparent' the logics of their complex, felt, ordering.

I am not interested in the kinds of 'dramatic' questions that circulate around aggression against passivity or nurture or nature here. Nor am I quite interested in this because I prefer co-operative sheep over competitive ones in the way that the ethologist and anthropologist Ashley Montagu, and Edward Bond the playwright, might have argued against the 'conflicteds', Konrad Lorenz and Richard Dawkins, some years ago. Don't misunderstand me; I quite like a feisty ram. But nevertheless I am, along with those drawn to the intensities of a sheep's appearing from the perspectives of animal organisation rather than classic ethology, interested in posing the question about the *collective that we form* and how we are to invest that collective with the intensity of appearing it demands – questions of community, in other words. I would ask along with Despret and Rowell: Do we prefer living with predictable sheep or with sheep that surprise us and that add dimensions to what being social means? I happen to think, along with a number of the animal watchers quoted here, that *cooperation* is much more interesting. And this is the thing that for Vinciane Despret 'makes the *social-living animals*, like humans and sheep, different and interesting, which we all agree that they are without having to be species exclusive'.[15] How to live together was more than the title of a film.

The transhumance allows me to get closer to something I would not otherwise see appear. It is faulty and banal but it is not nothing – and I have not only its interpreters, who I have been liberally quoting here, but also its recoverers, its theatrical re-stagers, its second-life curators to acknowledge for this opportunity. Indeed almost everyone who participates in this event annually in the Drôme, at the behest originally of the extraordinary writer and poet André Pitt (who has since passed away), especially those who sport the longest beards, the floppiest felt hats and look most like shepherds ought to look, are from central casting. They are paid actors and other extras, subsidised by the local Drôme tourist council to validate and make more 'real' a complex annual event of recovery from a practice that was abandoned more than fifty years ago, indeed just about the time that Richard Southern was broaching such animal/human matters for the first time in *The Seven Ages of the Theatre*.

To expand the repertoire of questions and hypotheses to the sheep, the wolves, the fakelore band in native costume, the Netto Supermarket selling choice cuts and all other participants in this matrix becomes the point. This begins to put into practice, rather literally but no less meaningfully for that, a theatre in the expanded field. Even the clouds in the blue sky at the end of our film spelt out a vaporous architecture worthy of some careful reading. It would be a mistake to ignore the appearance of these apparently untethered signifiers. This matter aspiring to form registers an infinite provisionality and imminence, of things yet to pass, ominous yet omniscient. 'Making Things Public' through appearance, as Bruno Latour and Peter Weibel showed exhaustively in their exhibition of that title in Karlsruhe that has so influenced the reading of these sheep, is not only about making them known; it is also about exploring the conditions for new ways of organising ourselves, which in turn depends upon us entering into polite, performing relationships with non-human appearances.[16]

I suppose, by way of conclusion to this chapter, and in the interests of circularity appropriate to transhumance, I should return to Oedipus and the shepherds. What happened to Sophocles' shepherds, the Corinthian and the Theban, in that play *Oedipus Rex*? Well, when Oedipus discovers he was passed as a baby in the woods on the mountainside from one shepherd to the other, he has the gall to blame it all on Cithaeron, the shepherd. He says in front of the townsfolk of Thebes that make up the chorus: 'Cithaeron! Why did you accept me? Why/Did you not take and kill me? Never then/Should I have come to dwell among the Thebans'.[17] The philosopher has always had their simple foil, their scapegoat for stupidity in the character of the shoemaker; the dramatist it would seem has their simpler shepherd to blame for the world's pollution. This is the lost shepherd, consigned to playing their predestined part as a dramatic device, a fall guy, for the tragic confusions of the Greek aristocracy.

This recovery of an abandoned practice that I have been discussing here, which was the founding *mise en scène* of Western dramatic literature, was a first step towards participating in and perhaps understanding something about the commonplace performance of the meek. This is a pastoral figure combining the shepherd and their sheep, in the practices of their anthropological movement, that is neither wholly human, animal, nor godlike, but *something*, a patient performance that does not need to inherit the earth, theatrically true as it is, to its own, immanent, charged nature.

Third Approach
Theological & Historical

The Strand, in central London, running between Fleet Street to the East and Trafalgar Square to the West, was the seventeenth century's Las Vegas. Just over the river, from where the Globe manifested a conception of a theatre that had retained its broadly social purpose since Classical Greece, a Commons at work, on the Strand public space had been relocated into the equivalent of the private sphere of the casino, a site for performance and spectacle, vistas of trompe l'oeil urbanism, surrounded by everyday shopping and consumption. If ancient Greece and its tragic theatre join to Renaissance London via Shakespeare's Globe in this way, as the cultural geographer Kenneth Olwig has suggested, then post-Renaissance, and for the purposes of this chapter, I would like to say a *postdramatic* tradition stretches from the scenography and architecture of Inigo Jones, the first British architect of significance, on the Strand, to that of the celebrities and their cults at the court of Las Vegas today.[1] Imagine fight night, with sporting royalty, watching the boxers Vladimir Klitzchko and David Hay crossed with a Karl Lagerfeld catwalk show with the sovereign Philip Green and courtier Kate Moss looking on, and looked upon for whom they are looking on.

Within the masque-making work of Inigo Jones, Kenneth Olwig suggests there has been a process of inversion in which the encircling, emplaced and embodied materiality of older forms of theatrical experience (not least those discussed in Chapters 1 and 2) come to be encompassed within an abstract, *perspectival* space, thereby transforming theatre into a performative spectacle, as much to do with its landscape surroundings as its interior. It is from this inversion that I would like to develop some arguments about the relations between performance and theatre through the always entwined braiding of the theological and the historical. It is no coincidence that it is precisely this early modern phase of an 'organised stage' that Richard Southern makes the fulcrum for *The Seven*

Ages of the Theatre, which like the circulations of the transhumance has been revolutionary in its own way.

The problem in weighing up the significance of these acts from our perspective today is that, never mind the justified but almost overweening presence of Shakespeare in British and North American cultural production, we have become obsessed with the apparent democracy of the Globe, its groundlings and its ultimate accessibility, its humorous low-life scenes and its 'universal' tragedy. The Arts Council of England would have loved it for its demographic reach; it ticked some boxes, as indeed it does now. I wonder how Inigo Jones's court masques would have fared with the box tickers?

The masque was an art form in support of a sovereign arrangement, as Clare McManus has shown in a series of decisive works, including her invaluable *Women on the Renaissance Stage* (2002), preceding, and in some ways preparing, the aesthetic ground for opera, involving practices of text, music, song, dance and posed performance in a mélange that would excite those for whom the combination of the arts has always been considered a relatively recent phenomena. The masque developed, as McManus puts it, from the 'pageant form', particularly those events identified with twelfth night, carnivalesque and courtly revels practised by members of the royal court and the nobility (the principal exponents of the masquing tradition). The masque initially involved the movement of its performers between a collection of carnival-like pageant cars (or floats) upon which were created sculpted models of different symbolic environments (mountains, caves, buildings and rocks, which were ubiquitous in masques as we shall see).

'Access issues' there then, for the good officers of the Arts Council should they have been considering the nation's first architect and engineer of monarchical spectacle, Inigo Jones, for revenue funding. But beginning with Jones's *The Masque of Blackness* in 1605, as Kenneth Olwig has argued, the masque came to be fixed within theatre's newly developing perspectival space and was focused upon the spectacle of changing scenic illusions on a stage at one end. The masquers, instead of moving bodily between and upon different sculpted topological material shapes, a flow that imitated the pastoral performance itinerary explored in Chapter 2, were now largely subsumed as spectators within the spectral, linear space of perspectival illusion, though a remnant of them also performed upon the stage. Through these events, Inigo Jones, consistent with his avowedly European architectural tastes, thereby created for the first time in Britain a centre for what Olwig calls an avowedly European theatre, a performance space that has since become the standard theatrical performance space, appropriating the encircling, emplaced and embodied materiality of older forms of theatrical experience, as exemplified by the earlier Revels and Shakespeare's contemporaneous Globe.

It is for this reason Richard Southern places Inigo Jones's innovations at the heart of his book, as the tipping point between a distributed and a located theatre. Performance thus encompassed, for both Olwig and McManus, on the one hand actors whose profession was to 'personate' others and on the other hand non-actors who posed and danced, blurring the line between the realm of the actors and performers in social spectacle. It is here, rather than in 1970 as Hans-Thies Lehmann in his seminal work *Postdramatic Theatre* (2006) suggests, that the boundaries between theatre and performance, reinforced in my opening, introductory columns, began to mutate.

Let's take a moment to look at a fragment from the archival record, as documented by Stephen Orgel and Roy Strong in their magisterial work *The Theatre of the Stuart Court*, of a masque event from the mid-point of that tenure, by no means as lavish as the later spectacles of Charles 1st, but indicative nonetheless:

Artenice

Date: February 21st 1626

Place: The Hall of Somerset House (formerly Denmark House), Strand, London

Occasion: The Queen's Shrovetide fete

Honorat de Bueil, Sieur de Racan

Designer: Inigo Jones

Actors: Henrietta Maria and her ladies

Cost: 'Works Accounts October 1st 1625 to September 30th 1626: payments for making a lardge theatre at the upper end of the hall and performing sundry other works for the scene of the pastoral there, along with soap for the engines of the pastoral. Warrant for payment May 20th 1636 [sic]:

"That is to say, First to George Gellin Taylor, for making nineteen gownes for the Queene, and the Ladyes that attended her in the said Masque [...] five and forty ellns of canvas for stiffening [...] eight pound of silke [...]

Item to Richard Miller Mercer, for three hundred thirty and two yards of Florence satten [...] one hundred seventye seaven yards Demi quarter of Florence taffatye [...]

Item to George Binnion, for one thousand foure hundred seaventie and five ounces of gold and silver bone and passamme lace to trime the said gownes [...] two hundred and twenty nine ounces more of gold and silver lace to trimme twelve suits hats budgets shooes and other such like necessaryes for the Said masque [...]

Item to John Sturton and Arthur Knight, for thirteen Bever hats with gold
and silver bands to them [...]

Item to John Walker for Lawrell wreaths heire and beards [...][2]

If that summary and abbreviated listing from the archival record give a taste of
the opulence and polymorphous perversity of the masquing practice, you might
be forgiven for concurring with Francis Bacon's well-known criticism that these
masques were mere *toys*, playthings of the powerful, devoted to flattery. But
in this chapter I would like to suggest that there was something indefatigably
modern, as distinct to *early* modern, about the masques and their relationship to
Inigo Jones's architectural, engineering and design work on the Strand in West-
Central London, between 1612 and 1642. I would like to suggest that those who
support all that is experimental, innovative and avowedly contemporary within
performance today, as outlined in that column to the right in the Preliminary of
this book, would recognise the true precursor of their interests, the postdramatic
theatre, within this work. Characteristics I might even heretically suggest that
are wholly at odds with the *dramatic* tradition that, thanks to Shakespeare's
exceptional yet peculiar talent, still, to a large extent, holds sway in the popular
Anglo-Saxon imagination when theatre is at issue. And I would want to insist in
a chapter devoted to the slippage between the theological and the historical that
it was precisely through the work of Inigo Jones, in the postdramatic tradition,
that a 'Divine Right of Kings', the holy legitimacy of sovereignty, segued into a
historically identifiable ceremonial acclamation of a secular nature, one that has
remained intact as we encounter performance and celebrity today and without
which Karl Lagerfeld and Kate Moss would not have any purchase on the public
purse of investment.

These processes of theological and political import are of course commonly
attended to and accessed by Renaissance scholars through Shakespeare's Roman
Histories, *Coriolanus, Julius Caesar* and *Anthony and Cleopatra*, but my contrary
choice of Inigo Jones as a mediator of the theological and the historical is a
conscious reminder of the tension between theatre and performance as figured
so far in this book. Shakespeare does almost everything very well, but as a
performance lover for me this brilliance has very little to do with a relation to the
real. Stage fighting would play no part in Shakespeare should reality be remotely
relevant to the proceedings. In this respect I was struck some years ago, as Hans-
Thies Lehmann was, by this comment from the philosopher Walter Benjamin in
his *Elective Affinities*, and I have never really recovered from reading it, much to
the chagrin of my textually literate colleagues:

The *mystery* is, on the dramatic level, that moment in which it juts out of the domain of language proper to it, into a higher one unattainable for it. Therefore, this moment can never be expressed in words but is expressible solely in representation: it is the 'dramatic' in the strictest sense.[3]

And it is this strange 'jutting out', this tension between theatricality and reality, that has fuelled my interest in contemporary performance since that time, in the 1980s, when I was seduced by Jan Fabre's production of *The Power of Theatrical Madness* discussed at the end of the Preliminary. A theoretical way of putting this would be something along the following lines by Hans-Thies Lehmann:

[…] what motivates the internally necessary exclusion of the real, which at the same time endangers the claim of the comprehensive mediation, is nothing less than the principle of drama itself […] Within this ethical problem […] there already slumber in the depths of the dramatic theatre those tensions that open up its crisis, dissolution and finally the possibility of the non-dramatic paradigm.[4]

In this sense theatre does not require performance to irritate and disrupt its pre-ordained practices; rather it dismantles itself from within in a process not unlike self-ingestion. Drama thus unravels itself in its failure to access the real, and it is the disappointment consequent upon this failure as I suggested some years ago in *Theatre & Everyday Life*, and as Matthew Goulish, Nicholas Ridout and Sarah Jane Bailes have all made clear more recently, not its virtuosity, that makes theatre so fascinating to watch for humans.[5] If you doubt this, consider how technically perfect juggling or tightrope walking can be so boring to watch. The point of the postdramatic during this *second* long Elizabethan age has been to make manifest that relationship, to put that disappointment, or at least that contingency, on stage, and it throws up an immediate problem.

We like the 'real' of Shakespeare's imagination; despite being so unreal as to alienate many a youngster, it occurs to those of us with higher feelings as *really real*, but as the playwright Edward Bond so movingly makes clear in his play *Bingo* (1973) that real has been finessed away into all sorts of poetic conceit in his plays. His actual theatre is just that, theatre; its realities are attractive for that very reason. Inigo Jones's 'Reals' are much more politically and ideologically, if not poetically and philosophically, challenging, for they force us to consider the Court, Jacobean, Stuart and Caroline, as not just a place of play, but much more than toys indeed. Rather than confronting the real of the Court in all its seeming and double-dealing, Jones was truly holding a mirror up to the nature of courtly culture and one in which that culture had spiralled out of all control at a time, at least in the Stuart period, when the economy was about as parlous as it is in the US and UK in the second Elizabethan era, post-*Lehmann Brothers*, post-*Northern Rock*.

It should not be forgotten that wherever Inigo Jones and Ben Jonson (his sometime writing partner) finished up, which was inevitably down, on the journey they climbed very high indeed in their early seventeenth-century day. Both had their origins among skilled artisans rather than the educated classes or the nobility. But they put this artisanal experience to work on a peculiarly immaterial, essentially *ethereal* art. Jonson in the end fell out with Jones because of the apparent collapse of hierarchy between the enduring text, the 'soul' of the work, and its machineries and effects, the spectacle. In keeping with this argument, in postdramatic theatre, at least as it is signified in Karen Jürs-Munby's excellent introduction to Hans-Thies Lehmann's abridged yet still indispensible English edition of his work, *Postdramatic Theatre*, staged text might have no place in the arrangements. If text is staged, then Lehmann emphasises it is part of a quite different formal economy than that commonly thought characteristic of everything we have come to expect since Shakespeare of the dramatic tradition. Text might well be one component as Lehmann describes it with gesture, music and visual elements all operating in and around the written word. But in this relative subordination from its previous hegemony it is now, or at least as signed by the postdramatic it is now, the relations of the total composition that become moot. This is what so enraged Ben Jonson. But Jonson was no Shakespeare, whereas Jones *in his own way and within his chosen profession* was at least, heretical as this may seem, Shakespeare's equal, and perhaps more influential in the shaping of the hyper-real Vegas landscape that defines commodity cultures today.

There is a long history to the postdramatic as conceived by Hans-Thies Lehmann in the book of that name that I am drawing upon here, a much longer one than the precedents he sets from the 1970s to the present day.[6] For Lehmann the relationship between drama and the 'no longer dramatic' forms of theatre, which have emerged at that time, marks a paradigm shift from a textual culture to a mediatised image and sound culture. It is no longer text but *theatrical means* that is the focus of postdramatic theatre for Lehmann. The postdramatic theatre is the first to turn the level of the 'real' explicitly into a co-player – and this on a practical, not just theoretical level. The irruption of the real becomes an object not just of reflection (as in Romanticism) but of the theatrical design itself. This manifests itself on many levels but most interestingly for Lehmann at the level of *undecidability* for the audience as to the status of the theatre act itself, a conundrum that has equally befuddled commentators on the significance, or not, of the masques of Inigo Jones and his contemporaries.

I would concur with this premise of 'undecidability' for all performance, and so would these artists who I have accompanied in my writing over the last three decades: Forced Entertainment, Bobby Baker, Goat Island, Rimini Protokol, Elevator Repair Service, Shunt and Societas Raffaello Sanzio, for instance. Each avowedly problematises the constitution of a dramatic fiction, and world in general, and with it confounds any immediate reference to social reality. This is no epochal 'post' in relation to the dramatic, nor a chronological 'post', but a more profound *rupture* with the dramatic itself that is underway here as Lehmann insists.

Lehmann's writing, as Karen Jurs-Munby outlines in her comprehensive introduction to his intellectual pedigree, might be considered a response to the celebrated Hungarian philologist Peter Szondi in his book *Theory of the Modern Drama* where from Ibsen and Strindberg to O'Neill and Miller a tension is noted between the formal requirements of Aristotelian drama and the demands of epic, social themes. Here, as Lehmann himself points out, drama is a time-bound concept, something that arose in Elizabethan England, where we began this chapter, seventeenth-century France and Germany during the classical period, where the dominance of dialogue and interpersonal communication excluded anything exterior to the dramatic world. All this came into crisis for Szondi, as Lehmann sees it, at the end of nineteenth century from Chekhov and his contemporaries onwards.

On the contrary, and to distance himself from this analysis, for Hans-Thies Lehmann this Aristotelian/Epic (Brechtian) tradition is limiting and needs to be dislodged from its common gatekeeping role on all that is admissible to the room that is radicality. Bertolt Brecht and the epic itself, in Lehmann's proposition, are equally to be brought into question; they cannot escape scrutiny for ways they perpetuate dramatic as distinct to postdramatic arrangements. Lehmann after all wants to show how theatre and drama have drifted *apart* in the twentieth century. I, in turn, would not wish to contradict Lehmann's seminal work but rather to extend it, to insist this happened 400 years before Lehmann suggests, at the very moment that the dramatic tradition from which it departs is marked by Shakespeare's inclusion of a masque within the latter stages of *The Tempest* whose opening was on 1 November 1611. It is this play within a play that hints at the end of an era for theatre and the opening of a future for performance.

But if I am to convincingly shift attention back four centuries, from the 1970s, it would be as well to identify the features of postdramatic theatre I might find in the seventeenth century, cited and summarised without undue injury, I hope, to Hans-Thies Lehmann's comprehensive catalogue:

PDT valorises performance
PDT spectators are asked to become active witnesses
PDT is a theatre informed by cultural practices other than traditional drama
PDT no longer represents the world as a surveyable whole
PDT is self-regarding and reflects its own processes
PDT is an attraction of the combined forces of 'speed and surface'
PDT foregrounds and problematises its status of illusory reality
PDT is a theatre of energetics and intensities
PDT is not conducted through action but states
PDT is the replacement of dramatic action with ceremony
PDT is a theatre of tableaux of metamorphoses and of landscape
PDT creates a time of the gaze
PDT is neo-mythical

This is clearly a far more convincing range of characteristics than I was able to offer either theatre or performance at the outset of this book. But if you attend again to the right-hand column offered in the Preliminary introduction, the five senses of performance in that list, you would be able to map each quite adequately over those listed above.

For instance, in what I have construed as Lehmann's last axiom (PDT is neo-mythical), a performance artist such as Robert Wilson in the US, and internationally, is figured as part of a much longer tradition that might include the acclamations of liturgical ceremony, the semiotics of the baroque theatre of effects, the stage machineries of the seventeenth-century European theatre, the ordering principles of Jacobean masques, the effects of Victorian spectacular theatre, the huckstering appeal of the variety show and the circus of modern times, all of which have always irreverently and effectively incorporated the depth of myth as much as the attraction of mythical clichés into their vocabulary. It is these continuities between theological acclamations and audiences to postdramatic (historical) forms that surface the most compelling questions in my view.

Furthermore, I am not sure all contemporary icons of performance are repeating history, the second time as farce, but Gertrude Stein, the queen of postdramatic theatre in its modern form, might well also have been describing the masques of Inigo Jones when she conjured her celebrated notion of the *landscape play,* where the multivalent spatial relationships of 'the trees to the hills to the fields [...]' any piece of it to any sky', as Stein said, 'might be connected to any detail, to any *other* detail'.[7] Works that offer a public reflection on particular themes instead of dramatic action are symptomatic for the landscape of postdramatic theatre as characterised by Lehmann, but it was equally, without detracting from Stein's remarkable originality for a moment, these themes that were critical to Inigo Jones's early modern experiments in form.

And, decisively, given the centrality of dance to the occasion of the masque, according to Clare McManus, and to post-1970s performance experiment from Judson Church in Greenwich Village on, it is within the act of dance that the new images of the postdramatic body are most clearly visible for Lehmann. In dance we find most radically expressed what is true for postdramatic theatre in general in Lehmann's characterisation. From the pedestrian dance of Steve Paxton, Mary Fulkerson and Rosemary Butcher on, this choreography articulates at its most obvious level of affect not *meaning* but energy. Crucially, in keeping with Lehmann's taxonomy of the postdramatic, it represents not illustrations but *actions.* Everything here is gesture as it was in the masque. Ben Jonson was well aware of this inversion and could not tolerate its implications for the ascendancy of the written text. Previously unknown or hidden energies seem to be released from the bodies of the dancers of this generation. Well before Oleg Kulik began spinning as a human glitter ball on the opening night of *Live Culture* (2003), dance had become its own practised messaging arrangement while at the same time becoming exposed as the plaything of a new courtly caste with all the codes of an elite, at least as reified as that of Inigo Jones's day.

But perhaps most importantly for Hans-Thies Lehmann at least, postdramatic theatre is a theatre of the *present.* What is of critical interest about this 'theatre of images' from Lehmann's point of view, and I am citing him almost verbatim here, is not whether it is a blessing or a catastrophe for the art of theatre, or whether it is the last resort for theatre in a civilisation of images. Neither, despite the title of this chapter, is it important in a historiographical sense, whether its time has run its course and whether neo-naturalistic narrative forms of theatre are perhaps going to make a comeback. Rather it is a question of what is symptomatic about it for the semiosis and pedagogy of theatre by which Lehmann means to take seriously and to make performance *now.* I presume Lehmann here is referring to, *here,* the culture, the secondary pedagogic performance culture, the one that some of us are fortunate enough to work and study within, the Universities of the twenty-first century, to where I will return in the concluding chapter, rather than to serve an industry that coincidentally surrounds me in the form of the West End of London, where we will be going shortly.

Why bother with this kind of phenomena, Lehmann asks us, when so much of the performance we share as observers in the late twentieth and early twenty-first centuries cannot live up to higher artistic demands of depth and form, mere toys then according to Francis Bacon? The answer I venture, along with Hans-Thies Lehmann, is that it is worth pursuing because this search for modes of expression and behaviour, beyond established practices, is still superior to almost everything we might see under the abandoned sign of theatre, the most 'routinised' productions, as Lehmann calls them, that fill the commercial and bankrupted stages about to 'go dark' for want of a pulse – even taking into account the frequent failure of its artistic means. For apart from the noticeable pleasure in theatrical play, these performances, since *The Power of Theatrical Madness* for me, but for others from decades before, have had the good grace not to presume the instrumentality of a dogmatic, performative politics, but rather, through the mobilisation of complex affective strategies and tactics, guerrilla incursions and fleeting encounters made appearances appear in such a way I would have thought would interest a twenty-first-century student of the future, rather than a nineteenth-century mannerist of the past who is no longer available for recruitment.

On the Concept of the Face

In the light of this discussion of the 'long postdramatic' in which I have been responding to, and drawing upon, Lehmann's seminal work, and Karen Jurs-Munby's generous rendering of that work for the Anglophone world, I would like now to attend to something more recent with apparently postdramatic qualities where Lehmann's hopes for a performance of 'sadness, compassion and anger' were very much at work. I want to explore some curious theological connections between being in the theatre with Romeo Castellucci's apparently 'naturalistic' production of *On the Concept of the Face: Regarding the Son of God* that played throughout Europe and at the Barbican Theatre in London, where I saw it in 2011, and being *outside* the theatre, in history in the making, with the Occupy London movement that was in residence on the civic apron of St Paul's for four months from 16 October 2011 – an event so limpid in its political presence and performance impact that the word 'postdramatic' might have been invented for it. And, to ensure continuity with the outset of this chapter, I would like to do this with reference to an early example of postdramatic theatre from the work of Inigo Jones. Just to complicate matters, chronologically if not thematically, we will conclude this chapter, as I said, in the same 'Las Vegased' West End, with some reflections on the musical *Les Misérables,* which, for more than a quarter of a century, has dominated the world stage and which has its own post-historic if not postdramatic qualities. This admittedly is an expansive task, but the approach to performance explored in this chapter, namely the relation between the theological and the historical is well suited to such an inclusiveness, indeed my point here, will rather be that such an approach insists on such a historical range to carry the relevance and resonance that is its due.

Romeo Castellucci's production, *On the Concept of the Face* (2011), was essentially made up of two episodes in its London version: the first intense and almost interminable, 'postdramatic' some (if not Hans-Thies Lehmann) might say; the second, briefly, dramatic. An older man, perhaps in his eighties, or even nineties, is tended to in a pure white apartment setting (furnished from a *Ligne Roset* catalogue), by a son who can never quite catch up with his father's incontinence. Being Castellucci, the human waste has been lovingly prepared beforehand ensuring that the auditorium is gradually but inescapably filled with a familiar odour that here seems somewhat out of place. On the evening I was present, the wife of the Italian ambassador and her friends sitting in the row in front of me, and who on first sight of the minimally but expensively arranged stage must have felt at home, passed a perfume-drenched handkerchief across their line and chloroformed themselves from the olfactory experience.

The son's ministrations to his father are offered lovingly and with great tenderness, despite the discomfort this inverted relation brings for both parties. As with other Castellucci productions for Societas Raffaello Sanzio, the dialogue is pared back to its barest, with the fewest words possible passed between these two agents of the stage.[8] It is the action that fascinates and appals us, the remorseless support required by those in their third-age dependency. We are fascinated not only because of the theatrically unique nature of what we are watching, real old age and its effects, but because we ourselves will be old in some way soon. The pitiless stage on which these images do their work functions as a condensing machine for this projected time, bringing us all back into stark engagement with what we face (Figure 3.1).

The performance takes an abrupt departure towards its end, however, when a vast backdrop likeness of Christ emerges covering the entirety of the stage rear void and begins to bleed something through its pores which could be shit, but,

Figure 3.1 Romeo Castellucci, *On the Concept of the Face*, London, 2011

given my senses were so shot by this stage without Italian perfume to immunise me, I am not at all sure.

I could start, in the spirit of the theological-historical frame of this approach to performance, by pursuing a theological reading of this face that would render it meaningful within its own religio-iconographic terms. According to Paul in the Corinthians, the optical phenomenology of Glory unfolds in the following way. God, 'the Father of glory' (Ephesians 1:17), radiates his glory onto *the face of Christ* who reflects it and radiates it in turn like a mirror onto the members of the messianic community. Given Romeo Castellucci's oft-repeated assertion that theatre operates as a 'dark mirror' on its times, this reading might not be wholly irrelevant in this context. Giorgio Agamben suggests that the celebrated eschatological verse Corinthians 1, 13.12 should be read in this light: 'the glory that we now see enigmatically in a mirror, we will go on to see face-to-face. In the present, we await the "glorious appearing".'[9] In contrast to John here the stress lies not on the reciprocal glorification of Father and Son but on the radiation of glory by the Father *onto* the Son and to the members of the messianic community. At the heart of Paul's gospel, Agamben suggests, lies not the Trinitarian economy, figured on this stage as Father, Son and the face of three in one, but 'messianic redemption'. This is a dynamic more suited, I would like to suggest, to a theatrical occasion where we, as audience members, are the third, obtuse, angle of a triangulated arrangement. Given that Castellucci is sitting above us operating a lighting desk that calibrates the exact, uncannily familiar glow back onto us from Christ's face, one might be forgiven for asking what divine right he might consider appropriate to the Director on this earth. But there is, as far as I can see looking around the Barbican, no redemption here, unless one accounts for our freedom to leave as and when we wish, which should not be underestimated given carers of the incontinent elderly have no such exit available to them.

Theological or not, it remains that this Christ is shitting *through his face*. So I began also to think through some historical as well as some theological questions that might take more seriously the Christian protest that ensued when Romeo Castellucci played the production at the Théâtre de la Ville in Paris, which might serve to co-opt the conservative Christian orthodoxy at work in their actions. I want to explore what Slavoj Žižek calls the *perverse* core of Christianity that I believe Castellucci is working with, and which operates in excess of the spectacle, in history I would therefore presume, and somehow is so excessive it reaches out, beyond the bounds of this theatre volume, to the west face of St Paul's where the Occupy movement in London stopped short of Paternoster Square in October 2011.

The first thing I want to attend to is *that* face, and specifically respond to that face in its defacement. Mick Taussig's figuring of defacement goes like this: 'When the human body, a nation's flag, money or a public statue is *defaced*, a strange surplus of negative energy is likely to be aroused from within the defaced thing'.[10] The thing we have been witnessing at the back of that stage is in a state of desecration, as close Taussig thinks as we are likely to get to the sacred in the modern world. You could call this, after Hegel, the 'labour of the negative', but perhaps the point here would be less to explain as to characterise and to interpret this act as one of profanation through play (as discussed in the Preliminary to this book). But this is an act of profanation that releases something, literally, into the auditorium. Through performance something sacred, that is by its original definition separate, is dragged away from its glorification and back into play in the world with which it might expect to have relations of compassion for instance, or magic mimicry in this case. Like shitting father, like shitting Son of God.

We can never prepare for defacement because, by definition, it always takes us by surprise. Certainly so in *On the Concept of the Face*, where the desecration reminds us of how complicit such violence is with the violences we have been witnessing of daily life where incontinence is the standard state. In these processes of defacement Walter Benjamin recognised that a profoundly theatrical project is underway in which *truth* is no longer a matter of exposure which destroys the secret, so much as a *revelation* which does justice to it. A lovely phrase worth repeating in the context of a theatre act such as this: 'truth is no longer a matter of exposure which destroys the secret, so much as a *revelation* which does justice to it'.[11] The revelation must always, for Benjamin at least, and I would suggest for any theatre director worth their salt, do justice to the secret.

A form of unmasking is underway in *On the Concept of the Face* in which the beatific truth as mystery, as secret, is revealed not so much as a private secret but rather as a public secret. In other words, the peculiar way is which we somehow know what *not* to know. The public secret is that which is generally known but cannot be articulated – in this theatrical scene, your prayers as a son, as a father, as an audience member that the shitting stop, just for a moment, will not be heard. And for Taussig such a public secret is moot as he believes all our social institutions, the workplace, the market, family and state are founded in precisely such public secrets. You might want to add to that list financial institutions and banks, and the public secret that long shrouded their excesses, if only to make obvious how we might begin to reach outside this act of defacement to another just up the road. This public secret is the most mischievous and ubiquitous form of socially active knowledge there is, always at the edge of exposure but waiting always for a form of revelation that does justice to it. Waiting for good theatre I might suggest.

The public secret in this theatrical scene is made manifest; it appears like a mystic alphabet on the screen in the face of Christ in the closing moments of the production, shortly after what I have described as the shitting face. The script that bleeds through reads: 'You are *not* my shepherd'. We have watched for an hour as an old man cherished and cared for by his son is abandoned by the Christ figure looking down upon him throughout. We all know well that abandonment, religious observance is not in a spiral of decline for no reason; the returns on investment in prayer just have not stood up when it comes to incontinent care.

But before this naming of the public secret, the lord who is not our shepherd is outed for all to see; there is still some investment in the public secret that demands the betrayal, or the abandonment, is concealed in some way, is not named *as such*. It is the cut of defacement, literally as the face of the 'saviour' is punctured, that releases this surplus, the cut into wholeness and holiness that like montage in a film, but certainly more than film here, releases flows of energy. This cutting of the face makes this energy visible and active in the theatre and it makes it active through being performed. I don't mean that quasi-mystic 'energy', that 1950s excuse for pop psychology, I mean the force of the gesture of the arm of the human who is puncturing the face, quite visible to us. An observer who knows Castellucci's work very well, Joe Kelleher, referred to them as 'Ninjas' later in the foyer. Christ is literally here beaten up from inside. The two faces we have been watching for an hour, of father and son, are here joined by a third much less forgiving face, and one that is brought back to earth.

The face is of course the figure of appearance, the appearance *of* appearance, of secrecy itself as the first act of being present. The face is enigmatic, it is sublime, it should surely be untouchable. It has been separated from history by religious interest, made sacred, but here the face extraordinarily reveals itself as sharing something insouciant with certain pornographic images, a looking *beyond* the immediate subject of its care, to an assumed audience in the middle distance. It is the only nude thing on the stage. While the old man is often 'without clothes', he is only ever seen in the 'absence' of the clothes that one longs to have placed back upon and around him to protect him again from our fascinated look. The face is somehow always already barely there; when you think back you are not quite sure when it appeared as a vast enigmatic wallpaper. The mystery revealed in the defacement of all this composure may become more mysterious for some, that is theatre, expressed in phrases in the foyer, such as 'what the hell was that about', or, 'I wish he had brought the play he was meant to', or much *less* mysterious given Romeo Castellucci's pragmatic dramaturgy.

There was a great deal written in newspaper columns and internet blogs about that smell for instance, but at every turn Castellucci expressed surprise that anyone would wish to imagine this smell as anything but palpably created, chemically constructed; it was a theatrical act not a natural one. Audiences seem to have forgotten here the first rule of theatre enshrined in Plato's Cave with its strategically placed illumination, that this is a synthetic, constructed place. Castellucci was even asked by one journalist, in my earshot in the Barbican foyer in London, whether it was his own shit, or the shit of his cast or crew, to which Romeo answered gently: 'Well, why would we do that?' In this misunderstanding of Castellucci's heightened theatrical craft, there is a confusion as to its association with the quite fake really real peddled by invasive performance art of the last century, and the postdramatic of this one (and the early seventeenth century).

There was, however, very little commentary on the austere, moneyed surroundings of the old man, at sea in this luxury apartment of pale, off-white. Romeo Castellucci has been very specific, and pragmatic again, in this historical location. He understands that the capitalist religion with its ungraspable fetish furniture is itself a remorseless 'separating machine' of consumption, and he gives form to this apparatus. Here the spectacle of capitalist trophy is wholly inadequate to the soiled reality of a man in his older age. Here the destruction of the thing, the fetish object, the furniture, the definition of consumption in the twenty-first century after all, is desperately resisted as the son frantically seeks to obliterate the marks, the remainder and reminder of his father from the leather covers. In this remarkable 'ill at ease' task-based performance scene that makes up the larger part of *On the Concept of the Face*, there is the haunting image of a well-meaning young man who has consumed objects that have incorporated within themselves a peculiarly modern capacity, that is their own *inability* to be used. While these two men might wish to exercise their right to this property, they dirty them without defacing them, they are constantly wiped clean, and in this sense are somehow beyond profanation. In this sense the economy of capitalist consumption has learnt well its lesson from its predecessors in the history of religious and theological defacement by veneering itself with wipe-clean surfaces.

So that's a start, a bare start with looking at and reading a saturated image *in* the theatre, one about which there was some degree of incomprehension in European theatre foyers but which spoke very clearly indeed to the Christian protestors who came from outside the venue and occupied the stage of the Théâtre de Ville in Paris during the run of *On the Concept of the Face* there in 2011. And a very fine demonstration it was. It is fine by me if not the cringe-worthy list of theatre luminaries who protested about it – they seemed to have a problem with the audacity of an audience taking to, and occupying 'their' stage, as though a theatre had never experienced a riot before. It is fine by me because like Mary Whitehouse in the 1970s in the UK, Jerry Falwell in the US, Jeremy Collier in London in the seventeenth century, and all right-wing fundamentalists have always done, this protest *takes seriously the power of theatre*, the suffering of images, and it does not leave it, or them, to whither on the indifferent vine of liberal consensus. I mean, if you force shit out of Christ's eyes you might expect some sort of reaction, surely? I personally do not subscribe to such show-stopping protests, but a tone of incomprehension at the protestors' actions strikes me as being wilfully naïve.

The Royal Remains

But why did defacement attract me as a way *into* this theatre act? As an act it does shift between the theological and historical in resonant ways. But also because it gives me a *way out* to the 'Complaint of St Paul's', back to Inigo Jones where we began in the seventeenth century and to the site of the Occupy movement,

Figure 3.2 *Occupy London*, West Portico of St Paul's Cathedral, 2011

which calls me from the theatre to another site of defacement in the same, old, city walls of London (Figure 3.2).

When Inigo Jones turns the world of the theatre inside out his act is one that stretches directly from his masque-making in Somerset House to the Barbican on that day when the Ambassador's wife took out her handkerchief. In this inversion the perspectival space of the theatre interior, so central to Castellucci's scenography in this production, with its scenic façades is applied to the planning and construction of the facial façade of the outdoor theatre building itself, and the external environment of the capital surrounding the theatre. In this process a reorientation or reterritorialisation occurs in which the realm encompassing the theatre becomes materialised as a form of physical landscape scenery. This then became the landscape face, or façade, of the city as we know it (in this case the capital, or head city from *caputa* as in the head of the sheep in the previous chapter) and subsequently, after William Kent's gardening designs, deeply influenced by Inigo Jones, this inversion began to shape the British countryside as well. Landscape hereby ceases to be conceptualised as a region, or place, and becomes a perspectival scene, which is quintessentially *modern*; it is as though everything 'out there' has begun to be performed, or at least staged, in a vertigo of landscaped attractions. Las Vegas indeed.

Let's take a look at the archival trace from Orgel and Strong's work of another masque that bears out these 'landscaped attractions'; this relation between town and country, interior and exterior:

Entertainment given by Robert Cecil, Earl of Salisbury
Date: Between May 6th and 11th 1608
Occasion: Visit of James 1 to Lord Salisbury, to mark his appointment as Lord Treasurer
Place: The Library of Salisbury House in the Strand
Poet: Ben Jonson
Designer: Inigo Jones
Performers: Mr Allen, a juggler, a conjurer, several boy actors, including the Flying Boye and 'the 2 boyes that played fancy an Barrahon'
Cost: Ben Jonson, Inigo Jones and John Allen each received £20

Scenery: A Rock and an Archway. An arch to left with sculpted figures on it and two sketches showing craggy mounds of rocks probably lit by the glasses for the 'rocke and the 26 waxe lightes' mentioned in the accounts bought at a cost of £2 –14 – 0.[12]

By transposing the perspectival space of the theatre interior to the outside of the theatre, not least of all between the Banqueting House in Whitehall via the Strand to St Paul's, Inigo Jones effectively turned the space of the theatre, encompassing both stage and spectators, inside out. Now life was to be lived in a performance space, reterritorialised as the facial façade and space of the urban landscape according to the surveyed spatial principles of Jones's theatre.

The dramatic transformation that occurred with the advent of Jones's Moebian, inside-out architecture can still be experienced by simply taking a walk through each of these central London areas, the relatively short distance from the reconstruction of Shakespeare's Globe Theatre on the Thames to the nearly contemporaneous Banqueting House by Inigo Jones, across the river at Whitehall, up Whitehall turning right into the Strand, and then along to St Paul's. On this itinerary the Globe stands out, as Kenneth Olwig has said, as a disjointed bit of old England, with its rounded shape, its half timbering, its thatched roof over its seated audience and its centre open to the sky. The Banqueting House designed by Jones for the performance of his masques seems on the contrary not at all out of place in modern London. With its quadratic performance space (a double cube) and almost neo classical façade it slots perfectly into the planned gridded space of a modern city with its focal points, and their social and economic hierarchical scales, radiating outwards from central squares and places, as pioneered by Inigo Jones at Covent Garden. One's impression in *this* London is of a larger urban space within which buildings, perception and movement are structured as scenery on the blocked space of a stage.

The record of a third masque, again from Orgel and Strong's comprehensive account in *Inigo Jones: The Theatre of the Stuart Court*, from half way along this route, at Middle Temple exemplifies this oscillating urban-theatrical aesthetic nicely:

Middle Temple and Lincoln's Inn Masque
Date: February 15ᵗʰ 1613
Occasion: The Marriage of the Princess Elizabeth to Frederick, Elector palatine
Place: The Hall of Whitehall
Poet: George Chapman 'supplied, applied, digested and written by George
Chapman'
Designer: Inigo Jones: 'invented and fashioned with the ground, and special
structure of the whole work by our kingdom's most artfull and ingenious
architect Inigo Jones'.
Composer: Robert Johnson
Masquers: Sir Edward Philips, Master of the Rolls, and Richard Martine
of the Middle temple are cited as the cheife dooers and undertakers' by
Chamberlaine
Actors and other performers: Lincoln's Inn Accounts include payments for the
services of several composers for performing on the lute: John and Robert
Dowland, Philip Rosseter, Thomas Ford, and others
Total: £1182

Contemporary Opinion: Chamberlain to Carleton 18 February 1613: 'On Monday night was the Middle Temple and Lincolns Ynne maske presented in the hall at court, wheras the Lords was in the bancketting roome. Yt went from the Rolles all up Fleet-street and the Strand, and made such a gallant and glorious shew that yt is highly commended. They had forty gentlemen of best choise out of both houses rode before them in theyre best array, upon the King's horses: and the twelve maskers with theyre torche-bearers and pages rode likewise upon horses exceedingly well trapped and furnished: besides a doiusen little boyes, dresst like babones that served for an antimask (and they say performed yt exceedingly well when they came to yt), and three open chariots drawne with foure horses a peece that caried theyre musicians, and other personages that had parts to speake: all which together with theyre trumpetters and other attendants were so well set out, that yt is generally held for the best shew that hath ben seen many a day. The Kinge stood in the gallerie to behold them and made them ride about the tilt yard, and then they were reced into St James parke and went all along the galleries into the hall where themselves and their devises (which they say were excellent) made such a glittering shew that the King and all the companie were exceedingly pleased, and especially with their dauncing, which was beyond all that hath ben yet'.[13]

This extraordinary description of an event – whose 'anti masque' alone, a dozen boys dressed like baboons, would grace the repertoire of Oleg Kulik's *Zoophrenia* project discussed in the Preliminary introduction – combines so many elements of the postdramatic theatre that one cannot but marvel that the tradition of the Shakespearean textual canon has, through successive generations, eclipsed its claims to be the true precursor of performance as we know it today. But how might we account for, if not accommodate or incorporate, this anomalous work within the continuum of the theological and the historical I am exploring here? Again I will return to the material evidence of the site I happen to be working within as I write this chapter, at the axis, literally the crossroads of Strand and Fleet Street, the meeting point of the various movements being discussed here, the location of this very 'gallant and glorious shew'.

If I have a historical method, it is an archaeological one, as laid out in the first chapter in this book, concerned with pre-histories, and an anachronistic one, or one that contemplates the apparently anachronistic and its strange power; for instance, the way I adopt Lehmann's *postdramatic* frame and bring it to bear on an apparently inappropriate time. Let's take a historical moment where the tension between the conception of a sovereignty given form in monarchical order gave way to a Commonwealth through which those royal remains found new form in a conception of the Public – a moment that is interred just next door to my working environment now, at the heart of Inigo Jones's landscape, in Somerset House on the Strand.

If the old Situationist rallying cry was 'beneath the cobblestones the beach', what if one starts *with a beach*, which is after all what *Strand* once stood for, and still stands for? What would one then cry: 'Beneath the beach, the stones'? Three years ago, in 2009, prior to the re-purposing and development of the East Wing of Somerset House, from its previous two-century deployment as a tax office to a publicly accessible cultural space, I was taken to the basement, precisely the location of Inigo Jones's most decorous postdramatic masques, by the Pre-Construction Archaeology team who were surveying the site, to find out more about these stones, to appreciate their Saxon finds. I was more interested in a pile of stones heaped against the wall, and, to all intents and purposes discarded there as so much *infill* detritus, to be cleared back for the earlier and more significant finds to be fully revealed. Longer history here was clearly perceived as 'better history'. But I recognised these stones; they are what I call 'Jones's Stones', remnants from the first Somerset House that stood on this site between 1547 and 1775, before William Chambers' masterpiece that referenced many of Jones's formal innovations, and for which Inigo Jones, the seventeenth-century engineer of spectacle, monarchical impresario and first great English architect, had created a Chapel, River Stairs, Cistern and Royal Lodgings.

I chased the stones back down to Brockley, in South East London, where the Pre-Construction Archaeology team had taken them, and spent some time with the archaeological team, examining, and then on return to the Strand, classifying them, within Jones's architectural oeuvre as I am outlining it here. My Leverhulme Trust–supported project, *Engineering Spectacle: Inigo Jones' Past and Present Performance at Somerset House* (2010–2013), avowedly eschewed any hint of reconstructionism. I am not interested in the 'authentic' or 'original' Jones, nor indeed very interested in guessing at what things once might have looked like, to rebuild them at great expense now. Even if I had a fetish for the past, such spaces would be next to useless for performance and its futures. In other words I am the opposite of Globe-ism, call it localism maybe.

I might not be interested in the constructions of largely imaginary reconstruction therefore, but I *am* interested again in what the anthropologist Mick Taussig described as that process which occurs as a consequence of something having been *defaced*. As we know from considering his work in relation to the appearance of Christ's beaten likeness in Romeo Castellucci's production, his ethnographically informed survey of the strange powers that reside in, and can be released *from* apparently lifeless objects, suggests that 'a strange surplus of negative energy is likely to be aroused from within the defaced thing'. I was especially interested in one column that lay before me, for while the column had been dug from the ground beneath the East Wing of Somerset House, it was identical to another column just down the road at St Paul's, or Paules Church as the medieval edifice prior to Wren's Cathedral was known.

One column (or at least its substantial fragment) represented the remains of a ruin, from the first Somerset House, which over a century after the Commonwealth was allowed to deteriorate and decay. Inigo Jones had turned his attention from his building at Somerset House, in the final decade of his life after the production of the masques we have been discussing between 1630 and 1640, along the Strand and Fleet Street to designing and building this west face of St Paul's, in his capacity as Surveyor to the King's Works. The columns there were ruined too; there were constant complaints about their upkeep, but somehow they *remained* to become performatively and publicly significant, before and after they were torn down. In July 1650 the Puritan Order destroyed the statues of the two Stuart kings, James I and Charles I, that crowned the portico on the west front of St Paul's, a portico made up of columns like the one that lay before me beneath the East Wing of Somerset House.

The west front of St Paul's is coincidentally where the Occupy movement pitched their tents on 16 October 2011, and from where they were evicted four months later in January 2012 (see Figure 3.2). A City councillor described their action as a travesty and a 'defacement of a great institution' as though this particular theological institution was not used to such defacement. According to Vaughan Hart's comprehensive work, *Inigo Jones: The Architect of Kings* (2011), Inigo Jones's largest and most important ecclesiastical project had been his work on precisely this location, this face of the cathedral, his application of the surface of antique ornament to the Gothic Cathedral of St Paul in London between 1633 and 1640.[14] According to one contemporary report, the new republican authorities in 1650 went on to allow the portico's Corinthian columns, which had been erected only a few years earlier to be 'shamefully hewed and defaced'.

Clearly Jones's architecture, or certain forms of it, did not enjoy immunity from the Puritan animosity directed at royalist and religious iconography during the Civil War and its aftermath any more than Occupy considered the Cathedral to be off-limits to their cause. This conflict had brought to a head the underlying religious tensions and related aesthetic sensitivities that Jones had had to respect throughout his career, popularising the antique style of building. And Jones knew, 400 years ago, very well what Bernard Tschumi was later to describe as 'architecture as event'. But why deface these *columns,* specifically, and not as with other iconoclasts just the faces of the royal statuary?

This is one reason as proposed by Vaughan Hart. The observer of all Jones's work, from the masques to the façades, was meant to read the ornament and forms of buildings, through a vocabulary drawn from the antique orders: a 'rhetoric of eloquence' as Jones would have described it. Ben Jonson eventually branded Jones's work as 'Court hieroglyphics' and missed the obvious point that Inigo Jones's *image-driven* work was the spectacular and gestural future for performance, the postdramatic qualities that would later prevail across the live arts. As Hart points out, the Italian architect and writer Palladio had already likened the architect to the *orator* in 1567. The analogy between architecture and oratory is underlined by the need for ornamentation, which both arts have in common. In this way the architect-orator moved an audience through a work's style, its embellishment and, on suitable occasions, its splendour. This idea of rhetoric had been explained by Henry Peacham with regard to the composition of a garden layout in his work *The Garden of Eloquence* of 1593 which was said to contain 'the most excellent Ornaments, Exornations, Lightes, flowers, and forms of speech, commonly called the figures of Rhetorick'. Jones knew Peacham's son, also Henry, who published *Minerva Britannia* (or *A Garden of Heroical Devices*) in 1612 and recognised well that the purpose of images and styles of speech was to *persuade*. Jones's mission was to persuade as well – in his case through the use of ornament. His was an 'architecture of eloquence' according to Vaughan Hart; the Whitehall Banqueting House façade with its swags of flowers and fruits could be considered just one such garden of eloquence though cultivated on the grandest of urban scales.

Royal processions of the Stuart period that often began at the Banqueting House would commonly wend their way via the Strand and having followed this route would take in St Paul's as a key marker and destination. The west front of St Paul's was often used as a backdrop for chivalric displays of City armour. The hereditary banner bearer of London marched to the west door where the banner of the City, an image of St Paul, was presented to the Lord Mayor, a tradition stretching back for 800 years that was interrupted for the first, and only time, in 2011 when the exchange during the Lord Mayor's Show was removed elsewhere to the East side of the building to avoid engagement between the City fathers and the Occupy camp to its west.

Jones's portico was a fitting triumphalist setting for this ceremony, making permanent in stone, as Vaughan Hart puts it, what had been temporary manifestations of royal power in ephemeral masque form. The Stuart attention paid to St Paules expressed the wish to restore the cathedral's eminence over that of the Abbey. The old medieval church was constantly close to ruin and the famous seventeenth-century pamphlet, *Complaint of Paules*, was a critical part of that campaign written by supporters intended to draw attention to the significance of its upkeep. As Occupy always understood, it had long been more than a mere building. St Paules had always had the advantage over the Abbey having been established on a dominant *civil site* as well as royal processional route. Given the magnificent statuary and its royal relevance Jones's *refaced* cathedral represented the ultimate achievement of Stuart rule presented on this Strand route. This, for Vaughan Hart, was the restoration of the true ancient British theology and unity, here expressed in stone (Figure 3.3).

The two parts of my chapter, between theology and history, dramatic and postdramatic, bifurcated somewhat up to now, usefully come together in this

Figure 3.3 Inigo Jones, *Brittania Triumphans*, London, 1638

image. So far we have considered Inigo Jones's inversion of the interior of the perspectival space to the external urban realm, but here the dynamic is reversed yet again, with this representation of St Paul's and the urban space radiating from it providing the backdrop to the Masque *Britannia Triumphans* of 1638. Here, the restored St Paul's is seen to the rear centre of the theatre scene. It was interpreted as an emblem that 'might be taken for all of Great Britain'. The area in front of the Cathedral's west end, to which Jones's portico formed a dramatic backdrop, was conceived as a setting for the enactment of court rituals and public theatre such as the *Triumph*, but the *Triumph* with its central image of St Paul's was *also* staged in a temporary structure at Somerset House, bringing graphic depiction of those columns and orders to this place, and to what this was, a Royal Palace.

As Vaughan Hart makes clear, this architectural mobilisation of meaning, and imperial meaning at that, was not unusual as Inigo Jones was responsible for a series of new, ordered façades that fronted a traditional royal route at the centre of which was the Strand and which in some cases were applied to existing buildings. The Stuarts thus intended to signify the imposition of their rule on established medieval institutions. This work celebrated the King with the Banqueting House at Whitehall Palace, the encouragement of commerce by the court with the New Exchange and Covent Garden, the Queen with Somerset House, the City and its

Figure 3.4 Anthony Van Dyck, *Charles I, Henrietta Maria and their Children*, 1632

Companies with Temple Bar and finally the church with old St Paul's. Through employing the device of the column, with its harmonic proportions and ordered relationships, these new façades would have permanently embodied the virtues of harmony and solar enlightenment personified by the monarch (Figure 3.4).

All in all this amounted for Vaughan Hart to a massive project of Stuart *resurfacing*. In the context of this chapter we might want to refer to this process as one of *refacing*. And it was refacing with a political purpose rooted not just in a historical sequence of succession but in a *theological order*. Jones's expression of the traditional legal concept of 'the King's two bodies' through his decoration of court buildings was built upon the ranking of the columns articulated through their decorative character from 'poor' to 'rich'. At the pinnacle of this ordering of columns was the legal body of the Stuart King, the richest among men. The king's body was the ultimate pattern of Jones's columns; they represented the crucial power that the monarch embodied: this was their ability to make Law by Divine Right. The sovereign, after all, is the one who decides on the state of exception.

The fluted columns offer a clue to this and further multiply the multidirectional forces that we have already seen at work inside and outside the masquing house.

They had an outward aspect, an appearance of symmetry and order yes, but also an *invisible quality* based on ideal human proportions – both material and transcendent like the king's two bodies. It was this invisible quality that the Puritan forces sought to reach in their act of defacement.

What really happens when a column is brought down from one elevation to another? I would suggest a symbolic and material shift is taking place, epochal in its significance, a shift from the 'King's Two Bodies' to the 'Body of the People'. Here contemporaries witness the minimum condition for a Public to arise, a transformation of the body politic that can be seen for what it is as the column I found in the archaeological dig in the infill basement of the second Somerset House is turned through 90 degrees, which is how I found it lying amidst the Saxon finds. Remember what Mick Taussig said about how defacement releases a negative energy. Here, on the pulling down of the stone, the negative of the *vertical* orientation of the column, for the Puritans at least, a locus of sovereign transcendence and divine authorisation comes to be dispersed *horizontally* among the people.

If you are wondering about the veracity of all of this, you might recall having seen this phenomena quite recently with statues of Saddam Hussein who/which were brought to the horizontal plane to be defaced and slippered after his overthrow in 2003 and his execution in Baghdad in December 2006 (Figure 3.5). Of course as post-war Iraq has demonstrated all too vividly, but also in all such 'de-thronings' wherever they are, 'the people' with a lower case p, dispersed in their intentions until now, become a Public who are both blessed, and cursed, with a surplus of immanence. The negative energy has only one place to go, and it is into them, the Public and the Republic. As Eric Santner says: 'The new bearers of the principle of sovereignty are in some sense stuck with an excess of flesh that their own bodies cannot fully close in upon and must be managed in new ways'.[15] I don't mean that this inhalation and induction of sovereign surplus is a cause of contemporary obesity, though that might be worth exploring for its relationship to those royal remains; I am rather suggesting that we are all saturated with the effects of such sovereignty.

We should remember before getting carried away with all this defacement on behalf of the people that some monuments in Rome may have been ruined, like the columns I discussed from St Paul's, but their proportions were nearly always perceived as somehow still intact. Renaissance architects, including Jones, certainly considered this to be the case, indeed Inigo Jones's only completed and published treatise under his name was a study of precisely this restorative dynamic, a project for the rehabilitation of the vast but dilapidated monolithic

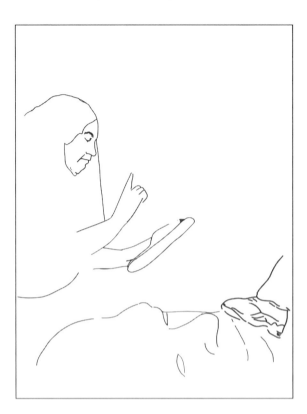

Figure 3.5 Statue of Saddam Hussein, Baghdad, 2003

ring called Stonehenge in the South West of England. Rather improbably he suggested this restoration should follow the 'true, classical, Tuscan Order' that was his architectural preference elsewhere, apparently blissfully unaware of the long history of the Druids at this site, and the Pagan roots of the stone circle.

As we will see in Chapter 5, Freud was later to make a great deal of this possibility of simultaneous pasts and presents coalescing in the form of ruins, and kept a favoured image of Roman ruins on his wall next to his print of Charcot ministering therapeutic hypnosis at the Salpêtrière. It was all very well for the Puritans to release this negative energy in the act of defacement of these columns, but as became obvious with the restoration and the building of Wren's masterpiece, St Paul's Cathedral, the continuation of theological *sovereignty* by other means, had a durability that the Puritan forces underestimated.

Indeed the royal *remains*, after all, whatever the Puritans and Cromwell thought they were doing, much closer to home than this Republican might have imagined. The Queen's relationship to King's College London, my place of work at the time of writing, the latest in a long line of royal engagements at Somerset

House from well before the Commonwealth and the demise of Inigo Jones, is surely fascinating and disturbing for those of us interested in the ceremonial of glory now. Ceremonial as an apparatus of praise and acclamation that, with the exception of David Beckham, Beyoncé and the cast of *Les Misérables*, has never quite recovered its potential for apotheosis since the era of Inigo Jones, when *this* site, the Strand and its environs, really was a theatre machine that generated images of true glorification for a grateful, subjected Public and a Court predestined to flatter those who might advance their interests.

I would be interested here in the degree to which we do not necessarily *need* the Queen to remind us that at King's and elsewhere across a broadly Republican culture in a neo-liberally-united-kingdom, the Royal remains. Quite *how* the Royal remains shape the kinds of public we are destined to reach, as distinct to those publics we might aspire to meet, if we have any interest in such a thing beyond ourselves, is for me here moot. The very questions of community that have threaded through the first three chapters of this book are precisely shaped by such considerations. The Royal remains not just through a fawning British submission to the enduring afterlife of monarchical power and privilege, it *is* that afterlife. But it would not be quite true to say that the equivalent of Inigo Jones now would be a royalist engineer of spectacle, Gary, or is it Sir Gary Barlow, say, who curated the Queen's Diamond Jubilee Concert in 2012, or the Mayor of London Boris Johnson who was the Queen's Pageant Master on the Thames on 3 June, parallel to what was once the Thames's north bank beach, the Strand.

No, in a wholly predictable but deeply unsettling inversion of what we might expect, the praise that was once due the sovereign is, I would humbly suggest, lived out now in *spectacles of the poor*, of the subjected, where the weak can be endorsed by our presence and the shedding of our tears on their behalf. My proposition would be that our newly minted, sovereign public enjoys their wretchedness as manifested in theatrical representation, just yards from where sovereign splendour was once king. It is Cameron Mackintosh, the British sovereign of spectacle, the truly world-dominant theatre producer, who has best understood and profited from this inversion and made himself king of all he surveys, from one end of the Strand to the other, which like some afterlife of its earlier centrality to the economic machinery of colonialism and empire, from Twining's Tea head offices at one end, to the favoured Royal bank Coutts at the other, still emanates an influence way beyond its apparently local limits.

Indeed Cameron Mackintosh's great Masque of the impoverished, *Les Misérables*, both the nineteenth-century novel by Victor Hugo (1862) and

Figure 3.6 *Les Misérables*, Queen's Theatre, London, 2012

the play that has dominated the late twentieth-century world stage, has been critical in the passage I am introducing, that is the shift from royal to popular sovereignty in the form of a public, from an essentially theological, divine right of kings, to a purposefully historical recovery of the people (Figure 3.6). Where royal sovereignty operated through a conjunction of political theological dynamics substantiated and sustained by Inigo Jones, *popular* sovereignty, the invention of a public is a bio-political operation, not just the management of a public's health and life, but the sublime 'life substance' of people who become the bearers of the royal remains in the 'democratising' processes of enforced investiture I have been describing. Indeed the Somerset House site on the Strand I have been walking and working throughout this chapter is the founding centre where an idea of such investiture of the people as a public was first invented and inscribed. Through the means of 'investiture', humans here for the first time became invested with authorities of a symbolic nature towards a public. Somerset House provided the first purpose-built public offices in the UK, and from 1789 until the *Performance Foundation* took up its new home in the East Wing of Somerset House, ushered in by her Majesty the Queen on 29 February 2012, that publicity machine has literally been creating manageable publics 24/7 for an unbroken quarter millennium.[16]

Performance is interested in such processes of investiture, from Inigo Jones via Somerset House to the Barbican today, in as much as such protocols are business as usual, further disturbances in the space of representation and appearance that are theatre's fuel. That is our ground and our expertise if we have one. And of course these representations connect with our capacity to feel represented in the social field, to experience the representations as viable facilitations of our vitality. The problem is that where in, and through, the mediation of the 'King's Two Bodies' the sublime flesh of the monarch underwrote and supported the operations of governance built upon it, the question of what might in a post-monarchical society secure the operation of the new bearer of sovereignty is critical, moot and in question.[17] One might ask, where is the flesh of the Monarch now? I can't tell you any more now than I could before 29 February 2012, when I was introduced to the Queen, because in the presentation line I took hold of a *gloved* hand. Gloves, for Walter Benjamin at least, heralded the human's disgust at 'touching' another animal.[18] But I already know this flesh quite well because it is this flesh that has been centre stage in all that is and was the postdramatic; from Marina Abramović to Franco B, it has been this *flesh* that has been contested and invented and examined assiduously through the postdramatic form, back to the early seventeenth century and Queen Henrietta who placed herself centre stage as one of the first women to dance, to perform, on the European stage, at her home, Somerset (Denmark) House.

While it is successive democratic governments that have *managed* this surplus that was once the King's flesh, it is performance, from Inigo Jones's magnificent costuming to Cosette's rags, that has most tenaciously adopted this terrain as its rightful place and perspective. With democracy the concept of the *nation* replaced the monarch and sovereignty was dispersed from the king's bodies to all bodies. With the old sartorial codes gone, Eric Santner suggests, bodies were less legible and a person's place in the nation became less clear. With royal columns crashing down it has become precarious to assume one's appropriate position at their base. And it is this lack of clarity that sets conditions for the precarity, the vulnerability, the dependency of the human now. And it was this precarity we were seeing played out most tellingly by Romeo Castellucci's production *On the Concept of the Face*. It is, I would suggest, the human's peculiar pleasure in immunising themselves from such vulnerability that accounts for the success of *Les Misérables*, seen by 60 million people in 42 countries, and explains why it has so many serially repeating fans for whom touching the hem of Jean Valjean is enough.

If the producer responsible for this fetish work, Cameron Mackintosh, really were the reincarnation of Inigo Jones today, he would recognise, I am sure, the magnificent irony that a production that has made its profits from assiduously praising the 'poor', we after all cry in sympathy for those starving on the far side of the barricades, has been generating those profits at a time when another cast of performers, the Occupy movement, has been drawing attention to the '99 per cent' at the very place, the West face of St Paul's, that Inigo Jones spent so long perfecting as an apron stage for seventeenth-century ceremony. The problem for Occupy activists, as they explained to me when I went to meet and talk with them at the Tent University in December 2011, is that they have no decent song to draw attention to the plight of the poor, and, unlike the cast of *Les Misérables,* they are rarely praised when they speak out demonstratively about the bankers and the Las Vegas casino economy we are all, somehow, now participants within. A public, that has truly paid, big time, for the gamble of all gambles.

If Cameron Mackintosh had Inigo Jones's genius for turning internal spectacle outwards towards its relationship with the urban realm, if he had an ounce of Jones's postdramatic instincts, he would have marched up the Strand on the day of their eviction from St Paul's west front and invited them into the Queen's Theatre to occupy those barricades where they truly belong, in front of an appreciative audience whose tears, for once, would not be driven by sentiment, but by sense. Having ensured everyone was happy with this arrangement, and there is no reason to think there would be any disappointment given it is the poor that are so conspicuously promoted to sell tickets to his show, Cameron Mackintosh would then lead his cast of *Les Misérables* back up the Strand from the Queen's Theatre to the West face of St Paul's. Then, having reintroduced the cast to today's equivalent of the barricades, some tents on the steps, Sir Cameron would simply have to count them in, 1, 2, 3, and stand back. The soaring harmonies of *Do You Hear the People Sing?* would ring out, and along the Strand, now a true Songline as well as a Strandline, a harmony that might be faintly heard now, if we could hear such things from our neighbours. At least we could trust that true to the film, these people would have found their *own* voices, but not so much 'singing for themselves' as the publicity for the cinematic spectacle puts it, as singing on behalf of others.

4

Fourth Approach
Digital & Technological

When Denis Diderot, the founder and editor of the *Encyclopédie*, was growing up in Langres, in the early 1700s, on a limestone promontory in North-East France, at odds with his cutler family and his local Jesuit College, he would have been a regular visitor to Saint-Mammès Cathedral at the top of town, just 100 metres from the gabled house in Place Chambeau where he lived (Figure 4.1).

Figure 4.1 *Saint-Mammès Cathedral*, Langres, France, 1710

In the far north-west chapel of that cathedral was a sixteenth-century stone-relief depicting the raising of Lazarus from the dead. Young Diderot would have noticed that Lazarus was having trouble with his hands. The 'paradox of the actor', the first secular theory of the actor, the apparent contradiction that a technically controlled performance might be a prerequisite for heightened feeling on the stage, must have come from somewhere. And I would suggest, it was here.

Lazarus, now, today, still without his hands, stands on his tomb, a solid stage-like platform, and is surrounded by a healthy audience of onlookers. The witnesses to this miracle are clearly divided down the middle and separated by an angel that delimits the horizon of the work. To the right, as you look up, are the disciples, all twelve of them, apparently bored with the apparition before them. They have clearly seen this kind of thing before. To the left are a symmetrical group of locals, but they are not bored. They are astonished and exclaim their amazement at the act with their hands to their faces and their jaws dropped. This fear is founded in the fetid; the stink of Lazarus is a mortal reminder of the temporal limits of the flesh.[1] The age-old signification of the ennui of the professional and the affective enthusiasm of the lay community is obvious (Figure 4.2).

Denis Diderot might have identified, in this sculptural depiction, a cloying sense that Langres and its limits could not hold him, and the capital called. But he took with him from this Cathedral, to the Tuileries in Paris, a memory of the paradox of the actor, who having been granted 'a life' on this temporary catafalque stage would generate concentration and distraction in equal measure. This is what I would like to call the Lazarus affect, the hopeful feeling that follows a theatrical effect that you know to be true.[2] That Lazarus has lost his hands to an accident of history suggests we might wish to explore this 'affect' for all its *digital* resonance, its two handedness. *The Paradox of the Actor* makes this clear: on the one hand there is an actor who is required to emote, on the other hand there is the expectation that this actor will remain in control of their feelings. And given, when this was written, when rhetorical meaning would have been made apparent largely through the hands, it is an invitation to move on from the previous chapter with its concentration on faces and surfaces to the gestures of the manual, the digital and, in the latter half of this chapter, the technological, conceived here as a prosthetic extension to the rhetorical reach of such bodies.

We should not forget in starting that we have the enthusiasm of the Parisians for theatre in the eighteenth century to thank for this first secular rendering of the art of the actor. The dialogue to which Denis Diderot gave the title

Figure 4.2 *Lazarus*, Terracotta Relief, Langres, circa 1450

Paradoxe sur le Comedien has reached an impasse when one of the antagonists, named Second, proposes to the other, First, that they might test their theory, developed at length and on foot, and 'repair to the theatre'. This interruption to the abstractions of conversation, this diversion from the path of speculation to encounter evidence, is a feint, a gesture towards theatrical practice destined to return us to the prose of the world, the writing, not the acting out, of experience. Diderot, the storyteller, looking on, describes what happens: 'Our two interlocutors went to the playhouse, but as there were no places to be had they turned off to the Tuileries. They walked for some time in silence.'⁴ In fact they are muttering to themselves, and Diderot insists he can only report on 'the ideas of the man with the paradox'.

The dilemma for Denis Diderot, at once First and Narrator who is not First, is the true paradox at stake in this episode, for these are 'incompatible places'.⁴ By definition one can only be in one place at one time, at least at this point in the eighteenth century that would be the case. By the end of the nineteenth century, and by the end of this chapter, a certain technological revolution will have made the potential of simultaneous co-existence quite compatible, but not yet. And not for Diderot for whom the split between emotions expressed here and now on stage and the rendering of such emotion in a technically realisable fashion was moot.[5]

This paradox, between the two incompatible subjects of Narrator and First, is marked by an act of enunciation with no part, and no place, and this paradox comes about because it is, precisely, a *paradox* that is being enunciated. As Phillipe Lacoue-Labarthe puts it more philosophically: '...would not the enunciation of a paradox involve, beyond what it has the power to control, a paradox of enunciation?'[6] The paradox of the actor is perhaps more accurately stated as the 'absence or suppression of any property', the *caesura*, or gap marked earlier in the neolithic caves where, in the midst of animals, to activate a propriety, any property, for the human is to recognise the human's marginality to animal continuity. It is therefore not just the disappointing man, the underachieving human that marks the actor, that would in the end be quite dull. Rather this paradox would suggest that the performing man and woman must be a 'man and woman without qualities', somebody who is literally beside themselves, their part played by those who have no part. Humans, like the under-boards of the stage space explored earlier, are indeed, for Peter Sloterdijk, 'hollow'. They mimic themselves, a chamber for ringing echoes, in the throwing of their ceramic vitrines and vessels. It is 'nature' that has given this sense of nothing to the human, simply, what Lacoue-Labarthe calls 'a perpetual movement of presentation'.[7] This gift, our birthright, is the gift to be improper through performance on every occasion. Again, and following our episode in the caves, it was precisely this dilemma that encouraged Plato to exclude poets from the Republic on the grounds that mimesis threatened the perceived coherence of 'self-identity'.

This vertigo against any such coherence, marked by the *incoherent* waving of the hands of First and Second in conversation, ceases for Denis Diderot with a decision, a decision concerned with affects. That is, when one becomes subject to affects, pre-eminently through performance, one *becomes subject*. The hollow human becomes resonant for others. This affect machine of performance, as conceived by Diderot, does not sound so alien to Marie-José Mondzain's conception of neolithic *Homo Spectator*, who through their digital reach realised themselves on the cave wall, and thus realised themselves. While Plato feared the vertiginous loss of identity through poetic semblance, it is precisely through the operations of just such an affect machine that subjects make an appearance from the hollow promise that is human. Let me explore one such manifestation of theatrical appearance through digital reach with respect to something, or at least, someone, closer to home.

Hands

I am at another theatre, not in the eighteenth century with Diderot's Parisian narrators, First and Second, but in twenty-first-century London, with you. It is me, and you, for reasons that I will explain in a moment. And, again, unlike First and Second we got the tickets. And Jonathan Pryce, perhaps best known for his portrayal of the Governor in *Pirates of the Caribbean*, is there too, and he is having trouble with his hands, as well. You could say, 'like Lazarus', but without the smell, though one would have thought nights spent on the blasted heath having been thrown out by his daughters would have taken their toll. Like Lazarus this is a digital problem, and one that goes to the heart of the relations being drawn in this book between performance and theatre.

So, Jonathan Pryce is having trouble with his hands. Or, Jonathan Pryce's hands are having trouble with Jonathan Pryce. Or Jonathan Pryce's hands are having trouble with King Lear. For this is what it is we are witnessing. While I am not quite sure about cause and affect here, what I do know is that King Lear's hands are not having trouble with Jonathan Pryce. Or at least, I don't think they are. These are decidedly not King Lear's hands I see before me. They are Jonathan Pryce's.

Jonathan Pryce's hands, his capacity for digital expression, are *not* what make Jonathan Pryce human, though philosophers for centuries, from Heraclitus to Heidegger, would like us to think so. For Heidegger the hand is intimately connected to thinking; we act insofar as things present are within reach of the hand, and in so doing we disclose what was once concealed. The marks and signs that are formed by the demarcating hand, the first acts in a digital world, these inscriptions, are what Heidegger calls 'writing'. It is this *handwriting* that makes visible the word, makes literature and, for Heidegger at least, makes Human Being possible. As Tom Tyler makes abundantly clear in his illuminating work *Ciferae*, Heidegger's thinking is not merely humanist; it 'displays a hauteur that is hyper-humanistic'.[8]

Despite what Heidegger suggests, there is good reason *not* to stake humanness on hands, identity on the digital, whether we are talking about the eighteenth or the twenty-first century. There should be no presumption as to which way things will go for Jonathan Pryce's hands either. Over time his ancestors might develop more digits, or as snakes showed with digital regression, *less* might be more. So, I wouldn't want to mislead you in this part of a chapter on the digital and technological by letting you think for a moment that I associate humanity with hands. No more than I associate drama with the digital, or performance with people.

Nevertheless, in thinking about the digital in this perhaps unconventional way, in other words by initially eschewing computing machinery and virtual platforms (as I did with my earlier discussion of the ceramic tile) and concentrating rather on the outer limits of the human body, whether that be Lazarus's exhumed body or King Lear's exiled body, I have taken Judith Butler rather literally, when at the close of her essay *Precarious Life* she writes: 'If the humanities has a future as cultural criticism, and cultural criticism has a task at the present moment, it is no doubt to return us to the human where we do not expect to find it, in its frailty and at the limits of its capacity to make sense. We would have to interrogate the emergence and vanishing of the human at the limits of what we can know, what we can hear, what we can see, what we can sense'.[9] For me that limit in the twenty-first century starts with Jonathan Pryce's hands, as indeed in eighteenth-century France it must have done for Denis Diderot as he looked up to that broken figure of Lazarus from below.

I should here admit that, to be honest, I am not really interested in Jonathan Pryce's hands, in and of themselves. I must admit I have only ever been interested in theatre and its various parts as I have figured them through this book in so much as it permits me to feel, think, say and write things I might otherwise have felt, thought, said and written, *but more acutely*. In this sense performance has simply done what other arts are too coy to admit to. Performance is, in its genetic irritability, a register of the unbalancing of action and reaction, in other words the measure of *exaggeration*, modest acts of up-scaling that materially reduce the distance between things, bring things closer together in order that we might perceive them in the same place at the same time.

I *am* interested in these hands in as much as they allow me to think of a means by which we might move beyond Denis Diderot's *Paradox of the Actor*, towards the figure to whom someone gave the name Jonathan Pryce, *as a person*. Not as a human, nor a citizen, certainly not a character, but something that modulates between these various entities: a *person*. A person who acts. Or more accurately, an actor who in doing so becomes some sort of person, an 'other' person. Following an idea first developed by the linguist Émile Benveniste and picked up by the philosopher Roberto Esposito, I would like to suggest we call this figure, as we did at the outset with Oleg Kulik spinning in the roof of Tate Modern, not Jonathan Pryce, not King Lear, but a 'Third Person'.

What Jonathan Pryce's hands are telling me is that his *rôle*, a performance by nature of his situation, is also a 'performative', a form of language combining gestures and words productive of *real* effects. These effects, which are affecting me, have something to do with a continuously recurring separation between a character, given the name King Lear by Shakespeare, and a person to whom you might be inclined to give the name Jonathan Pryce. The *person* I witness, falteringy, emerging before me in *this* play, is striking me at *this* moment with the hands, as the more artificial entity among those present. This feeling is compounded by these hands, reminders of the human 'as a natural being', for whom the status of person may or may not be in question. To be the owner of this body, let us say these hands for a start, the person as far as I can see from the stalls cannot for some reason be coextensive with it. The person, in *this theatrical setting*, is specifically defined by the *distance* that separates it from this body, these hands. While close to Diderot's 'Paradox of the Actor', I would want to call this distantiation, disturbance or division, something similar, just similar: the 'Parallax of the Performer'. In being similar but not quite similar enough to be the same, this person and Jonathan Pryce (or at least his hands) would appear to have parted company. And I am discomforted by this distance, measuring my own distances to this stalling of identity from a distance, not least of all looking down at my hands. Never mind *Catharsis*, I suspect this 'looking away' from such theatrical split personality is one reasonable side effect of tragedy. As children, after all, we watched terror through the gap between our fingers so as to claim back editorial control over our earliest feelings of extremity.

This separation is amplified in the scene I am talking about by costume. Jonathan Pryce's hands sit at the end of a doublet and hose arrangement in universal beige that is the *sine qua non* of a certain kind of Shakespearean production. Meanwhile Edgar as Poor Tom in the same scene is unclothed above his belt and it is harder to identify where hand ends and arm begins, though his skin is the same universal beige, which further unsettles me.

The words Lear speaks are complicating this further. They are prose, not poetry, which separates them from what has come before, and while peripheral for me with regard to what makes this scene *theatre*, are nevertheless just surviving the hands that wave them our way:

> Thou were better in a grave than to answer with thy uncover'd body this extremity of the skies.

Poor Tom has just emerged from a fissure, a rend in the stage, a trap door in the earth.

> Is man no more than this? Consider him well. Thou ow'st the worm no silk, the beast no hide, the sheep no wool, the cat no perfume. Ha! Here's three one's are sophisticated; thou art the thing itself; unaccomodated man is no more but such a poor, bare, forked animal as thou art. Off, off, you lendings! Come; unbutton here.[10]

But why then do I insist on this 'naughty night' as the Fool puts it, on referring to Jonathan Pryce in the third person, or even *as* the third person? Surely at the theatre we have commonly figured the rest of the audience as the 'he', 'she' or 'it', the 'they', that is not you, communing as *you* are with the first person on the stage, the I (Jonathan Pryce) that speaks to you. But I want, in this chapter at least, as I did with Oleg Kulik in the Preliminary, to refer to him, them, actors up there, in this way, not to be disrespectful, but because they show me something crucial for our future about the *impersonal,* the potential of the impersonal in an increasingly personalised world. And it is the rend of performance in this most canonical of theatre scenes that allows for such an appearance – the sense that an increasingly personalised world has never, perhaps, felt more impersonal, where our supposedly defining human hands have provided the very means to *dehumanise* us. This 'digital data' epitomises and marks our age as avowedly as the digital database that accumulates, collates and centralises it (Figure 4.3).

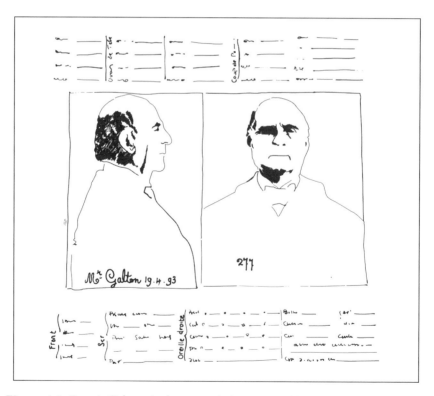

Figure 4.3 Francis Galton, *Anthropometric Apparatus,* 1887

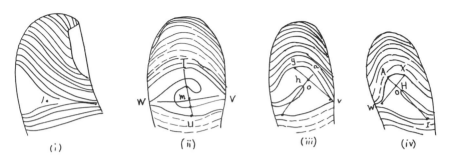

Figure 4.4 Francis Galton, *Fingerprints*, 1889

This dehumanisation begins, perhaps ironically, with Charles Darwin's cousin, Francis Galton, who in the 1870s began to work on a fingerprinting classification system which would allow for criminalisation without recognition of a person's face, a system that was specifically designed to apprehend what were described as 'natives from the colonies' whose physical characteristics tended to be confusing and appeared indistinguishable to a European police eye, and to apprehend 'prostitutes' of the time whose 'long hair', according to the authorities, 'made measurements' difficult to take accurately' (Figure 4.4).[11]

As Giorgio Agamben, whom we encountered in Chapter 3, has pointed out, having refused to accept invitations from states where biometric data determine access through borders, for the first time in the history of humanity 'identity' was no longer a function of the social persona and its recognition by others, but rather a function of biological data which could bear no relation to it. In this process we literally lost touch with our own means of identification. Today the entrance to high school cafeterias prepare children as young as my daughter, and her friends, for their fate in this respect, installing regulating means of biometric apparatus upon which students distractedly place their hands while busy insisting, in archaic conversation, that they still recognise each other and those who are serving them sustenance.

But back to the theatre, and to *King Lear* and to the performance that has become so irritating (in the best possible way).

In a binary world of the theatre in which actors and audiences would appear to take precedence, this *third person* is critical, and not least of all because it is through this figure of the third person that we can begin to understand something more of Denis Diderot's 'paradox of the actor' through the 'parallax of the performer'. And this is possible because the third person is not *actually* another person, with respect to the first and second, or First and Second as

Diderot characterised it, but rather *something* that extends out of the logic of the *other* persons there, the audience, in favour of a different regime of meaning. The actor, like Maurice Blanchot's 'neuter', is thus not another person to be added to the first two but something that is rather neither one, nor the other. It defies all dichotomies founded on, or presupposed by, the language of the person.

For this reason actors like Jonathan Pryce in my view are not located at any point in the expected proximate relation that we think of when we say theatre, but most definitely outside interlocution, actors become an 'outside'. Actors are not similar to anything; they are just 'similarness' itself. Given this radical breach of the two-way dialogical model we have presupposed theatre to inaugurate, various *theatre* approaches would seem to have attempted to tame its excesses for all its disruptive affects (actor training that involves concepts of centring, sub-text and intention are prime examples). Meanwhile *performance* has of course contrarily, though not always, relished the disruptive effects that my characterisation of a third person initiates, without carefully enough considering its binding, conserving and often conservative implications.

I am beginning to sense if not understand why Jonathan Pryce's hands were causing so much trouble and it is a condition not wholly disconnected from Lazarus's hands as witnessed by Denis Diderot. His hands of course, any actor's hands, represent the obvious opportunity and most obvious means to reach out towards us, even to touch us, or *be* touched. But more importantly than this rather obviously romantic observation, an observation that has been fetishised in a century or more of attempts to reduce distances between audiences and performers, from Sergei Eisenstein in Moscow to *You Me Bum Bum Train* in London, a process that will be discussed in some detail in Chapter 7, we should not ignore the rather obvious point that I am making here for the first time in this book (and we should delay no longer given we are about half way through) – that any relation through theatre is as likely to be one of the registration and measurement of degrees of *immunity* as celebrations of *community*.

Now, this is important to me and I think should be important to us all if performance is our serious interest. For it is this person, the one with the hands that are causing so much trouble for me in the economy of representation, who does not identify themselves through their gestures, but chooses not to reach for us but rather away from us, rather makes what I would like to call using a painter's term, a 'rend' in the stage image through which I can begin to perceive, faintly at first, sometimes with a blow, often partially and with much peering though not enough touching, possibilities that might be open to persons in such situations, concrete ones such as this. This is how I think performance is working in this theatrical scene. Not what is inside that will take care of itself, but the rend itself. The rend in the fabric of theatre is, for me at least, as I have understood it in the theatre and in this book, the work of performance through which the possibilities of persons are played out – the potential, and importantly the impotential of personhood. And it is this rend that will run through this chapter, a rend that I hope you will not take at face value, but put into doubt as I try to locate it.

By way of approaching this 'rend', I could re-register what I have just said *theatrically*, using Jonathan Pryce as a rather impersonal prop at the very point of such personhood, and I could emphasise the nature of such a performance personality by introducing some animistic terms to the argument. If I contest this third person is as much some*thing* as someone, what could that mean in this theatrical context?

Just as humans do not need hands to be humans, persons do not need humans to be persons. Humans *become* persons at various moments in which their rights are recognised but can just as quickly become 'less than persons' as the history of the twentieth century revealed. Indeed human rights are no longer extended to individuals because they are citizens, but rather because they are *persons*. The category of the person in the twenty-first century now appears, for Roberto Esposito and Giorgio Agamben at least, to be the only one that can unite human beings and citizens, body and soul, law and life, but it is nevertheless, performance notwithstanding, a category at the heart of which is an almost wholly unquestioned assumption.

Performance, whether you call it *King Lear* or Franco B, *The Three Sisters* or Marina Abramović, if it is concerned with anything, is concentrated almost wholly on a life's entrance into the regime of personhood, not as an unquestionable value, but as something that is *put at stake*. This would appear to be what the sculptor of the ceramic relief depicting Lazarus (now, but not originally, without his hands) was figuring on that wall of Saint-Mammès Cathedral.

It is perhaps a horrible irony that simultaneous with the scandalous loss of personhood across the globe that escalates today through local examples such as strip mining in Nauru, oil-powered levelling of communities in Nigeria and genocidal militarism in Syria, there has been an equivalent and reciprocal expansion and extension of personhood to any number of previously organic and inorganic things, from animals to oceans. The issue is not, to put it crudely, whether these animals and others are people too. The issue, rather, as Anthony Kubiak has argued recently in an essay on which this animist analysis is built, is to recognise that the impulse in humans towards recognition, something called 'personness' (not mere subjectivity, or, worse, 'subject position'), is an impulse that is not necessarily bound to notions of what constitutes the human of the humanist traditions, the one with hands.[12]

The *recognition* of personness, for Kubiak, grows out of the propensity to be concerned about, precisely, an 'other'. Not a bad starting point I would have said, for both an interest in theatre and also an understanding of why performance itself is a critical touchstone for any university of the twenty-first century that takes seriously a grave problem. Judith Butler was precisely speaking about the university when in *Precarious Life* she wrote:

> The structure of address is important for understanding how moral authority is introduced and sustained if we accept not just that we address others when we speak, but that in some way we come to exist, as it were in the moment of being addressed, and something about our existence proves precarious when that address fails.[13]

That sociology can tell us about alienation, that psychology can tell us about anxiety, that medicine can tell us about arthritis, is not in doubt in the twenty-first-century university. But few if any of these disciplines can encourage us to *care* in quite the way that performance links evidence and experience in uniquely affective ways. We will return to the performative role of the university and the imperative for tactical critique in Chapter 7.

What precisely is at stake then in the turn to *animism* Anthony Kubiak and others are advocating here, for that I am afraid is what I am touching on through the first part of this chapter in which the inorganic of the ceramic relief meets the organic gestures of Jonathan Pryce, which in turn become petrified in their apparent distance from me in his greatest moment of need as a homeless father? It is certainly not, as Kubiak warns, an invitation or recommendation to return to the 'old animism': a return to some atavistic belief in spirits that inhabit inanimate objects. This might be helpful in getting to grips with certain world views, as Kubiak recognises, but it is simply wrong and is a misinformed view of those world views. Rather animism now pulls together recognition of the inter-being of the world in a way that would not have been alien to those residents of the caves that we started out with. The animist stance is just that for Kubiak, a stance, an attitude of openness a fundamentally affective and thus aesthetic world view but one which comes about through the partial, and temporary suspension of ideological or categorical states of mind. The new animism is for Kubiak less a view or belief system than it is a conscious enactment, a performance of an inherent relationality infused with awareness.

I think that describes what performance brings to the theatre, but I am afraid for the romantic and the communitarian in me; this has to start with the potential of the *impersonal*, or the *impotential* of the personal, if it is not to subside into solipsistic self-regard.

It is in this climate of simultaneous retraction and expansion, proximity and distance, personal and impersonal that any conversation concerning the merits or not of performance might be conducted today. There are many of us at work at this front: Anthony Kubiak has mobilised the term 'animism' somewhat provocatively but effectively, Claire MacDonald has called it 'radical inclusion', Bruno Latour has called it the 'collective', Roland Barthes in his first lecture series at the Collège de France called it 'How to Live Together'. And many others such as David Williams, Jen Parker Starbuck, Tuija Kokkonen, Baz Kershaw and Lourdes Orozco have insisted through their pluralising efforts that such endeavours might be worthy of recognition in the performance field.[14]

So what do we do from such an animist stance as we watch theatre in a digital age? What is worth doing under this sign of performance: this is what begins to occur to me in the Almeida Theatre watching Jonathan Pryce's hands.

In this theatrical scene involving Edgar, as Poor Tom, and Lear, I find myself thinking about Jonathan Pryce's hands by way of diversion from what I have been invited to look at through something that some directors do, though by no means all directors I must stress. This work of the director is called *blocking*. Much of this administration of the stage, this manual labour, is, quite happily for me, because I enjoy these complications at the theatre, getting in my way, or getting in the way of some sounds which include words but might also be poetry.

In the case of these hands I am drawn to them because they are about as far away as I can look from the actor Jonathan Pryce, by which I mean his vast beard, without simply giving up on the thrashing figure in front of me and turning my attention to the walls, which at the Almeida Theatre in general, and in this *King Lear* in particular, are really, well there is no adjective for it other than, 'wally'. The stage is just full of walls and there are walls as far as you can see. There are hands and walls. On this night, in this show, I am being *disturbed* by hands and walls. Animism thus moves us away from the central semiotic image of *consuming* culture, there is far too much happening on this stage to presume I could consume anything; rather what I am describing here is an intense phenomenological state of *dissolution*, subsuming and being subsumed within ever-widening spheres of responsibility. Here, there are walls, touched by an animist's sensibility there are you could say 'walls that talk', and there are hands that reach out for those walls.

Waves

If the digital as figured above is the handiwork that incorporates a spectrum of practices between Heidegger's conception of handwriting as an essentially human revealing of the concealed, to the gestures, lost and found, of Lazarus and Jonathan Pryce, I wanted to ask the most obvious question in the second part of this chapter that arises from such close encounters. At what point in human history did such proximity give way to relations at a distance, at what precise point did humans understand the possibility of their presence and its effects on others prior to their being there? This would, it seems to me, be the critical precondition for any arguments we might wish to mount regarding the special quality of theatre in its 'live', proximate relations to us. The wave, while it might describe the gesture of the hand, provides us with the ethereal link we might need.

If the *techné* of technology is again as Heidegger would have said, a 'revealing', as with his conception of the digital act of handwriting, where was it that the fundamental closeness of human speech gave way to the mobility of network relations that we take for granted now? Where the theatre stage is just one social platform among many? The answer I believe lies with the emergence of *telegraphic* communications in the early nineteenth century, but not simply because the telegraph initiated the fundamental shift from here to there, the stage coach had already done that, but critically, through the telegraph, time and space collapsed into each other in a manner that parallels the disturbance I have described in the theatre confronted with the multiplying walls against which were foregrounded Jonathan Pryce's hands. It is the telegraph that from the 1800s begins to move us from the Ceramic Age of the glazed screen encountered in Chapter 1, or at least bypasses that screen through the voice-throwing wave of radio-phonics.

To locate the beginnings of this movement you could do worse than take a close look at some more walls. Not ostensibly a theatrical arrangement this time, but no less shaped, framed and ornamented by humans for that. Walk west from Hammersmith Bridge, along the north bank of the river Thames where London gives way to its suburbs, and there you will encounter unlikely architectural neighbours. Jostling between the paupers' graves beneath Furnival Gardens, the Dove public house and the carcass of the boat-house of the 'Men of the Thames' remodelled in oligarch-kitsch by its billionaire Russian owners is a single Georgian building of architectural and historic distinction, and a squat two-storey workshop of unprepocessing charm. Here is a speech site where a history of orality reveals something more than oral history, a *location*

Figure 4.5 Kelmscott House, Hammersmith, London, 2004

where *locution* might be amplified through technological innovation in order to discern an ethics of speech, a place for performance, before and after the telegraph (Figure 4.5).

As you cut down, away from the river, by the Dove Pub, Kelmscott House will greet you first on your right, five storeys of symmetry and elegance that, in the nineteenth century, once housed William Morris and his London-based works.[15] Let us turn away from its 'technologised' neighbour for a moment in order to read between the lines of a stone in the elevation that records: 'William Morris Poet, Craftsman, Socialist lived here 1878–1896'. From here Morris, the writer and designer, conducted his interdisciplinary and avowedly digital, that is *manual* enterprise (Figure 4.6).

Morris was an uneasy but inveterate public speaker, concerned equally with politics, art and the environment. His holistic views on architecture and design, expressed most notably in lectures such as 'Gothic Architecture', might not

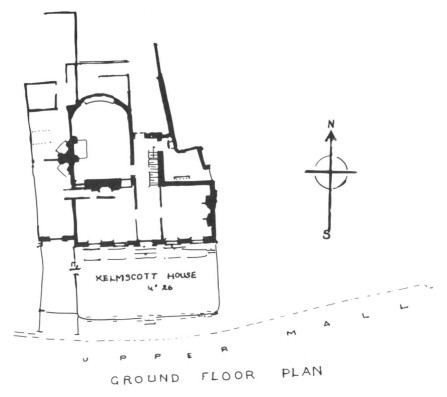

KELMSCOTT HOUSE
N° 26

GROUND FLOOR PLAN

Figure 4.6 Kelmscott House, Groundplan, 1895

seem too distant in their organicism from some of the concerns of this book and its concern for theatre in the expanded field. Morris did after all say: '…a work of architecture is a harmonious co-operative work of art, inclusive of all the serious arts …'.[16] However, in the same speech are serious reservations as to the possible relations such architecture might have with technologies or constructions of the future of any kind. Indeed the absence of what Morris called an 'Art of Architecture' signified a 'transference of the interest of civilised men from the development of the human and intellectual energies of the race to the development of its mechanical energies' (Figure 4.7).[17]

William Morris's move to Kelmscott House in 1878 coincided with just the moment in the life of this metropolis where the suburban was being enveloped by the urban. Hammersmith had just become connected to the newly built underground system of subway trains linking the western fringes of the city to its centre. As a writer, in works such as *News from Nowhere,* Morris was as preoccupied with this long future towards the city as the medieval past away from it.

The Oxford and Cambridge Boat Race 1892

Figure 4.7 Kelmscott House, Boat Race Day, 1892

News from Nowhere is a utopian work with a contemporary social purpose which through its multi-layered disorientations in time and space projects the personal as political in ways reminiscent of a much more contemporary critique, say in the prose of Iain Sinclair or the filmmaking of Patrick Keiller. First produced in a serial form for the journal *Commonweal*, the narrative is structured through two river journeys, one East into London, from Hammersmith, the other out of London, West towards Oxford and Morris's other riverside dwelling Kelmscott Manor. In an ironic self-portrait, William Guest, the protagonist of the story, is rowed downriver by Dick the boatman through a sequence of urban villages surrounded by green and space.

This is a dream-work where in a post-revolutionary state Marxist processes of history (towards the city) are offset against instinctive 'needs' (towards the country). While the power of roots is never far from Morris's itinerary, there is little real challenge to the power of place; indeed, Morris's own indifference to machinery denies the narrative any technological dimension which might have threatened the bonding power and persistent claims of the priority of place over the vectors of space. It was not that Morris could be described as a Luddite, indeed given the central place of *patterning* in all his work, and specifically in wallpaper and carpet design, this would be contradictory. But rather that for Morris the role of machinery and technology within the workplace might threaten the relationship between the worker and their product which, for Morris, was to be one of *joy* if it was to be of value.

However, before we are irretrievably lost to the claims Morris makes as the favoured son of this site, we should avert our eyes just to the left for the sake of this chapter on the digital and the technological. Attached to the side of the headquarters for Morris's work is something of an anomaly. A squat two-storey coach house grows from the side of the house as though flying in the face of its freehold. The coach house carries its own legends. In the upper part a stone is inlaid and inscribed: 'The first electric telegraph eight miles long was constructed here in 1816 by Sir Francis Ronalds's F.R.S'. The modernity of this inscription is its first appeal. Here was produced for the first time a practical means of conveying messages instantaneously through space. Here was manufactured the prototype for the device through which humankind might precede themselves in space, arriving orally before they appeared physically. And here begins a history of cultural complexity and hybridity, with people knowing about you before you appeared. The stereotyped and simplistic meetings beloved of children's books, of Captain Cook and the Aborigine, Amerigo Verspucci and the Amerindian, on their respective pristine shorelines, are superseded by a hyper-speeded version of that classic meeting of familiars: 'Dr Livingstone I presume'. It is all jungle from now on – a twisted braid of knowingness that intertwines identities and colombines previously distinct national boundaries.

It is in this complicating spirit, rather than a heritage crocodile trail, blue-plaque performance, that I suggest we examine this site to see and hear for ourselves what else these walls that make up a house might tell us about two contiguous histories of speech – to consider how such walls are not *representative* of anything beyond themselves but rather marked memorials to the melancholy loss of a means of speech, the manner and material of saying something, now, after another fashion.

You will have noticed that inscription's contradictory expansiveness, its evocation of an object *eight miles long* within a workshop barely 20 feet by 40 feet. How could that be, and why is this apparently arbitrary distance worth recording for posterity? It is doubly ironic that this message to modernity should sit above the portal of a home for the previous apotheosis of communication: the horse-drawn coach. Until then the coach was the vital means of cross-country delivery of mail and the fastest secure physical communication link between one voice, in script, and another.

Within weeks of taking the lease on Kelmscott House, Morris had filled the coach house with looms; it became the site for the production of his celebrated woven 'Hammersmith' carpets, and he subsequently converted it to the lecture room for the local branch of the Hammersmith Socialist League. So to summarise, this was a coach house which never housed a coach, which had once been a workshop which never housed the 'wire' that was to supersede the coach. The telegraph was, in fact, manufactured in the garden, to the rear of the house, and as each resident comes and goes now from this leasehold home, the turning of the soil reveals another section of that historic remainder to voice-throwing.

If Morris's biography is somewhat familiar, Ronalds's lifeline is now almost completely eclipsed by the prior claims of Morse in the US and Wheatstone and Cooke in England to the invention of the first telegraph. A simple technical resistance has removed Ronalds from the place in this history he deserves. He maintained, long after his competitors, a faith in the power of 'static electricity' that was to become unfashionable, and then unworkable, with the rise of constant current and the use of the battery that his competitors espoused. A library of electrics compiled through his European travels, two small monographs, a portrait in the National Portrait Gallery in London and the stone on this coach house are the only signifiers that record his endeavours. So what were they? Considering this man is the founding father of our telecommunications revolution, it was strangely difficult to find out.

Having studied physics in the east London suburb of Walthamstow, which was also coincidentally the family home of Morris, he had conducted his first experiment in North London – 'the blowing up of a large hydrogen gasometer in the breakfast room of No 1 Highbury Terrace', from where he transferred his studio to a small cock-loft over the coach house: 'Here through a round hole or window, in the south wall, I introduced one end of a long wire extended down the fields towards Holloway... I made a few unimportant observations ... and only mention them because I think that the idea of transmitting intelligence by discharging an insulated wire at given intervals first occurred to me while thus occupied'. In the end, Ronalds discontinued the work: '...because the neighbours were occasionally affrighted by very loud detonations and said that they should be killed by "the Lightning which I brought into the place". In fact two or three of my neighbours were killed; but these were only unprincipled rats, experimented upon, dwellers in the Hay Loft, devourers of my poney's corn'.[18]

So Ronalds's early work accounted for one of the first crosses between vivisection and execution, an initiation of electricity's complex relationship with discipline, death and 'famous last words', which was to prevail in language from there on until the last use of the electric chair in the US in the late twentieth century. At this time, in 1813, Ronalds, now sited here at Upper Mall, acknowledged that he had moved to a 'more elegant hay loft'. It was during this year and the next that he experimented with Deluc's 'dry column', obtaining

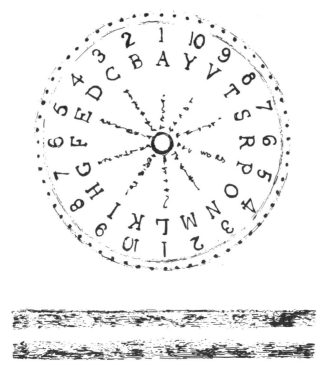

Figure 4.8 Deluc's System, Francis Ronalds, 1816

discharges between the smallest possible conducting masses, and, with the help of a watchmaker, adapted Deluc's system with a pawl and ratchet mechanism through which the movements of a pendulum caused the rotation of a pointer round a dial. Here Ronalds was establishing the first means to read the discharge of electricity down a wire, as text. Being alphabetical, this was so far so digital, but the wave patterning of this current was to initiate the significant shift between that digital past and an analogue future (Figure 4.8).

Ronalds describes himself among 'scoffs and jeers and a few imputations of insanity', constructing his first electric telegraph in the garden of Upper Mall. The garden, now truncated by the pulsating A4 road west from Hammersmith towards Heathrow, was at that time 600 feet long. Ronalds transformed this into 'eight miles' by suspending his overhead wire on multiple lattices suspended by silk from hooks in horizontal bars. His generator was a frictional cylindrical machine and at the end of each line was an electroscope and balls, which collapsed when the line was discharged. Dials were set at the sending and receiving stations, which rotated synchronously by clockwork. Each was marked with the alphabet covered by plates with a single letter-sized aperture. When the

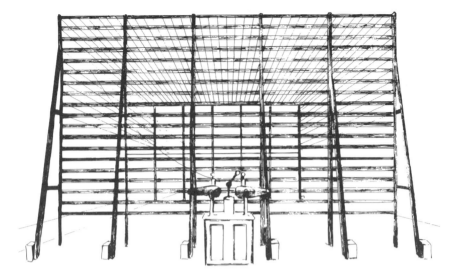

Figure 4.9 Telegraph 'Eight Miles Long', Kelmscott House, 1816

desired letter appeared on the disc the operator discharged his line, the receiving station noted the visible letter as his electroscope collapsed (Figure 4.9).

Ronalds's first overhead construction, which had created distance in concentrated parallels, was then superseded by a subterranean experiment where a trench 525 feet in length, and four feet deep, was dug down the garden, secured with a trough of wood in which was laid glass tubes carrying the conducting wires. It was this experiment which has emerged, piece by piece, over the years. In 1862 the first sections were dug up and passed via the Pavilion at Brighton to the Science Museum in Kensington where, if you ask to have them brought from storage, you can see them now.

If these were the experiments, what implications might they have for our consideration of the reverse shift being described in this chapter, between an earlier digital that gives way to a later technological, from the hand-held to the wave?

Well, if cultural hybridity starts from the eclipse of coach-bound communication by the wire, so does the demand for a post-colonial anthropology of technology. For if 'being here' and 'being there' are now intertwined through the possibility of speaking to 'there' before arriving from 'here', an innocent arrival scene, once beloved of anthropologists in the field, is no longer adequate nor possible. From here the journey of the visitor is always one in debt to their host; the guest is known about, thought about, expected and theorised before they can open their mouth. In technological terms, foretold is forewarned.

The coalescence of the signatures on this site here becomes confused and interlaced. Morris was concerned in the nineteenth century with the colonial implications of the Stanley explorations in Africa and resolutely opposed their triumphalism in print and speech. Stanley's adventurism in Africa in the 1870s and 1880s occurred to Morris as the brutal act of 'colonising capital' bolstering the capitalist system in Britain. The celebration of Stanley's London-speaking engagements, by the press, was anathema for Morris. Yet the communication conditions for Stanley's mission to the Congo, to the 'heart of darkness' with the illuminating force of Christianity coupled with colonial geography, had been set by the invention of the telegraph. On his return to Europe, Stanley was able to perpetuate myths of his endeavours through the media of his day and to prey on the residual jingoism of a nation that had in reality tired of his brutalist exploits in the name of their nation. Indeed, Stanley's adventurism was itself constructed with the funds and complicity of print journalism. *The New York Herald* had funded his expedition to 'find Livingstone' and The *Daily Telegraph* to follow the course of the Lualaba in a monumentally ill-conceived expedition.

The implications of the relation I have been sketching out between a prior digital, demonstrative drama and a technological distribution amongst others cannot be underestimated in this virtual age. Nor can its influence be underestimated for the geography and demography of the city. From here there was BT and AT, before the telegraph and after the telegraph. It is not so much the graph in the title that announces the disruption of a logocentric history of communication as the 'tele', which alerts us to its electronic means, the fundamental leap from digital script to the wave structures of electronic analogue code (Figure 4.10).

Where the 'digital age', for all its contemporary sounding urgency, had in fact long ago been initiated by the invention of the alphabet (digital refers to information representing a set of fixed symbols such as letters or digits), it was analogue, the means of the electric wire, which used a continually varying *wave* form quantity that more profoundly marked two dynamics of distance.[19] Cities now could co-exist as relational concentrations of communications platforms, by-passing the hinterlands between what once had to be crossed in a grounded reminder of the root of the word 'country', that is 'contra', against and in distinction to the urban.

This audio revolution, in broader terms what Paul Virilio called 'the last vehicle', had technically begun with the first experiments in telegraph in 1794 that had preceded Ronalds's work, and following Ronalds's was to continue with the telephone of 1876, the phonograph of 1877 and the radio of 1894,

Figure 4.10 *Animal Alphabet*, Hermione Read, 2002

revolutionising what could be considered the 'means of communication'.[20] As we have seen, visual systems had previously predominated with Robert Hooke's demonstration of visual telegraphy to the Royal Society in 1684, setting the dynamic of signing which reached its apotheosis in Claude Chappes's 1852 system of 556 semaphore stations across 4800 km of France. These towers bore signs which were telescopically viewed at relatively high speeds, but although 500 miles could be covered in three minutes, this was not the zero point of instantaneous communication that was so sought after.

While the earliest telegraphy system was proposed in 1753, static electricity, the source of its invention, was more widely used at the time to entertain philosophical gatherings of friends than it was considered a serious contribution to communications. It was a common amusement to transmit a shock through 30 or 40 persons, each holding hands with the next, by means of a simple magnetic device. This experiment was repeated on a grand scale by Abbé Nollet when a shock was passed around a one-and-a-half kilometre circumference circle of 200 Carthusian monks linked by iron wire lengths. What these amusements *did* prepare for was a common understanding of the instantaneity of the medium irrespective of the span of the circuit. These were the first demonstrations of hand-conducted wave patterns, where a digital history literally 'handed' over to the circulating patterning of waveform over extended distances.

It was this sense of 'knowing now' rather than then, or sometime, that shaped this avowedly modern geography of speech. The instantaneity of the telegraph set the model and pace for what might after its inception have been considered the 'speed of speech'. One response to this acceleration of speech might be to wonder at the loss of space, the contraction of the world, the 'death of distance' as Frances Cairncross has called it. Another would be to accept that throwing one's voice does nothing to annihilate distance but reinforces the very separation of subject and discourse; it literally brings people together in mutual misunderstandings. I would suggest it was this faculty that ensured theatre would not only survive the technological revolution being described here but also would thrive amidst its misfires and performances; it would act as an archaic reminder of a rhetoric of proximity, a carapace of closeness.

As a pamphleteer, a typographer and public speaker, William Morris was himself, in the midst of this technological revolution, reinventing the relations between political writing and speech. But for him, living to the side of this lecture hall and above a drawing room theatre (which we will come to later), *proximity* was the essence of meaning. What constituted the 'with' of communication, talking *with* someone, what constituted the history of that 'with', and its possibilities for social change, did not allow Morris to recognise the potential power of the technological means that lay beneath his garden, despite the fact that the very means of this revolution would have, from time to time, emerged in the top soil of his vegetable patch.

Morris's scriptural energies travelled by other means; they were profoundly digital in their orientation. While it might be anomalous to think of him enduring the pollution of the early London subway system, recording with some delight his thoughts about the novelty of travelling by underground train, he considered tapestry weaving itself a kind of movement therapy, what he described as 'the dear warp and weft of Hammersmith'. His Hammersmith carpets, produced within these walls, were only part of a range of responses to designs of the East and Persia which Morris described as 'carpeteering', orienteering towards an Eastern model. Each carpet was a textual reminder of a geography of elsewhere, read through motifs of the locality, and in Morris's house, as elsewhere, were

Figure 4.11 Lecture Hall, Kelmscott House, 1895

not only used to walk, and sit on, but to drape over and surround the whole domestic environment. These walls were thus digitally enabled, screens of warp and weft for perceiving foreign fields. Morris called himself the 'word spinner' and though, as his biographer Fiona McCarthy points out, he was verbally inhibited in public, the more one looks at this site itself a different history of his spell-binding emerges (Figure 4.11).

Outside, below the stone memorial to the telegraph, lies another plaque complicating in assertive upper case the textual cacophony of this apparently mute site: 'GUESTS AND NEIGHBOURS, ON THE SITE OF THIS GUEST-HALL ONCE STOOD THE LECTURE-ROOM OF THE HAMMERSMITH SOCIALISTS. DRINK A GLASS TO THE MEMORY! MAY 1962'. The text is from *News from Nowhere*, Morris's futuristic work which, when discovered beneath the modernity of the wire announced above, appears singularly dated. In fact, the plaque was mounted on the coach house in 1962 and though the Red Flag had long flown over Hammersmith Town Hall, almost directly north of this house, away from the river, the vision of socialist debate the script promises had passed from the site even before Morris's death in 1896. The history of guests speaking in this venue in the latter years of the nineteenth century reads like a 'who's who' of founding socialist voices. As well as George Bernard Shaw, there was Keir Hardie, a miner and founder of the Scottish Labour Party, Pietr Kropotkin, the leading Russian anarchist, and Beatrice and Sidney Webb, all of whom spoke in this long but intensely focused assembly room with a spectral light illuminating its small platform from above and behind. What Donald Sassoon has called 'the most anomalous Left' in Europe found its voice right here, overwhelmingly middle class, idiosyncratic and divergent from the Social Democratic Foundation and the Fabian Society of the day. The Socialist League was nevertheless unable to outlive Morris's own lifetime. As Morris joked in the opening passage of *News from Nowhere*: '... there were six persons present, and consequently six sections of the party were represented ...'.

William Morris was a consummate storyteller, a romancer from the Nordic tradition of the sagas, and he was above all else, through necessity if not desire, a 'public speaker'. He chose to speak of architecture, art and the city as well as write about it. It occurs to me that choosing to speak about each of these three complex and mutable objects is an invitation, as people concerned with theatre in the expanded field of such endeavours, to become inscribed within them and responsible to them. We do not have to share Paul Virillio's technological dystopia to begin to wonder whether amid the hype, the promises of the wire here pale, for the possibility of speaking at a distance and with a degree of anonymity *could* be perceived as an unwelcome invitation to remain discreet from questions and their implications. But how might one theorise the question of distance in a more nuanced way, neither noting its death nor submitting to its dominance?

Readdressing this site through the work of that 'botanist of the asphalt' Walter Benjamin, in that space between his two now very familiar texts of the same year, 1936, 'The Work of Art in the Age of Mechanical Reproduction' and 'The Storyteller', further opens out some of the complications of speech in this location. The shattering of tradition that Benjamin recognised in the mechanical reproduction process, the end of the auratic quality of the live and unique encounter, was precisely the potential for the reinvention of artistic practice as a mass phenomenon. The historical decline of the aura, from Diderot's handmade rhetorical flourishes, was most assertively premised for Benjamin in the culture of film. For Benjamin film was associated with the masses, cinema's urge was to bring things 'closer', spatially and humanly and in so doing to deconstruct the 'distance' on which aura depends. Here Benjamin memorably referred to the masses destroying the aura like 'prying an object from a shell'. Thus distance was associated with the unapproachability and status of the cult object. For Benjamin, technical reproduction would bring the art object closer to the beholder, meeting the viewer halfway. So far, so Ronalds. Indeed Ronalds's telegraph not only announces the destruction of the 'original' encounter, but his graphic machines – which he made as an aesthetic sideline to his scientific work – were invented precisely to dispel the aura of the artist as a privileged arbiter of perspective.

But the spectre of Morris returned in the other key text of that year, 'The Storyteller', in which Benjamin discusses the disappearance of the storyteller's art.[21] Here space is reversed with Benjamin arguing for the power of the distance inherent in the storyteller's craft. And here perspective was coming to an end, literally the means through which experiences might be exchanged. Thus storytelling is for Benjamin, as for Morris, a fundamental part of subjectivity. There could be no greater contrast with the faith in the technical means of production than this celebration of the individual experience in *communitas,* the significance of dialogue. This well-known and observed dialectic in Benjamin between proximity and distance, reproduction and originality is played out between the two buildings and their inscriptions. And it would seem the one determines the fate of the other.

The end of storytelling is harboured, for Benjamin, in the proliferation of information which gains precedence over intelligence in its infinite revolutions. The class control of the media of communication, including the wire, ensures the responsibility of this information to advanced capitalism. Here Benjamin, perhaps like Morris, distinguishes between information and story: 'The value of information does not survive the moment in which it was new. It lives only at the moment; it has to surrender to it completely and explain itself to it without losing any time. A story is different. It does not expend itself. It preserves and concentrates its strength and is capable of releasing it even after a long time'.[22] Benjamin proposes something akin to the 'slow release' efficacy of a narrative vitamin – a reminder perhaps of why *News from Nowhere* retains its signifying power long after the more copius ministrations of Morris and his Socialist League colleagues have been immersed in history's folds.

The disappearance of the storyteller vacates a space where rumour can flourish. The political word-spinners of Morris's coach house, George Bernard Shaw, Keir Hardie, each worked their own crafting of narrative containers which were themselves socially and politically constructed. These stories, of course, were not only describing political process but making movement and practice possible in the first place. To move into a place, there is always the need for a story about it. This goes for the oldest of seafaring legends as it does for the narratives of cyborg culture in virtual space. Stories furthermore by their presence resist the flourishing of rumour: 'stories differ from rumours in that the latter are always injunctions, initiators and results of a levelling of space, creators of common movements that reinforce an order by adding an activity of making people believe things to that of making people do things. Stories diversify, rumours totalise.'[23] Rumours here begin and revolve around the river. Morris was well aware of the suicidal allure of the river, the nearby Hammersmith bridge as a site for vertiginous valedictions.

On his landside deathbed on 3 October 1896, Morris is reputed to have said: 'I want to get the mumbo-jumbo out of the world'. This went for everything between discourse and design and returns us to this Hammersmith home. As Shaw said in 1880, on visiting Morris's house: 'Nothing in it was there because it was interesting or quaint or rare or hereditary'.[24] But of course the eternal contradiction in which Morris is held is the wealth that enabled this paring away of the irrelevant. Morris could do little about the entrance to his house being bordered by Ionic pilasters, and indeed he never liked the house in which he lived. In Morris's lecture at Burslem Town Hall in 1881 on 'Art and the Beauty of the Earth', he said: 'Look you, as I sit and work at home, which is at Hammersmith, close to the river, I often hear go past the window some of that ruffianism of which a good deal has been said in the papers of late. As I hear the yells and shrieks and all the degradation cast on the glorious tongue of Shakespeare and Milton, as I see the brutal reckless faces as figures go past me, it rouses recklessness and brutality in me also'.[25] Here Morris recalls the good fortune that began with the inheritance from his wealthy father that has placed him on the far side of the glass among the books and works of art in his library.

But how might one read the gap between Morris and this world, between the digital and the technological by way of conclusion to this chapter? Again by looking up at the house. Between the two tablets marking Ronalds's and Morris's lives and works is a third, darker, and more solemn tablet etched in classical script noting that: 'George MacDonald Poet and Novelist Lived Here 1867–1877'. His tenure joins the two ages of Ronalds and Morris, the digital and the technological. His current obscurity (except among literary fantasists and game theorists for whom he has always been a prophetic figure) invites us to avert our eyes once more. There is little point in seeking a comprehensive biography of this building through these walls despite what Vilém Flusser encouraged us to do at the outset of Chapter 1 of this book. That would hardly be possible given that Rosetti in three days here was said to have fallen so intensely in love with a sixteen-year-old that he would have given the whole of the rest of his life for that stay at Kelmscott again, or that Lewis Carroll wrote *Alice Through the Looking Glass* in the garden that had once been overlaid with wires. Rather than these anecdotal biographies of a building, the task might be to reflect back on the two modes of speech we have already been examining with the entry of a third voice, to conclude, as we began, with a 'third person'.

MacDonald, who lived in this house in the years between Ronalds's death and Morris's arrival, is the biographical, historical and conceptual link between the digital and the technological I have been discussing so far in this chapter. MacDonald was a poet-preacher, religious novelist, modern mystic and future fantasist from the Scottish congregational church background of radical non-conformism. In works such as *Robert Falconer* he awakened a new popular interest in what working among and 'for' those people in poverty might be and he was one of the few writers of his generation to turn the reading classes' heads Eastwards towards the slums at the edge of the city.

At 'The Retreat', as this house was then called, he came into the city circle of Burne-Jones who, at the Grange in nearby Fulham, was to become a close associate and working partner of Morris. MacDonald believed in the growing reform of the stage and as Joseph Johnson notes in his hagiography of 1906 'the elevation of the public taste by the introduction of pure plays performed by acts of high character'. Here fantastical 'juvenile tales' were dramatised by his children and acted out in the drawing room of the house with its natural proscenium break, and annually these occasions became an opportunity to gather large numbers of people together from across the social divide. Each winter there was an open day for Octavia Hill's 'model dwellings for the poor' at which the MacDonald children acted out plays and ended their celebrations with bouts of country dancing. These were gatherings of the impoverished alongside intellectual and artistic philanthropists such as the Reverend Samuel Barnett, the founder of Toynbee Hall. In 1868, Ruskin, Morris's mentor, had attended the first of these receptions. These amusements were said to blend and almost imperceptibly grow into reverential service. The garden played host to a visit of the American Jubilee Singers, and Mark Twain also visited the house around this time.

MacDonald was known in his day as 'the Interpreter', and there is a sense in which his work in fantasy such as the 'faerie romance' *Phantastes* and *The Princess and the Goblin* (enduring through the work of C.S. Lewis and Maurice Sendak) is as persuasive a medium as Morris's social tracts or Ronalds's technologies as a means to imaginative transformation. Here the hermeneutic link between the digital and the technological might be worked through. It is MacDonald's mystical allegories that have become the ubiquitous architectural structuring device for the return of digital play in the late twentieth and early twenty-first centuries, it is his non-conformist apocalyptic overtones coupled to grassroots social observation of injustice that seems most closely echoed by today's eco-warriors whose environmentalism might once have been expected to mimic the secular Marxism of Morris's speeches or the technological utopias of Ronalds's far-reaching wire. In the labyrinthine warrens of those environmentalists, 'Animal and Co', zig-zagging beneath England's 'green and pleasant land' through the turn of a century, *Climate Camps* occupying common ground across its razed surfaces, *Platform* making international grids of power visible (see Chapter 6), there has been at work one of the only visible resistances in Britain to the spoiling power of capital that this post-Millennial moment can summon. But the means of resistance in this subterranean network, its baroque filigree and rococo languages of resistance is conducted in pulses, 'through the wire', in and around 'social networking platforms' 'with' the enemy of nature, 'between' comrades through the erudition and weaving of fantasy and fact, drawing precisely on the technologies and traditions of speech afforded by MacDonald as much as the medium of Ronalds and the political pedigree of Morris.

In the, perhaps inevitable, return of the digital, now arithmetic not alphabetic, it is no longer Lazarus's misplaced hands that sign the distances of touch, but rather the filigree of fibre optics that multiply those glass prosthetics to communication, that Ronalds once buried in his garden, across the globe. Here at the speed of light that most basic of speech patterns calls out across the divide: 'one two, one two'. As though conveyed on the voice of a continuous and infernal sound check, shouted into the microphone wherever you are in the world by a roadie who remembers his vocation from Plato's day, information now accelerates in exponential proportion to communication. But this is nothing new. The porcelain overload that Diderot must have experienced from below in Saint-Mammès Cathedral in the early 1700s would have been one for which the word 'relief' could only have stood as a mocking irony.

Is there not something to be gained then in the interests of complexity from rereading these signs of the street as a dialogue with each other, *between* the digital and the technological, a sedimentation of pasts and futures, rather than a succession of stuttering incidents, a contradictory impasse to thought? They are already, and anyway, in states of mutual coalescence for the dates are strangely inconsequential, or even misleading. The Hammersmith house dates from the 1790s, Morris bought the lease after the decade of MacDonald and brought it to commercial life in 1878; the stone in its classical antiquity speaking of the future of communications is dated 1816; the socialist message is inscribed in a text of 22 November 1892 while looking forward to the final meeting of a socialist group in 1962 which may or may not have occurred. The apparent nostalgia of a socialist ideal here becomes the more up-to-date message, while the true future in the form of telecommunications predates this rootedness by almost a century.

If there was a living image of what Jürgen Habermas describes in his resistance to the facile announcement of the end of modernity, this site might provide its most fruitful illustration. What price the baton charge of history when faced with this accretion of reversals to fortune? Here, the epigram we began with from Hal Foster regarding the circulatory of approaches taken in this book, the 'complex relay of anticipated futures and reconstructed pasts', comes well and truly home to roost (having never gone away). The story would appear to run: first there was the word, and the word was made electronic and man needed no more to travel to be heard, except when the other did not listen to his threats. Or, first there was the word, and the word was made locally and confusion reigned under the guise of universal emancipation for all those who could not understand each other but felt that their oppression might be shared.

Between these two apparent poles is a spectrum of positions from which one might construct a politics of the location of locution, which neither lionises stability nor celebrates the insecurities of hybridity. Walter Benjamin understood this tension when, in speaking about the art of the storyteller, he characterised the archaic representatives of the genre: the resident tiller of the soil, working the land by hand and plough, and the figure destined to travel afar, who from a distance returns with stories from elsewhere. Characteristically nuanced, Benjamin avoids settling with either, understanding that in our continuous historical state of emergency, the significant blows would be struck left handed by those complex figures whose sense is never one of being quite at home.

There is only one record of William Morris's direct personal engagement with Francis Ronalds: towards the end of his life in 1896 and after Ronalds's own death in 1873. It is recorded, in a single source in the archive of the Science Museum, and there is no verification of this in Morris's letters. A man called W. Kemp approached Morris with the aim of placing a memorial stone to Ronalds on the house: 'The suggestion met with wrath. Morris declared that for their brutalising influence upon humans, telegraphs were as much to be blamed as railways'.[26] Modernity prevailed, however, and with Morris's 'full approval' the tablet was placed on this coach house, where it is to be seen now complicating and confusing any pedestrian's sense of the past as 'back then' with a present sense of 'here now' and a future invitation: 'where to?'.

Fifth Approach
Psychological & Legal

Two offices and two desks might provide a means through which the psychological and the legal can be brought together in one place to consider theatre in the expanded field. Questions concerning what it might mean to 'assume office', the performance of such investitures, the work that accrues to such office from the surface of such desks and how that work is 'staged' become the motor of this chapter. The first office is Sigmund Freud's workplace, at Maresfield Gardens in London; the second is that of Daniel Paul Schreber, at the Higher Court of Dresden, where he was president, and then at the window of his asylum room in Sonnenstein where he was removed, when he could no longer adequately act on behalf of the law. While the first was occupied by Freud in 1939, where he reflects and writes upon his earlier analytic experiences of the 1890s, the second was where Schreber suffered the 'nervous illness' that in Sonnenstein became his *Memoirs,* which found their way back to Freud's desk in the first decade of the twentieth century. The circulatory shape of this looping influence is by no means coincidental and becomes the performative structure of what follows. It is, what I would like to call after the sociologist Niklas Luhmann, the *autopoietic* quality of social systems such as the psychological and the legal within which performance plays a critical part.

Why autopoietic? Are we not appealing, through such a discredited word to the threat of interior systems, the kind of dereferentialised, 'desolate theology' of old appeals to the self-contained, the structuralist and the semiotic that denies anything we might have learnt in the last chapter? Surely in such an appeal any hopes this book might have had for community are long gone? Well, not quite. Social systems require humans for their existence, that much is clear to Niklas Luhmann. But, social systems such as those exemplified in this chapter through the practices of psychoanalysis and law are not simply a matter of aggregates of individuals for which the phrase 'community of interest' might once have been coined. Indeed they are no more aggregates of individuals than were that most peculiar of aggregates – that 'audience' I sat amongst at that performance of *The Power of Theatrical Madness* in Nancy in 1983, which led to this way of thinking about theatre in the expanded field (see Preliminary).

While on the one hand the work of the psychoanalyst concerns what others cannot see, or hear about your thoughts, and feelings, one might say in legal terms a 'contract' entered into with another, the social sphere of the legal process has to be somehow evident to those subject to it. It is a procedure after all which is imposed on us independently of what we might wish. Luhmann was insistent that in considering such processes people should be placed in the *environment* of social systems rather than inside the thing itself.[1] This rend between office (location) and office (rôle) provides us with an opportunity in this chapter, as it draws attention to the part performance plays within the expanded field of disciplinary practices, both as a mediating device for the functioning of those practices, but also perhaps more controversially, as the *precursor* to those practices. Performance is the genetic link between the gestures, practices and protocols of psychoanalysis and law.

To be placed in this way, in an environment (let us call it an office for the moment), as distinct to within 'systems' (of psychoanalysis or law themselves), demands that communication, and of course I would say performance, plays its part as an active and reactive mechanism, facilitating on the one hand the rhythm, exercise or conduct of the system and on the other hand the human individual's place within that process. Continuing with Luhmann's view of these processes, both the psychoanalytic and the legal domains are ones whose 'operational closure' generate the conditions (or operations) that they need in order to generate operations in the first place.[2] This circular sounding process is what Luhmann described as *autopoiesis* which distinguishes these processes from other everyday practices, which do not share these properties. It is not that law and psychoanalysis are unique in this respect therefore; there are many self-perpetuating machines at large from cell structures to capital's state functions, but they are not as distant from each other either, as one might have imagined in at least their foundational arrangements. For a start, that description of psychoanalysis as equivalent to contract, as distinct to law, rests upon an agreement entered into 'freely with another'. As we shall soon see, there is no such thing as 'free' therapy.

A practice (or praxis) is for Luhmann something that has meaning *in itself*; a practice is a practice because it is meaningful 'as such'. Swimming would be a good example; in all circumstances, with the exception of sport or survival, swimming lacks instrumentalism. On the contrary *poesis,* as Luhmann understands it, produces something *outside itself,* namely 'a work'.[3] Theatre is perhaps an act of this kind, which is why Aristotle wrote a *Poetics* for its right form. But in Luhmann's phrase, autopoiesis bridges these two phenomena, a process that describes a *poesis* that is its own work, and a system that is its own work. Thus the autopoietic act is something more than just a practice that is able to reflect upon itself (theatre in the hands of companies such as Forced Entertainment and Elevator Repair Service do that very well) and it is that 'more' that interests us here.

While the approaches taken to performance so far in this book have been largely compatible, beyond the coincidence of the shared offices above this chapter has perhaps foolishly drawn together two social systems that well and truly strain the binding of the ampersand between them. It will soon become apparent that I have had to deploy a historical conceit, and perhaps, given this is a theatre book, not surprisingly and I should admit it, a trick, to bring these two systems into the same space. The fact that Freud provides the connection between the two, about three pages into this chapter, should come as no surprise given that Freud's work could be deployed to suture any number of diverse practices between 1889 and 1939 (the broad historical half century of what follows). But the mobilisation of Freud in this case has less to do with his property, as was the case in the last chapter in our reflection on the shared home of William Morris and Francis Ronalds, as the *propriety* of office, where his property and his investiture within a social system meet.

As with other chapters in this book, but perhaps acutely so in this case therefore, such considerations, despite fears at the outset, are ones also of community. For it is through such offices, literally the places and locations under consideration here, that the relation between the public and the private is played out. What might that thing be that all communities have in common and that such offices inscribe? The ancient and originary meaning of community, from *communis,* certainly provides an opening, for community describes 'he who shares an office (*carice*) a burden (*carico*) a task (*incarico*)'.[4] From here the philosopher Roberto Esposito suggests that *communitas* is the totality of persons united not by a property but precisely by an obligation or a debt. He or she who instead is *exempted* from such responsibility, one might say who does not feel the need to 'assume office', might be said to have been granted immunity to others. Here can be contrasted something of what we understand by the public and the private, but also the relation between *communitas* and *immunitas,* community and immunity itself. If *communitas* according to Esposito refers to he or she who is required to carry out the functions of an office, then it is logical to assume that the one who is immune in such a situation is the one who either has no office to perform or, I would suggest, has had such office *removed* from them if such an extraction is possible, or, perhaps better, that they are removed from said office – a condition of forced removal that applies to Schreber and one that nicely describes a recurring tension between compensations and dispensations in the record of his 'loss of office', his *Memoirs*. Esposito glosses such a situation with the term 'ungrateful', as though as to suggest that the resistance to or inability to receive the gift implied by the *munos* of community leaves those beyond such gift-giving and receiving as inevitably unable to demonstrate gratitude. In such a lack the gift of response-ability, or responsibility, to be or become 'beyond oneself' that community might require as a precondition for functioning is evacuated, or as Esposito puts it 'vacated' from the scene.[5]

But if this is the semantic origin of community, inasmuch as Espositio has traced it, where might performance, psychoanalysis and law relate semantically? Let's take the psyche first. For a start, I would suggest, performance and psychoanalysis are offspring of the same ancestor: the placebo effect. Despite transgressive signs to the contrary, where irritation of the stability of identity and resistance of the unconscious to interpretation would appear to be paramount, both in their own ways seek to please, to be acceptable, and both are characterised by their psychological rather than their physiological effects. The relationship between the two was first consummated on a fine evening in 1889 when Sigmund Freud took a night off from the 'Congress in Hypnotism' he was attending in Paris to see a performance artist. Since that fateful evening the two have been artificially sundered to protect the scientific legitimacy of psychoanalysis in its flight from its origins in hypnotic performance. But despite seeking medical authority, and the status of a 'treatment', psychoanalysis might here be reminded of its debt to a performance tradition. If, since Chaucer, to 'play at the school of Placebo' has meant to flatter with servility, the task in the first part of this chapter is to contest the intellectual sycophancy shown to psychoanalysis by practices in search of a spurious theoretical rigour, in order to reassert a prior place for performance in the psychoanalytic turn.[6]

Performance and law on the other hand would, at first sight, appear to be the remotest cousins, if related at all, divided by their distance from the consequences of their actions. In the case of performance, affects are all; in the case of law, effects are all. But just four years after Freud's fateful encounter with performance artist Yvette Guilbert described above, Daniel Paul Schreber, a district judge in Chemnitz Germany, wrote something that might suggest our presumption as to affects and effects be reordered with regard to performance, psychoanalysis and law.

In 1893, Schreber had just been promoted to the elevated position of *Senatspresident* to the Reichstag. It was on hearing this news that Schreber, by his own hand in his *Memoirs* of 1903, began to 'suffer from the nervous disorder' as a 'result of mental overstrain' that would have him readmitted to the Leipzig clinic he had left some years earlier, and thence removed against his will to the Sonnenstein Asylum, overlooking the River Elbe in Pirna in East Germany. The connection between the first short history I have offered you and the second is of course the use Freud made of Schreber's *Memoir* in his only writings on Paranoia, an unusual task for Freud given he was in no position to analyse Schreber, but rather encountered his writing from afar, in the mode of a literary critic and clinical diagnostician.

Schreber's view of his own condition was not that of a layman conducting a lay analysis. It is the view of an *expert* witness, who by the time he writes these words has already spent a decade oscillating between an inside and an outside of legal identification, recognising the peculiar paradox of the law. All law. That is the performative paradox of the self-generating *limits* of law identified by Nicklas Luhmann, the autopoietic way law contains itself as, paradoxically, *only ever in the present*.

It takes a performance person to fetishise this peculiarity of law, its *presentness*, but I will insist on the implications of such presentness for what follows. I will insist on it because the system of law, as with any system of performance, is only ever actualised through its operations. In law as in performance, only what happens happens. Everything that happens in the legal system and in its environment happens at the same time, as it does in performance. The legal system is, in this sense at least, an autopoietic, operatively closed social system, and it is this defining quality that I want to capture in my title for the second part of this chapter: *Homo Juridicus*. But first:

Homo Psyche

Let us begin with the peculiar way in which psychoanalysis closes itself as a social system, through the means of performance. The senses in which psychoanalysis was in it earliest manifestations already and always performance might illustrate ways in which the 'and' in 'psychoanalysis and performance' can operate more critically, especially given the role we would want psychoanalysis to play in the second part of this chapter.[7] There we will see how psychic and social structures become tied in a structural couple, or a coupling (to quote Luhmann's preferred phrase for these processes) that becomes the pre-condition for their very survival.

In an age of Prozac and the resurgence of a pharmaceutical mind field, Jacques Lacan, Freud's best-known successor, has become the midwife of psychoanalysis beyond the impulse of treatment and cure, beyond the pale imitation of medical integrity. His project returns us to its origins, located closer to the hypnotist Carl Hansen than to Hippocrates. As Adrian Dannatt says: 'Just as painting exploded in entirely unprecedented, unimaginable directions when photography took on the burden of realism, so psychoanalysis will revolutionize itself in the wake of its freedom from the "cure".[8] But the return to performance, while hastened by Jacques Lacan, has always been inherent in Freud's formulation of the field he invented. Like all good revolutions this promises to be as much a reprise as an advance, and it is the degree of the return, measurable as the uncanny refrain of stage hypnotism within the talking cure, that will remind us once again in this book of the inherent interdisciplinarity of these practices.

Installation

Such thoughts come to mind once again on foot, as in other pedestrianised chapters here where performance provides the wayfinder in the expanded field, amidst a temporary installation by the French-born artist Sophie Calle at 20 Maresfield Gardens in Hampstead, London, Freud's last home and workplace, and now preserved as the Freud Museum. Here Sophie Calle has followed in a tradition of other artists, including Susan Hiller and Cornelia Parker, by installing her work between the folds of the museum's artefacts. Calle's project, *Appointment*, takes the form of a sequence of thirty short text pieces interspersed with related objects, some of which draw upon the Freud archive itself (Freud's overcoat, wedding ring, etc.) and some constructed scenarios introducing new but equally mundane objects to the collection. As a spectator you are never secure that the identities being discussed in the small texts refer to Sophie Calle or someone autobiographically close to her, whether it is the six-year-old who took to stripping in the elevator on the way to her grandparents' sixth floor apartment or the twenty-seven-year-old stripper whose blonde wig is torn off by a colleague in a fight. Some of the sequences are sombre; others are apparently lighter, but with a touch of foreboding:

> At 30 a woman recalls her father thought she had bad breath. He sends her to a doctor who turns out to be a psychoanalyst. On visiting the doctor the woman says: 'This must have been a mistake. My father is concerned I have bad breath and he sent me to a generalist.'
>
> 'Do you always do what your father tells you to do?' replied the man.
>
> 'I became his patient.'[9]

The joke is a good one (as is the Freudian slip) and within this specific setting – for this is a site-specific performance, albeit a staging of the absent aura of the analysand. Memories and characterisations from a related past accumulate in this building and permeate its already redolent ether with inscriptions of its myriad consultations.

My interest in this installation is the attention it draws to the performative qualities inherent in the architectural cradle of psychoanalysis. This would be by no means the first time Sophie Calle has provided such a hermeneutic bridge between disciplines. Indeed Peggy Phelan rounds off the opening of her celebrated essay 'The ontology of performance', in her collection *Unmarked*, discussed in the opening pages of this book, with a rhetorical ploy recruiting Sophie Calle from the 'other arts' to verify the draw of performance, the problematic of reproducibility: 'Calle demonstrates the performative quality of all seeing'.[10] But Calle, though a very interesting artist, is not a recruit who can bring credence to special claims made for performance's ontology, from beyond performances's own boundaries, as she is at odds with the very categories of artist that Phelan herself identifies. She is clearly not a painter or even a 'photographer' (although she uses photographs in her work, these are only ever the record of a deeper performative strata). She is a time-based artist working principally with durational projects of simulation and surveillance, which implicitly places her within a performance tradition quite distinct to object-based work that can be physically assessed in space and time. And she is a performer whose very stock-in-trade is the kind of reproducibility that Phelan is questioning on behalf of performance. 'The performative quality of all seeing' is in fact a problem in the phenomenology of perception, which has very distinct historical traces precisely tracked in this book that are all about reproduction as well as representation. It is these reproducibles that make Calle's installations so engaging and it is on this ground that some historical questions of the relations between psychoanalysis and performance might be worked through.

The perception of any space, never mind something as loaded as an office, is always structured by this historical accretion, but for Peggy Phelan 'performative seeing' suggests perception differs on each and every occasion, that it is new every time. The political force of Phelan's 'ontology of performance' comes into question in this very place where the apparently irreducible, unreproducible moment of the playing out of the talking cure participates all the more actively within the circulating energies of the exchange of capital between analyst and analysand. There is no performance without this exchange; here there is no liberty from the 'fee for all'. In this re-constructed second site of psychoanalysis, Freud's London consulting room, a mimesis of his original Viennese study, all transactions are in the end ones of capital, where money is at the heart of the matter. This is not so much a world of free association as one of fee association. Hence my insistence that what we are describing is an *office* and its works.

Circulation

There are a number of circulations at work in this place that make the question of the return of reproduction inevitable and playful and that do nothing it seems to me to impoverish the status of what might have occurred here as performance and indeed enhances the sense of that activity and its history. Let's keep in mind Sophie Calle's work, but look beyond the specificity of this installation towards some of its terms of reference within a historical context; that is, the specific cultural history of the emergence of psychoanalysis itself from within this site of performance. In the process of so doing, it might become possible to notice the reproducibles stacking up alongside the representations without disarming for a moment the power of the multiple performances within this history.

From the outset it is worth recalling the complexity of the professional's role at the end of the nineteenth century, when the distinctions between physician, surgeon, charlatan, dentist, barber and performer might have appeared less determined than they are now. You might call this the era of the open plan office. The terms on which professional alignments were organised on one or other side of a disciplinary divide do much to situate contemporary practices, and their conditions of relating in ways that, Bruno Latour suggests, might never have been separated.[11]

In this context I am interested in Bertha Pappenheim's (Anna O.'s) little quoted likening of the talking cure to 'chimney sweeping'. Setting aside banal Freudian associations, one may wish to draw from the phrase an intriguing sense of historical location coupled with domestic science, an image of architectural purgation brought about by the character who in local lore delivered good fortune and a dose of theatricality to the hearth. As in Herman Melville's short story 'I and My Chimney', narration is set off by proximity to the chimney, the 'centre' of the home both in its structure and function. For Melville's unreconstructed narrator the chimney has the added benefit of listening, for 'it did not like his wife "talk back"'.[12] At 20 Maresfield Gardens the hearth, which has heard it all, is mute for other, more mundane, reasons.

The first thing one notices on entering Freud's study is not so much the couch, for that has disappeared under a woven rug, which in turn has been temporarily covered by a white wedding/night dress and elegaic textual accompaniment left there by Sophie Calle, but the way the arrangement of the couch and the analyst's chair at its head rest against what would appear to be a chimney breast. On easing back the tapestry that drapes the hearth, it becomes apparent that the fireplace has been blocked in. The chimney still rises to the roof from this point, and is clearly visible from outside the house, but it is no longer open. At the head and foot of the couch are radiators. The museum caretaker tells me that Freud's architect son Ernst had, on arrival at the house in 1938, fitted a diesel-fired central-heating system that was 'revolutionary' for its time. The expiatory systems of hearth, fire and draft have here been replaced by an internal system of circulating waters, a new age of comfort and technological rationality. But it had not always been this way. Above the couch and proud of the chimney breast hangs an image of a performance masquerading as diagnosis that points to a history of psychoanalysis prior to this centralising moment, when whispering eddies of the interdisciplinary were still at play in the field at large (Figure 5.1).

The theatricality of the talking cure, its performative origins in mystic speech, the confessional apparatus, possession and exorcism has long been noted by commentators seeking to disturb the originary myth of Freudian analysis. The recovery of an early Freud, just prior to the revisionism of *Studies in Hysteria* (1895), is therefore the recovery of psychoanalysis within the province of hypnotism, magnetism and somnabulism, in other words from within a performance tradition. And lying, masquerading and malingering play an inevitable and overtly performative role within that tradition.

The trajectory of the talking cure from Freud's couch to the confessional platform of the day-time television of Oprah Winfrey, Vanessa Feltz, Jeremy Kyle and Jerry Springer (with all their recent admissions of fake characterisations and simulated scenarios) is a distinct paradigm of durational performance – albeit punctuated by the regime of the fifty-minute hour and of generic site-

Figure 5.1 Freud's Office and Consulting Room, Maresfield Gardens, London, 1939

specific domestic performance that, if temporarily unleashed from its mitigation 'as treatment', might reveal a legacy of unexpected delinquencies from within the heart of the analyst's domain. In this performance legacy, the long derided 'innocents' of analysis, contained and constrained by Freud's rhetoric – Anna O, The Rat Man and The Wolf Man – become the self-possessed forebears of the icons of the rhetorical flourish: Eleanora Duse, Antonin Artaud and Josef Beuys. Whether the placebo of performance 'did them good' is not my question; rather are we willing to acknowledge the place of performance within psychoanalysis?

These borrowings from the regime of signs associated with performance do nothing to destabilise the efficacy of the cure itself – Prozac is doing that in the twenty-first century – nor do they intimate that the 'mad business is show business'. Instead, in the interests of interdisciplinarity, they once more seek redress for performance in the face of disciplinary disempowerment.[13] Michel de Certeau suggests that psychoanalysis 'moves forward over lands that are not its own ... it becomes a "novel" within the foreign field of erudition' and considers it a 'fragile discourse because its postulate is the non-place of its place', and this suggests that the terms of its endearment usurp the very grounds for performance which it occupies and empties. So, though de Certeau concludes that psychoanalysis can only be a 'fantasy', the reality of that fantasy for performance is a lost opportunity.[14] Adrian Dannatt believes it is not too late for performance: 'Psychoanalysis guards a unique space that does not exist elsewhere in social relations, neither in the closest friendship nor the psychic's parlour, and it is in this defiantly indescribable zone that its continued importance lies, as a laboratory to explore the unthinkable'.[15] But if this unique space sounds precisely like a zone contested and fought for in the cycle of theatre avant gardes of the last century, from the site-specific constructivism of the 1920s to the intimate autobiographical live art of the early 2000s, how has this coalescence come about?

Location

Let us leap to an end, which inevitably is also a beginning in order to find out. By spring 1938 the complex conditions necessitating Freud's departure from Vienna and the Nazi threat had been realised. On arrival in London Freud took up residence in temporary accommodation secured by his architect son Ernst. In June 1938, referring to this house in Elsworthy Road, Hampstead, Freud said: 'It is difficult for us to live vertically instead of horizontally'.[16] In the latter part of this configuration, Freud was referring to the single-storey accommodation that his family had occupied at Bergasse 19 in Vienna and in which Freud had conducted his analysis and writing for forty-seven years, including the work on paranoia, and of Daniel Paul Schreber, which we will come to in the second part of this chapter. While Freud's premises in Vienna are now empty, simply adorned with the simulacrum of the photographs of what was once there, the Freud house in London is a more replete, uncanny mimesis of that original site of psychoanalysis.[17]

As Ernest Jones records in *The Life and Work of Sigmund Freud*, Bergasse 19 was not Freud's first office. Freud had originally occupied premises in a newly built block on the site of the Ringtheater in Vienna which had burnt down in 1881 with the loss of 600 lives.[18] Freud and his fiancée Martha reputedly had tickets for the fateful night, 8 December, but had spent the evening elsewhere. Part of the rental proceeds from these apartments went to recompense those children who had been orphaned by the disaster. Setting aside the extraordinary poetic neatness of psychoanalysis's birth in a block, which came to be called the Suhnhaus, the 'House of Atonement', there are more directly performance-related associations to be drawn out. It was after all at the Ringtheater in the early 1880s that mesmero-hypnotic fever had gripped Vienna, and Freud himself had first recognised the power of hypnotic suggestion through the stage practice of Carl Hansen. In his 'Autobiographical Study', Freud writes about his concern for the efficacy of treatment, his loss of faith in electrotherapy and yet his confirmed interest in hypnotism:

> With hypnotism the case was better. While I was still a student I attended a public exhibition given by Hansen the 'magnetist', and had noticed that one of the subjects experimented upon had become deathly pale at the onset of cataleptic rigidity and had remained so for as long as the condition lasted. This firmly convinced me of the genuineness of the phenomenon of hypnosis.[19]

Why this condition convinced Freud where it left others sceptical he does not elaborate, but he does note that 'professors of psychiatry' continued to declare hypnotism to be fraudulent and dangerous. Freud had seen hypnotism used in Paris as a method of 'producing symptoms in patients and then removing them again'; the Nancy school had used suggestion and hypnosis to great effect and Freud notes how it became his 'principal instrument of work' in the early days. He locates the need for this approach topographically; working in a large town in private medical practice, Freud comments on the 'crowds of neurotics' who hurried with their troubles unsolved from one physician to the next. But apart from this utilitarian purpose Freud notes something more salient for my performative argument: '... there was something positively seductive in working with hypnotism. For the first time there was a sense of having overcome one's helplessness; and it was highly flattering to enjoy the reputation of being a miracle–worker'.[20] This ur-showmanship remains with Freud even when the strategies of hypnosis are replaced by free-association. Freud acknowledged this debt in retaining, like some cod-certification, the image of Charcot conducting hypnotic masterclasses above his couch. As Freud said:

> Hypnotism endows the physician with an authority such as was probably never possessed by the priest or the miracle man, since it concentrates the subject's whole interest upon the figure of the physician; it does away with the autocratic power of the patient's mind which, as we have seen, interferes so conspicuously with the influence of the mind over the body, such as is normally to be observed only as an effect of the most powerful emotions.[21]

Freud comments that it was not until later that he discovered the drawbacks of the procedure, a procedure that was in effect the recognition of the power of the mind over the body – the placebo effect.

Elaboration

While one might concur with the political reclamation of complex identities for 'Anna O' from Freudian misinterpretation, these are understandably sensitive, but often defensive, reservations with regard to her *own* claims that she 'performed' her symptoms. For this debate between authenticity and simulation obviously extends deep into the rationale of the psychoanalytic act itself and as such unsettles those faithful followers of Freud the clinician, not Freud the impressario. As John Forrester says, 'The context for the elaboration of an ad-hoc but sophisticated epistemology of lying by psychoanalysis is to be found in the medical practices of the late nineteenth century'.[22] In Forrester's reading there is no moral implication to this lying but an opportunity to examine the trust that underlies the institution of truth-saying, the distinctive connection between truth and lies that operates through psychoanalysis (an economy that I proposed in my third distinction between theatre and performance at the outset of this book as being fundamental to their relations). He traces a history of hysteria leading doctors on a wild goose chase from Sydenham's definitions as early as 1681 where 'organic disease of the nervous system is mimicked', to Falret's observation of 1866 that '[t]he life of the hysteric is one perpetual lie'.[23] He outlines a range of concomitant professional strategies, from physiological attempts by doctors to outwit this deception, giving rise to the lie detector, to the collusion of the doctor with the patient, 'playing the same game' as Forrester puts it, and deceiving the patient through the use of hypnosis.

Hypnosis may have been the stage on which pains and symptoms could be suggested away, but also it was intended 'as a sure physiological technique for the duplication and reproduction of hysterical symptoms, as in Charcot's work, which met the reproducibility requirement of science by using the theatrical techniques of rehearsal and staging'.[24] It is the idiosyncratic place of reality in the psychoanalytic scene that encourages the patient to surrender the relationship between speech and sense, and it is the reality principle that announces the impossibility of the patient not conforming to rhetorical structures: 'This dialectic of lying, deception, and truth was played out between doctor and patient in a malign form in hysterical malingering, in a more benign form with hypnotism, both against the background of a search for an ultimate truth of the disease'.[25]

In the context of a discussion of performance we might side-step the implicit moral question associated with the axis between malingering and authenticity, between reality and simulation, and reflect on the terms of this debate and on how in the fields of psychoanalysis and performance there was a simultaneous preparation for acts which were *neither* real nor simulated but, to use Mikkel Borch-Jacobsen's term, were 'surreal'. As Jacobsen says: 'Bertha, playing her role [her second 'personality'] on the stage of hysteria, was also watching from the wings, as spectator of her own theatricality.' The paradox of the trace (of hysteria) is nothing other than the 'paradox of acting', as Diderot put it after stepping back and away from the Lazarus relief at Langres that we looked up to in Chapter 4, which is why Bertha concluded that 'the whole business has been simulated'.[26]

Simulation

From the hypnotic domain let us compare these claims with a document of 1891 by a Dr Foveau de Courmelles who, at the heart of a work on hypnotism, poses questions about the significance of simulation. Courmelles begins by defining simulation in judgemental terms as a word 'applied equally to persons who "feign" in order to deceive others, or who are themselves labouring under self deception'.[27] He is at pains to prove the possibility of feigned effects on the part of 'nervously affected subjects' in order to sustain an argument about the reality principle that all somnambulists maintain, keeping them safe from the two key dangers of external suggestion, criminal acts and submissive complicity with rape. These twin figures were the recurring threat to stage hypnotism in the nineteenth century and return in almost all dialogues about its safety and moral rectitude.

A specialist by the name of Dr Gerard is recruited by Courmelles to give an extreme account of the neurotic's motives: 'A woman suffering from neurosis has no will-power, but something replaces that absent faculty; she is a liar in every comprehension of the word ... Every hysterical subject craves for a pedestal, whether it is a velvet cushion, the foot-lights of a theatre, or even the prisoner's dock'.[28] Courmelles is more reserved in his judgements. In the interest of justice, he is concerned to detect simulation in hypnosis, to counter what he describes as the medical man's tendency to see in every case 'lunatics rather than criminals'. The deeper search is to distinguish between consciousness and unconsciousness, the voluntary and involuntary: 'Someone has said that it required great ability to play the fool, and that is by no means paradoxical; but criminals have often enough intelligence to play such a part'.[29]

Freud's colleague and mentor Bernheim had admitted that his own 'great therapeutic successes by means of suggestion were only achieved in his hospital

Figure 5.2 *Un Léçon de Charcot a la Salpétrière*, Lithograph, Eugène Pirodon, 1887

practice and not with his private patients.[30] The invitation to performance within the setting of the hospital as distinct to the invitation to therapy within the dialogue of the consulting room is reinforced by the image on the chimney-breast at 20 Maresfield Gardens. Freud understood well the performative allure of hypnotism and directly alludes to its sublation in the talking cure by marking its genealogy directly above the couch from which he practiced (Figure 5.2).

Here was, and still is (thanks to the care of Anna Freud and the family maid Paula Fichtl), a lithograph by Eugène Pirodon of Charcot lecturing/performing for an audience of students at the Saltpétrière, entitled 'Un Leçon de Charcot a la Salpétrière'. It is an image of a painting by Andre Brouillet exhibited first in the Salon of 1887, then to great acclaim in the Exposition Universelle Internationale of 1889. The print is, in its own right, an uncanny restoration of the painting, miniaturised and greyscaled. It shows Charcot with his patient Blanche Wittman who is in the familiar and weekly process, 'the Tuesday saga', of being demonstrated as a hysteric in hypnosis to doctors at the Salpétrière Hospital.

Charcot opened his clinics on hysteria and hypnotism not only to physicians but also to the non-medical public. As Axel Munthe, an English physician, noted in his record of the Latin quarter and the Salpétrière at the time of Charcot:

The huge amphitheatre was filled to the last place with a multicoloured audience drawn from tout Paris, authors, journalists, leading actors and actresses, fashionable demi-mondaines, all full of morbid curiosity to witness the startling phenomena of hypnotism [...][31]

With his literary colleague from this audience, Guy de Maupassant, Munthe had travelled to the Nancy clinic under Bernheim and was convinced of the fakery of what he described as 'the stage performances of the Salpêtrière', a 'muddle of truth and cheating'. Among the 'true' somnambulists there were 'frauds, knowing quite well what they were expected to do, delighted to perform their various tricks in public, cheating both doctors and audiences with the amazing cunning of the hysteriques'.[32] Munthe's purple prose has to be placed in the context of his own banishment by Charcot from the Salpêtrière for attempting to 'liberate' under hypnotic suggestion a young woman who he believed would recover if returned to her family in Normandy.

Nevertheless, the contemporary witness to a scene that Munthe described as 'the Tuesday gala performance', a scene that Freud was very familiar with and chose to situate as a window to the origins of his own work on the couch, and above the couch, is in performance terms of great interest. Worthy of actors undertaking Grotowski's transformational exercises, or Oleg Kulik pushing *Zoophrenia* to the limits, Charcot's *grande hystérie* 'would crawl on all fours on the floor, barking furiously when told she was a dog, flap her arms as if trying to fly when turned into a pigeon, lift her skirts with a shriek of terror when a glove was thrown at her feet with a suggestion of being a snake'.[33] Munthe likens the whole affair to a 'suggestion en masse' and there appeared in the newspapers of the day denunciations of these public demonstrations of hypnotism as spectacles unworthy of the traditions of the Salpêtrière. But from the perspective of performance it is clear that this was *all* these events were – the iconography clearly indicates their performative nature and the image that Freud chose to oversee his couch is a further exaggeration of this theatrical tradition. This, of course, is not to deny for a moment the efficacious *placebo* effects these operations might have wrought on their subjects. But that is a claim and a gain for performance, not for the promised empirical, scientific 'cure' of psychoanalysis.

Innovation

In his only overt writing on theatre, the essay 'Psychopathic Characters on the Stage', Freud takes the Aristotelian line on the purpose of drama: '... the prime factor is unquestionably the process of getting rid of one's emotions by 'blowing off steam'.[34] Character and 'acting' are presumed to be central to the performer–audience relationship in which 'someone other than himself … is acting and suffering on the stage …'. It is, after all, Freud notes, 'only a game, which can threaten no damage to his personal security'.[35] Freud's economy of theatre expects that suffering should not be caused to the audience, that drama should know how to compensate its spectators and that 'Modern writers have … often failed to obey this rule'. But here, as Theodor Adorno and Rosalind Krauss would remind us, lies Freud's symptomatic distancing of the contemporary in the reassuring embrace of the canonical.[36]

However, the modernity of Freud's own practice, the degree to which the talking cure was already and had always been to some degree a game, played equally knowingly by analysand and analyst, has an echo in his real interest in performance. From the 1880s to the 1930s in Vienna, Freud had time for only one contemporary stage artist *in practice*, and she had little to do with the Shakespearean canon he espoused in his writing and displayed in his office. Yvette Guilbert was a celebrated singer whose annual performances in Vienna were typical of her chameleon, hybrid style, a style that has more to do with a legacy of solo performance-artists working across sexuality and gender today than with any dramatic tradition whose effects were to 'blow off steam'. She sang in a vast variety of personae, prostitutes and schoolgirls providing the most predictable of many more unorthodox axes of identity morphing. And she was to visit Freud's house, and office, at Maresfield Gardens shortly before his death (Figure 5.3).

Her signed photograph nestles in the library shelves behind Freud's desk as another reminder of a repression of a contemporary counter-tradition in the formation of psychoanalysis. Guilbert's work explored a new realism within the conventions of the 'Chat Noir' singer and had an unusual preference for representing the 'low life' of the city. The description of *diseuse* does not convey the formal experiment of her work combining songs with intellectually demanding lectures honouring figures such as Baudelaire and Verlaine. Guilbert was loved by Eleanora Duse, who recognised the advanced physicality of her gestural range. Freud was an ardent 'Guilbertian', his interest dating to 1889, the precise moment of his fascination with hypnosis, and recorded at the time as worthy of comment: 'That year, while he had been attending a Congress on Hypnotism in Paris, he had yielded one evening to a friend's urgings to go to hear a new caf'-conc' singer – "for relaxation". Instead of relaxation, however, he had experienced that night a deep excitement that he never forgot'.[37]

From this point on Freud describes a clear rupture in the formation of his field, from the 'cathartic' method, the discharge of symptoms through the hypnotic procedure and 'psycho-analysis proper': 'So I abandoned hypnotism,

Figure 5.3 Yvette Guilbert, Maresfield Gardens, London, 1939

only retaining my practice of requiring the patient to lie upon a sofa while I sat behind him, seeing him, but not seen myself.'[38] From this juncture Freud describes himself as 'set free' from hypnotism (if not gender-limited descriptions) and begins almost immediately to denigrate hypnosis's screening from view the true interplay of forces that would provide him with his theory of 'repression', the repressed impulses of the unconscious and their conversion into symptoms. By 1900, hypnoid states had become 'that unfortunate idea that had been forced on me' and in 1901 that 'superfluous and misleading idea'.[39] Here the task of analysis changed dramatically from a process of abreacting affects which had 'got onto wrong lines' to uncovering repressions and replacing them with acts of judgement. The juncture is recognised by Freud in a change of name: 'I showed my recognition of the new situation by no longer calling my method of investigation and treatment catharsis but psycho-analysis.'[40] This is the date from which the psychoanalysis that is performance has to become the psychoanalysis that might have relations with performance.[41]

The reminder and remainder of the hypnotic history of this space of consultation were retained by Freud directly above the couch (see Figure 5.2).

The detail to the upper-left edge of the Charcot image is a drawing based on the work of Paul Richer whose illustrations of the 'contortion' stage of hysterical attack were well known in their day. If ever there was a 'compulsion to repeat', that uncanny performance is played out here. Blanche is 'striking attitudes', no less potent than Lady Hamilton's classical poses or the 'poses plastiques' that followed them in nineteenth-century acting styles, constructing for the attentive onlookers a 'typical hysterical attack' which resembles the image opposite. This image, as Forbes Morlock has conclusively shown, is, in its own turn, an uncanny replication of a photograph, which, for the purposes of securing a clear exposure, would have required a still pose of twenty minutes duration.[42]

Charcot described himself as a photographer fixing through clinical descriptions his observations, while the multiple refrains at work here deny any definitive fixing of source and influence. Where in this scene is the 'original' disturbance, and where is its repetition and refraction through the conventions of photographic portraiture and hypnotic staging? The fixing gaze is that of a male audience while the 'Napoleon of the Neuroses' and his faithful aide, Babinski, stand by. While Babinski appears to gaze into Blanche's cleavage, a nurse's hands reach out to redeem her for the stretcher. Any 'ontology of performance' is destabilised by this show, counter-show and representation within reproduction.

The *poses plastiques*, which gave rise in the nineteenth century to the first exhibitions of 'nude statuary', body-stockinged performers posing for audiences, were not so far from the disarray of Blanche Whitman. Freud's daughter Mathilde said of the lithograph:

> It held a strange attraction for me in my childhood and I often asked my father what was wrong with the patient. The answer I always got was that she was 'too tightly laced', with a moral of the foolishness of being so. The look he would give the picture made me feel then even as a very young child that it evoked happy or important memories in him and was dear to his heart.[43]

One might extend Forbes Morlock's penetrating analysis of the image of Charcot to the consulting room and to Freud's office itself. There is a move from the visibility and demonstration of practice to the absence of seeing in the talking cure and therapy, the reproduction of the hypnotic scene or the location is replaced by acts of memory and remembering. Here the performance of the talking cure moves beyond reproduction to a paratheatrical state where the surreality of simulation through multiple 'fictions' is, as Hélène Cixous says in her reading of the uncanny: 'Neither real nor fictitious, "fiction" is a secretion of death, an anticipation of non-representation, a doll, a hybrid body composed of language and silence that, in the movement which turns it and which it turns, invents doubles, and death . . .'.[44] This consulting room and office, which is neither 'real' nor 'fictitious', evoke the deadly double of the uncanny. The performative allusions of Sophie Calle thus serve to remind us of just such haunting theatrical illusions in the place of psychoanalysis.

Restoration

In *Civilization and Its Discontents*, Freud had summoned a fabulous representation of Rome in which incompatible places would coincide: '. . . in which nothing that has come into existence will have passed away and all earlier phases of development contrive to exist alongside the latest one. If we want to represent historical sequence in spatial terms we can only do it by juxtaposition in space'.[45] This has often been read as the rendition of the psychoanalytic act itself, but more prosaically it provides a means of reading the uncanny accretions of this speech-site with its lineaments in stage hypnosis, solo cross-gendered performance and durational live art acts. Here, in Freud's last year, text and site become one. With reference to Freud's final edit of his last work *Moses and Monotheism*, Michel de Certeau constructs a symmetry of textual and biographical space:

> In *Moses and Monotheism* the old man Freud has become will gather all of his essential theses around the idea of repression which had been '. . . the true point of departure for our extended study of psychopathology'. In sum he entirely recomposes *the* place that he had made for himself – psychoanalysis . . . But when he collects all of the furniture around him that proves the establishment of his own place, the other returns in the inevitability of an effacement; that is of filiation and of death. When Freud makes his inventory of acquired goods, he is really packing his bags.[46]

According to Freud's diary, his son Ernst had 'transformed the house into a ruin in order to restore it anew in a more suitable state for us. He is building in a lift making two rooms into one or the other way round. Sheer sorcery translated into architectural terms'.[47] The sorcery of the uncanny had begun earlier with the building of the house itself. Designed by the architect Albert G Hastilow in 1920 it was already a reflection of an earlier more sedate architectural period that Ernst, not wholly accurately, described as Neo-Georgian. So the façade of the house is already a recovery from an order of the past in a play of associations that writes large the accretions of the images in the study: 'The apparently irreconcilable demands for the absolute negation of the past and full "restoration" of the past here meet in their inevitable reliance on a language of architectural forms that seem, on the surface at least, to echo already used-up motifs *en abime*.[48] The ruin that Ernst mimics, one of the earliest acts of gentrified 'knocking through' in North London, is itself a palimpsest of Freud's previous locations, simultaneously reproduced and rendered in this final resting place. It is this very specific reproduction that makes a visit to that office at 20 Maresfield Gardens such an uncanny encounter.

The fireplace in the wall might be bricked in, discreetly veiled by a tapestry, but delinquent drafts eddy around the couch. The chimney acts as a conduit that blows both ways. It might let out the mutterings of the analysand like an amplifier to the ether of other voices on air, but it also draws down unwelcome house-guests to the hearth of a discipline in disarray. The uncanny reminds us this is no simple haunting but the revisiting of powers that have long been thought dead: '… at any moment what seemed on the surface homely and comforting, secure and clear of superstition might be reappropriated by something that should have remained secret, but that nevertheless, through some chink in the shutters of progress, had returned'.[49]

The compulsion to repeat, through representation and reproduction, is not only at the root of mimetic behaviour, of restored behaviour and of the twice made of performance; it is also inherent within the very setting in which those acts take place, at the heart of the psychoanalytic tradition. In Freud's consulting room it is the restoration to their rightful place of a myriad antiquaries, books, masks and images that construct a setting in which he might 'pack his bags'. He describes the composition of *Moses and Monotheism* within this setting in recalcitrantly conventional theatrical terms. Close to death, on the publication of this final work, in 1939 Freud noted in his diary: 'Quite a worthy exit …'.[50] In the Latin rite Freud's departure would have been accompanied by Vespers, an *office* for the dead, or in the ecclesiastical word originally given to such soulful songs, a 'placebo', a pleasing performance of passing through such an office.

Homo Juridicus

In 1911, Freud had set about his 'Psycho-analytic notes on an autobiographical account of a case of Paranoia (dementia paranoids)'.[51] He was writing these notes in Bergasse 19 in Vienna, well away from the room, the 'office' in a clinic in Sonnenstein, where Daniel Paul Schreber had composed his account during the preceding decade, and where I am standing now. On 14 April 2011, one hundred years to the day after Schreber's death, I look up at a shuttered window where Schreber was incarcerated for a decade, knowing that his history here is the lesser of two evils. The notoriety of Sonnenstein is not so much due to Schreber's influence, though an intense psychoanalytic interest remains wedded to his cause, but rather as the 'birth' place of the Nazi 'Euthanasia' programme, sometimes referred to as 'T4', after the site of its first development in the 'fourth' facility dedicated to this purpose in Berlin's Tiegaarden. Any looking back at the longer history of this site in Sonnenstein, to the relations between psychoanalysis and law, requires visitors to peer through a past without discounting, euphemising, or belittling the greater force of that which lies between. It is Daniel Paul Schreber through his written and phantasmic responses to the 'crisis of investiture', between *Homo Psyche* and *Homo Juridicus*, who resisted the 'totalitarian temptation' as Eric Santner puts it in his work *My Own Private Germany* (1996), a resistance that any visit to Sonnenstein today makes apparent through the exhibition of the conjunction of the two histories that played out there in the late nineteenth to the mid twentieth century.

While Schreber's *Memoirs of My Nervous Illness* have, since Freud's interest in them, generated an industry of their own, representing as they do a remarkable testament to identity mutation and ecstatic illusion, precisely the 'resistance' to the totalitarian impulse in response to a perceived threat, real or imagined, to one's security or borders, there has been little commentary on the precise performative relations that exists in the *Memoirs* and Freud's reflections on them. It is my view that these relations are ones born of an autopoietic system that frames the symmetry of the two offices in this chapter. Where we explored *Homo Psyche* with regard to an architectural volume, the office of memory in Maresfield Gardens, we will here reflect upon *Homo Juridicus* from the literary site of Schreber's *Memoirs,* where an office of investiture joins a lawyer's chambers to an asylum.

Identification

If Schreber's own writing retains its force for a performance-minded person, it might be the following lines from his essay of 1900 that provide our best point of departure. The question he poses is: 'In what circumstances can a person considered insane be detained in an Asylum against his declared will?' And Schreber's answer provides me with the autopoietic link I am looking for: 'The answer to the above question offers not inconsiderable difficulties as only a few or no explicit regulations exist *in law*, and what can be described as existing law must mainly be derived from general principles'.[52]

As I suggested at the outset of this chapter, this is not the legal opinion of a layman. It is the view of an expert witness who has been oscillating between an inside and an outside of legal identification for more than a decade, recognising the peculiar paradox of the law. That is the paradox of the self-generating limits of law, those *general principles* described by Schreber, the way law contains itself as, paradoxically, only ever in the present. Indeed as an autopoietic system law is only actualised through its operations. In law: only what happens happens. Everything that happens in the legal system and in its environment happens at the same time.[53] According to Aristotle, in *The Poetics*, tragedy has peculiarly similar features which does not excuse our bringing such diverse systems together, but might alleviate our guilt at doing so on the grounds of classical precedence.

It is precisely within this peculiar chronology of the law that Daniel Paul Schreber identifies the chronology of his own circumstances. We know that he knew this much as he spells it out in the fourth chapter of his *Memoirs*. There he writes: 'I have suffered twice from nervous disorders and each time as a result of mental overstrain. This was due on the first occasion to my standing as a candidate to the Reichstag and on the second occasion to the very heavy burden of work that fell upon my shoulders when I entered my new duties as Senats president in Dresden'.[54]

Well I suppose we know what he means when he says 'shoulders', he means his desk, but the precise way his desk couples with *himself* to feel the inordinate pressure of work. We will come back to the arrangement upon that desk in a while. Eric Santner put these relations very elegantly some years ago in *My Own Private Germany*.[55] He described them as: '... shifts in the fundamental matrix of the individual's relation to social and institutional authority, to the way he or she is addressed by and responds to the call for official power and authority'.[56] Santner is describing the peculiarly performative way an 'office' is taken up. These calls, as Santner continues, are 'symbolic procedures of investiture', a new social status accompanied by a symbolic mandate and via a 'performative magic' the individual assumes an identity, they *become who they are* via such 'names, titles, degrees, posts honours and the likes'.

I have no argument at all with this 'performative magic', but would like to flesh it out, historically and specifically within the law with regards to such offices. My qualifications to do such a thing are tenuous; I am certainly not trained in jurisprudence. My expertise rests upon having played the role of Azdak, the garrolous judge, when I was seventeen years old in Bertolt Brecht's play *The*

Caucasian Chalk Circle. If you know the play you will know that the drunken, lecherous layman, Azdak, has a remarkable, and not wholly deleterious, impact on his community for someone who has essentially donned the robes of law out of expediency and self-preservation. He appears in the latter half of the play, *Der Kaukasische Kreidekreis,* which has been framed at the outset from the perspective of a pair of competing Russian communes where the retreating Nazi forces in the late days of World War II have left a landscape of disputation over the rights to farm. Through a series of mock trials and counter intuitive if common sensical judgements, Azdak gains the preferment of the Grand Duke, who, at the cusp of his hanging, pardons him and invests him with judicial power. This order of investiture is met with a paradoxical retort, wholly in keeping with the spirit of this chapter, by the Ironshirt to the Corporal whose office requires him to officiate: 'I beg to report that His Honour Azdak was already His Honour Azdak'. Azdak thus essentially, by the end of the play from whence he slips away unnoticed with no apparent identity having lost a double identity, has *become himself* through the processes of law.

It was obvious for me, as a long-haired drop out, about to be 'invited' to leave my school for failing to encounter at any serious level the best part of its curriculum, that assuming this role of Azdak spilled out from the aesthetic domain of a school play into my immediate social realm. 'They are us', Socrates was right to point out in *The Republic* when observing those tethered to the illusions of spectacle, and Plato justly feared theatre for all its doubling deception and its potential for distraction from the one job I was meant to be doing, being a diligent student. This performative magic of unseemly doubling was so potent that my curtain call and its transition from 'play world' to 'social world' could barely operate as it was, and is, designed to function. Nicholas Ridout describes such identity stallings in his work *Stage Fright, Animals and Other Theatrical Problems*. In the curtain call the representational machinery of the theatre stops whirring quite so furiously and allows for the passage of the 'still costumed' actors back to the far side and the reestablishment of social and personal contacts with those for whom the previous three hours have been a most peculiar experience, simply at the level of credibility.

I went through my own crisis of confidence, a suburban miniature of Schreber's cataclysmic dissembling, immediately following this forced investiture, through the dogmatic operation of casting. A crisis that was complicated by the fact that while I appeared to have played the part of Azdak in the long final act, 'The Chalk Circle', according to the lavishly Gestetnered programme at least, the role had been played in the longer, and dramatically more significant *penultimate act*, 'The Story of the Judge', by someone else entirely, with a similar but typographically inept name: Alan Reid, with an i, not an a. I remember quite forcefully the retrospective anxiety this modest secretarial mishap caused me at the time, given I had considered that story '*my* story', and while I was later in life to become a performance specialist, I was never to get back onto a stage again in quite the same way for fear of misattribution.

What I understood about law I learnt through playing that part, not really by any other familiarity with its systems. And I learnt that because in playing that part, of a judge, I began to recognise for Azdak, yes, but also for me, that it really did not mark quite the difference I might have expected to enter the law, to take up its office, costumed in this way. It was, that is, as if the law was already peculiarly familiar. I was 'made for it', as I contend we all are. This is what I infer by deploying the French anthropologist Alain Supiot's term: *Homo Juridicus*.

My sensitivity to that misattribution might not however be wholly irrelevant. Alain Supiot reminds us that human beings are not born rational, they *become* so by gaining access to meaning shared with others.[57] This is, I suppose, the precondition for Freud to be able to do his work, and for the office of psychoanalysis to exist. If we are to enjoy thinking and expressing ourselves freely in language, we must first submit, says Supiot, to the limits that give words meaning; without this consensual constraint, we would have no autonomy. But, before I arrived at my own awareness of my being through speech, certainly well before the speeches I was to make as Azdak, I had already been named, and situated within a lineage, a lineage that went by the name of 'Read', as in to read a book, not Reid as printed in that programme, or indeed any other name, for now. A place was assigned to me within a succession of generations. This was complicated by the fact that, like, but not quite like Bill Clinton, the sometime President of the United States in the 1990s, my father had died six months before I was born in 1956. So I was a 'posthumous' child coming after the event that others, sympathetically but misguidedly, thought should define my life. The projected naming by my parents was to be subverted by my mother who changed my planned name, John, to that of my father, Alan. But she had never condoned that in place of that A, in the name READ, there should have been an I, that would just not have been us.

I take it from this post-natal anecdote that before we can dispose of ourselves freely and say I, as in '*I* played Azdak', we are, as Supiot would suggest, already a *subject* of law, we are bound, *subjectum*, literally tied to responsibilities, duties and debts, we are 'subjected to' by becoming 'subjects of' words that can only have meaning, even if mistaken, for others. Contracts not wholly of our own making, and sometimes not of our making at all, require the ties of law and speech to relate and engage in some meaningful way. Alain Supiot would suggest that it is the shape, form or symmetry of such relations that not only become a 'new born' member of humanity, but more, to enable that life to become endowed with meaning, in other words to exist as a subject amongst others. Again, I presume it is upon these bonds and their disruptions that psychoanalysis does its work. Wherever people are cut off from their fellow creatures, Supiot contends at least, they are condemned to idiocy, in the etymological sense of that term, from the Greek, *idios*, 'confined to oneself'. As are people who cannot envisage that universes other than their own exist and are therefore unable to arrive at a consensual representation of a world where we would each have a place, a condition that clearly describes the predicament of Daniel Paul Schreber. The aspiration to justice is thus, for better or for worse (and this is why Supiot describes us as *Homo Juridicus*), a fundamental anthropological fact, and not a mystical leftover from pre-scientific modes of thought.

It is, Supiot suggests, by transforming each of us, not quite into an Azdak, but into a *Homo Juridicus* that, in the West at least, and he is diligent in his separation of juridical process in those cultures that do not subscribe to the Western legal canon, as he would wish us to learn from these 'others', the biological and symbolic dimensions that make up our being have been linked together. The law for Supiot has an anthropological function because it connects our infinite mental universe with our finite physical existence, and in so doing fulfils the function of instituting us as rational beings. In this process it is *law* and the *psyche* that provide the twin motors of the anthropological machine. Between the archaeological realm of the caves of Chapter 1 of this book, to the theological and historical realm of the early modern period of Chapter 3, animality, humanity and the divine are registered, compared and distinguished at every turn. Now here within modernity, psychoanalysis and law, it is rather prohibition, identity and investiture that are what is at stake.

I think, given the above, that there may be a problem with making too much of the diagnostic correlation made by Daniel Paul Schreber, that of the chronological link between the assumption of his legal responsibilities and his nervous disorder. Such an admission might begin to suggest there is a state that could be somehow described as pre-law, or 'before the law', or preposterously 'outside the law'. For there to be a performative process of *investiture* and entry into such a new 'social status' we would have to subscribe to some sort of *extra* legal domain from which one arrives to be made into such a thing. It was not as though I had not forcefully felt the power of discipline prior to being cast as Azdak. Indeed, a cursory reading of the short stories of Franz Kafka would disabuse us of any such hope. You might want to argue that it is the rôle, as in a theatrical rôle, that is the problem and precisely the elevated, heightened legal rôle of *Senatspresident* that causes Daniel Paul Schreber *his* problem, indeed he says as much so why not take his word at face value? But I would wish to remain true to 'performative magic' here, and make a play for exploring the degree to which we are all lawyers now, and have always been (despite the disappointing evidence that we are not being paid at their rates).

Prohibition

So far so relevant to the individual biography of Daniel Paul Schreber, *Homo Psyche* meets *Homo Juridicus* indeed. But the anthropological link between law and identity is one which, once detected, can of course be threatened and even anhialated. Looking up at Schreber's window in that place, Sonnenstein, on that anniversary of his death, is to bring forcefully to mind one of the lessons that Hannah Arendt draws from the experience of totalitarianism rooted in this very place. As she says: 'The first essential step on the road to total domination is to kill the *juridical person*'.[58] Brecht's quasi mythical setting for *The Caucasian Chalk Circle* does after all follow the historical materialist Prologue, the *Nazi* occupation and withdrawal from Russian valleys. It is with particular regard for that context that the figure of the 'lay' judge is put into play in the absence of law created by totalitarian measures.

Hannah Arendt is of course not alone in making these links between the extermination of the juridical being and the threat of Fascism. Alain Supiot makes clear that to deny the anthropological function of the law, as he would figure *Homo Juridicus*, in the name of what he calls a 'supposed realism grounded in biology, politics or economics', is characteristic not only of Fascisms but of any and all Totalitarian projects. Hearing those 'guides' in the basement of this place called Sonnenstein, remembering, memorialising and marking the machinery of the 'Euthanasia' programme, forty years after Schreber's residence there, is to be brought, face to photographic face, with the industrial pursuit of just such extermination. This lesson, Supiot believes, seems to have been forgotten by the jurists who today argue, in the interests of 'human rights' even, that the legal person is a 'pure construct' bearing no relation to the concrete human being. Indeed, at a wholly mundane theatrical level, this apparent contradiction is one I chase around the stage in Chapter 3, in pursuit of Jonathan Pryce's hands, and the problem of 'personhood' this provokes. The legal person is just that, a construct, as I was before, and after, being Azdak, but in the symbolic universe that is our lot, everything is, of course, a construct *not* a unified character. Legal personality is certainly not a fact of nature, for Alian Supiot, but rather a certain *representation* of the human being that posits the unity of that body (hands) and that person (in the form of a character) at the same time as it formulates a *prohibition*: that the human being should never be reduced one-sidedly to either.

It is in the wake of this totalitarian history of the twentieth century, a history in which Sonnenstein, Schreber's place of incarceration, played such a central part as the home of the 'T4' Nazi Euthanasia programme, that it was deemed necessary to extend legal personality and the prohibition it contains to every 'person' wherever they may be. It is this prohibition, Supiot makes clear, that is really being challenged when people today seek to disqualify the subject of law, and treat the human being as a mere accounting unit, like a commodity, or, more or less the same thing, as an abstraction. By materialising this threatened 'abstraction', those hands of Jonathan Pryce as Lear gesture against the 'accounting' of his daughters that follows his own demand that they 'account' for their own stake in his Kingdom. The schism between the office of this unfair trading and its bureaucratic fruit, the dispossessed person, runs like a demon of writing, the power of paperwork through the modernist literary tradition and was of course precisely the rend within which Franz Kafka worked in those 'fictional' offices in the years between the moment of Schreber's residence at Sonnenstein and the arrival of the Euthanasia programme in its cellars.

Operation

Homo Juridicus then operates within a law that is made up of a braid of precisely human, performative operations that deserve more attention than are ever given to them. In a temporal sense, operations, whether legal or performative, are events. That is, they are realisations of meaningful possibilities that, as soon as they are realised, disappear again. Legal events are *no* different to performance events in this operational sense. They are quite different in other obvious ways (we should count ourselves lucky, all the world is *not* a stage given the appalling evidence of post 'Homeland Security' justice at Camp X Ray in Guantanamo Bay) but I won't go there until the next two chapters.

Operations, as events at least, have no significant duration, even if there is a minimal duration in which they can be observed, for instance the time it takes to pronounce a legal judgement, or literally to 'hand down' a judgement from judge to court clerk. Hence as they have no duration they cannot be changed. While we might wish to interrupt a legal summing up from the public gallery, or a performance from wherever we are, it is highly unlikely (given the reasons already offered in this book regarding the immunity of the audience, and the impersonal operations of the 'third person' performer) that any such action will lead to anything but ostracism, rejection and eviction. One only need here reflect upon Sir Peter Hall's notorious (yet wholly apposite) critical 'commentary' on the final scene of *Uncle Vanya* at the Vaudeville Theatre in London in 2012, a 'shout out' as much as a critique, and an interruption that he had to pretend was the consequence of sleep induced by his 'older age', to recognise the draconian policing regimes of spectacle. I am not convinced, as I have made clear in *Theatre, Intimacy & Engagement* (2008) with regard to the drastic limitations to Augusto Boal's 'Forum Theatre' and the wild claims to democracy of interactive and immersive theatre, that anything like 'change' is at work in such events, especially when such change has the qualifier 'political' before it. That said, like all performance, such court judgements are as good as they can be, given what is available to them at any one time or place.

The problem is, and what might induce mental anxiety in the strongest of constitutions, that in reality, or what passed for reality for Schreber when he took on that legal rôle in that office, operations had to be understood as *creating a difference*. This is where law in its 'effects' departs quite acutely from performance and its 'affects', in which the definition of an operation, as my caveat above suggests, might as well be that absolutely *no* difference need happen, nor will ever happen; so marvellously, instrumentally disfunctional is performance. But in any law (worth its name of course) something has had to be *changed* after the operation and has been made different by the operation. Here one could think of filing a legal action or simply of referring to a question of law in everyday life. It is this discriminating effect of the operation which, given a sufficient duration to the operation, and the opportunity to weave its outcomes into a recursive network of further operations, thus creates a difference between system and environment; or as Niklas Luhmann puts it, an operation that 'differentiates a system'.

Observation

But as any performance scholar would insist, an operation *can* be observed and described in many different ways. The filing of a legal action can be described as the suffering of an indignity, by Daniel Paul Schreber say, or as providing a welcome ground for the final breaking off of social relations, divorce papers issued by Azdak say, as permitted by law. If one wants to know how an operation is observed, as theatrical practice makes clear, one has to observe the observers. This is what Richard Yates pictures so beautifully in his novel *Revolutionary Road* (1961), with which we began this book, when our attention is drawn less to the stage, where April Wheeler is beginning to self-combust in the Laurel Players' dissembling production of *The Petrified Forest*, and more to her husband, Frank, towards the back of the auditorium, eating his fist in empathetic distraction. Here as the shattered audience make their isolated way from the event to the parking lot outside they are defined as much by the distances they keep as the proximities they share. From the outset Richard Yates has made clear the aspiration of this group is something more, much more than theatre, it is 'community' that is at stake, and it is community that cannot cohere.

Simultaneously just to mix things up a bit, and Richard Yates is an acute observer of this process as well, the observation of the act is, itself, an operation, a *new* condition of the system, and this is as true for theatre as it is for law. As regards operations that are specific for law we shall find that self-observation oriented by the *distinction* between law and injustice is indispensible, while in performance self-observation between expectations and realisations, between conventions and departures from orthodoxy and engagement or ambivalence are indispensible as they are the mechanisms that allow us aesthetic response-ability. It is also, critically, these processes that form the minutae of the immunising principle we described earlier as the defining quality of the modern audience.

But you will already have noticed a problem, and it is one that Alain Supiot believes is critical to our understanding of *Homo Juridicus*. The concepts of observation and self-reference that we are dealing with here, both in the theatre and law, imply each other. On the one hand observers can only observe when they can distinguish between themselves and their observation instruments, their distinctions and designations, and so manage not to keep confusing themselves with their objects. On the other hand this is precisely what *self-reference* is needed for, and it is this self reflexivity that has characterised almost all theatre at the edge of performance for at least the last half century since Richards Southern and Schechner began to articulate their relations. The first chapter of Richard Yates's *Revolutionary Road*, structured around a theatrical failure, demonstrates a phenomenological acuity precisely because the author employs these registrations of distance as a means of calibrating the embarrassments his subjects suffer in the face of performance collapse.

We might now need Diderot's *Paradox of the Actor*, First and Second on their walk through the Tuilleries (as discussed in the last chapter), to lead us back through the problem that this 'paradox' presents to us. That is the gap between one's observations and one's checking of these experiences against one's own 'sense of self'. For Daniel Paul Schreber, self-description, and a *Memoir* might well be the highest form of such a thing, is a paradoxical enterprise because it deals with internal descriptions, in the case of Schreber's state of mind highly mutable ones, as if it were an external description capable of reporting objective matters. This has to be the status Freud gives to the work in order to build his theory of Paranoia upon it in some way. But this version of a paradoxical problem is only one of many. The code of the system, whether that is legal practice ('law as a social system' as Niklas Luhmann characterises it), or performance practice ('theatre in the expanded field' as I have been discussing it), turns into a paradox at the point at which it is applied to itself. For instance, the efforts of the legal system to come to terms with *justice* as a formula for conduct hides the fact that it is concerned with unfolding a paradox: a ceaseless oscillation between two opposite positions which Luhmann describes as: legal/illegal, internal/external or equal/unequal. And each of Luhmann's characteristics of legal process is rather reminiscent of a series of oppositions well known within performance study: audience/performer, inside/outside, illusion/reality. We said at the outset of this book that in solidarity with Rosalind Krauss who never feared naming binaries, we would not be shy in registering some of those binaries here. For what such binaries obviously set up are the parameters for oscillation between poles of conserving force that I recognise as definitive to these fields, however disturbing that might be for a field that announces the end of such reductiveness with appeals to ambiguity, hybridity and plurality.

This *oscillating* between binaries is significant because it returns us to the everyday lives that we live, it returns us to the system as a problem of everyday behaviour, by which of course I also imply Schreber's everyday behaviour, just as much as Freud's, or ours for that matter. Imagine Schreber's desk, his legal desk I mean in his new rôle. And here the desk differs quite markedly from the stage in its resistance to the clutter of its own, unmanageable history. The reality, of legal proceedings in courts and parliaments, not least of all caricatured by Charles Dickens in the first outrageous, mud-bound pages of his legal novel *Bleak House* (1852–1853), differs widely from what is said, desired and intended. For instance the courts call what they are doing the 'application of law'.

The reality is quite different, according to observers such as Alain Supiot and Niklas Luhmann, who keep their eye on the desk not the dogma. The daily world appears to be approached through the goal of 'clearing the desk'. Dates and deadlines, files and distractions absorb the attention that one might have presumed would be dedicated to that 'application of law'. There is always

Luhmann notices – and his own academic experience might be amplifying this observation – something *to be* done in order that something *can be* done. This much would not appear to have changed since Jarndyce and Jarndyce practiced on Chancery Lane in Dickens's day. What the participants of the legal process see, from Esther Summerson in *Bleak House* on, is quite different from what is stipulated by the self-description of the system by those lawyers responsible for its promotion. It is in this gap of stated intention and reality that the novel unfolds, just as it is those gaps that orchestrate the dramas that follow hard upon Richard Yates's theatricalisation of dissensus in *Revolutionary Road*. Any analysis of how a system deals with its own paradoxical ineffectiveness, whether it is the reality of the poverty of the law, the poor law you could call it, or the poor theatre, will in the end expose mechanisms which are quite different to the mere logical and methodical ironing out of inconsistencies as though such paradoxical illogic could be fundamentally altered by sudden sense. It is the complicating effect of these mechanisms from which degrees of immunity and community first arise in performance.

Daniel Schreber would have seen countless clients frustrated by this system, the 'poor law', but it is the nightmarish fact of the system, and not just the Dickensian system, that no *actual* consequences follow from frustration, each case is treated as an individual case and somehow cannot take account of previous difficulties in the system. In the end we are all like Kafka's patient victim, waiting our turn at the door of the law as though someone will call for us soon and provide the answer we seek. The adjustments to such irritations of the system at this level will always, for Alain Supiot at least, take the form of idealisations. By definition reform cannot be admitted to be the work of a profession's critical attitude towards this system, the door cannot suddenly be thrown open to reveal the workings of this system. What is expressed each time, through the actual processes of law as distinct to the idealisation of an 'application of law', is the discrepancy and divide between different levels of communication in that system. The system must operate, Supiot suggests, 'acratically', contrary to common judgement, which means that it does not have sufficient means to control itself. Rather it is as though the whole system had become one characterised by Azdak's ministrations, rather than just his operations as a temporary irritant in the service of everyday justice. It really is no wonder if Supiot's anthropological analysis of the law laid out here is anywhere near the mark, and Luhmann's social systemics of law is taken seriously, why Schreber when confronted with paradoxes of this ever-widening kind effected an operation of *self-exception*. Schreber pursued this self-exclusion from the law in his own way, by submitting to the conditions that necessitated the removal of his office from Leipzig, to the more secure one, now above me, in Sonnenstein.

Immunisation

Is there any way out of this autopoietic system of self-perpetuating conditions and circulating paradoxes other than to submit oneself to the incarceration of the asylum in retreat from the lunacy of the law? Not surprisingly, having suffered the consequences of playing Azdak, or perhaps more accurately introjected the paradoxical virus of the law through investiture *as* Azdak, I would propose it is a peculiar kind of performance *within the system* that does the trick, that protects the social and the individual body from what Walter Benjamin once referred to as the 'out-law' dimension of law, that is 'law making' violence and 'law preserving' violence. In order for us to get to the 'social' and 'sensible' expanses offered by the next chapter, a welcome if temporary relief from these suffocating circulations, I will give this performance of protection the name 'immunisation'.

We have seen these kinds of operations of 'escape' from metaphysical madness, discussed most forcefully over the last decade and a half by the Italian philosopher, Roberto Esposito. Indeed in his work *Bios* (2008), this operative link is made explicit at the outset of his definition of what he means by the paradigm of immunisation: '… the category of immunity', he says there, 'is inscribed precisely on the tangential line that links the sphere of life with that of law […] Immunity in political-juridical language alludes to a temporary or definitive exemption on the part of the subject with regard to concrete obligations or responsibilities that under normal circumstances would bind one to others'.[59] Here Esposito as good as describes Schreber's conduct of self-exception from the office he could not tolerate under the 'threat' of the law.

Without stretching Esposito too far, law (and as we will see later, theatre) can also be seen as an apparatus of the immune system of any society within which it plays its peculiarly poor part. We are not here allowing ourselves to follow the biologists, arguing by analogy, and are certainly not using the concept of the immune system purely metaphorically, that is the telling move that Esposito has made on our behalf. We are also certainly not neglecting the *positive* potentials of an immunisatory system that, given the critical part it plays in the protection of the earliest life forms in the mother's womb, cannot be without merit. Rather here we are dealing with a general problem which is typical of systems that organise the construction of their own complexity on the *reduction of the complexity in their environment*, in the form of operative closure say, or structural coupling, the kinds of operation Niklas Luhmann has drawn our attention to and which I have ascribed to the psychoanalytic and the legal so far.

A 'system' as we have adopted that term from Niklas Luhmann cannot rely on its prediction of possible disturbances to defend itself against them; there is no equivalent of a Star Wars defence shield available to protect its integrity blow by blow. Counter-measures, or return fire in such circumstances, will never be able to take account of all possible angles of attack, however judicious the planning. In performance such a stricture might, for the purposes of illustration, amount to the director, Romeo Castellucci, having to preface each staging of his work *On The Concept of the Face* as discussed earlier with a litany of apologia as to its potential effects, from those in *Civitas* with Christian sensibilities to those immersed in perfumed muslin with fragile olfactory systems. Any such counter measures would effectively introduce an intolerable load from outside to within the system under pressure and ultimately that system would collapse under its own battery of defences. The ambiguities of art would simply fail and become a sub-division of academic second-guessing. Point by point, or feature by feature, relations between the system and its environment are feasible in neither a positive sense nor a negative sense, because this would reduce the difference between system and environment to that of being a mirror image of each other like a Borges map covering the world it is meant to represent rather than to replace.

What the immune system in fact does is to compensate for this lack of requisite, totalising variety. I have to make the obvious point here that this degree of complexity, that law cannot tolerate, is the complexity that precisely Schreber's *Memoirs* can, his prose can. It is law's problem, not poetry's problem, nor performance's problem, because, remember what we said, it is *law* not performance, that has the peculiar problem of having to make a difference; it is about effects not affects, as we agreed earlier.

The immune system, for Luhmann, does not correct, replace or excuse errors but 'cushions' structural risks. It is not, as he would have known from his work across the systemic qualities of a myriad disciplines, directed by the ideal of a rational practice that is free of contradictions or troubles. It has the 'good enough' about it in its modest specificity. Its function is not to eliminate misconceptions about what is right, because in that case any problem regarding the law, as caricatured from Dickens to Kafka say, would be easily solved (whatever the criteria may be). No, rather the immune system enables society to cope, to survive and even to thrive ironically with the structural risk of the continuous production of conflicts. The demand for an immune system is not, Niklas Luhmann insists, the result of poor adaptation to the environment (that would be ubiquitous to systems whose shared characteristic is human fallibility) but is a result of giving adaptation and its threat of infinite modulations a miss, in other words avoiding it for the sake of the protection of its lively but limited energies.

I would suggest, and the two narratives of the chapter come together here, it is this 'bypassing' quality of immunisation that might best describe Schreber's shift from legal brief to *Memoir* and Freud's shift from performance (hypnotism) to case study. Mental overstrain, as Schreber describes his condition in his *Memoirs,* points to a material condition that brings about what he then describes as 'nervous illness'. The condition has been brought about, if we take Schreber at his word, by the *unlimited* nature of the law. He describes a common way in which we might describe the corrosive quality of law, the way as Esposito says in his reflections on Kant, though it might as well have been Kafka, 'it breaks down our subjectivity'. This law imposes on the subject a statute of permanently being unable to carry out the law, the requirement to circumvent it with recourse to a community who might have in common this crisis of subjection.

Because, not despite all of this, it is the law in its various valences of violence, that after all provides us, and Schreber, with the possibility of talking about community, or, what is 'allowed' to be thought about community and the protections it might offer from such violences. But community isn't to be found outside the law, in some alternative violence-free idyll to the side of Rousseau's May-pole, community pertains precisely within the limits of the law, even if it is that interiority that precludes its realisation. Without Azdak the judge, irrespective of his qualifications, the matter of settlement, whether that be the destiny of a child, or the farming of a valley, cannot take place. The exodus of law from these Kolkhoz villages and valleys in the opening scenes of *The Caucasian Chalk Circle* has been precisely figured by Brecht as an enforced transhumance of the goats to the pastures East. It is this tension, contradiction or paradox that represents all those from Thomas Hobbes who have denied the question of community and those since Jean Jacques Rousseau who have tried to solve the problem of community through myth. It is not that community is impossible, but that 'impossibility' is itself community. As Roberto Esposito says: 'Community is the only one that men and women can experience if they accept its law: that of their finitude, which is to say, of community's impossibility'.[60] This is, in the end, what we really share: we are joined together, dramatically and otherwise, by the impossibility of community, by an impossible condition that is our common *munos.* This is *the gift* that is required of us, a gift whose exchange defines community, but whose debt inaugurates the will to *immunity* – an immunity that Daniel Schreber experienced and expressed as deriving from his always having been 'in debt to others'. This is, after all, the object of the legal community from which Schreber withdraws, the high office in Dresden, to enter another community, that of Sonnenstein whose foundations provided the conditions for the suspension of the juridical person.

The question at the outset of this chapter was: 'In what circumstances can a person considered insane be detained in an Asylum against his declared will?' As Daniel Paul Schreber discovered to his detriment, where all that is law is performed, poorly, and has to be. Here the impotential of performance (of law, of psychoanalysis) is writ large as the failure of investiture, the anhialation of performative magic. This is, in the end, what the community says to Daniel Paul Schreber (and to Azdak): that the *limit* of the law cannot be erased, nor in the end can one cross it. Both Schreber and Azdak are rather left, as Pierre Bourdieu has made clear in a different context, to respond to incessant calls to order, to office, to stay on the proper side of a 'socially consecrated boundary'. But in such abandonment to order, or interpellation through investiture, they are, as with all elites, 'destined to waste away when they cease to believe in themselves, when they ... begin to cross the line in the wrong direction'.[61]

In that Brecht play that so disorientated me, the chalk circle was, after all, one born of myth. It does not survive the transition back at the end of the play into the world of work, where the valley must 'go to the waterers, that it yield fruit'.[62] The rogue judge does not so much take leave of this community, as *waste away* at the moment of its coerced coming together. As Azdak takes off his robe for the last time he 'invites' those present, whose tribulations he has solved with a sequence of improvised judgements, to 'a little dance in the meadow outside'. As he signs the final divorce papers for the wrong couple, the dance music is heard. Azdak cannot withdraw his final clerical error, an error of office, because as he says: 'If I did how could we keep order in the land?' Azdak 'stands lost in thought. The dancers soon hide him from view. Occasionally he is seen, but less and less as more couples join the dance.' The Singer who has narrated the story of the chalk circle wraps up the occasion: 'And after that evening Azdak vanished and was never seen again./The people of Grusinia did not forget him but long remembered./The period of his judging as a brief golden age./Almost an age of justice'. The best law has to offer, in keeping with what has gone before, is still not 'quite' justice. As the couples dance off, Brecht's stage directions are enigmatic, but decisive; Azdak has 'disappeared'. The director's note to me, before the opening night in that school hall, was, I recall, something like: 'Find a way to disappear from view without attracting attention to yourself'. This, of course, was not how it was; I was after all, wasted. It was 'quite a worthy exit ...'.

Sixth Approach
Social & Sensible

I have a childhood recollection of a television programme on a small black and white screen in the corner of a suburban room in the early 1960s. A man, the fugitive, was running from bus station into a back alley, evading capture, and on the run righting the injustice that had been done to him. The law was letting him down, again. Like all good cliffhangers, time and space were intimately bound. The fugitive's face was a pale reflection of his troubled past and his foreclosed future, his proximity to a receding hope of justice. The time of his freedom was running out as the FBI closed in, while the space of his endeavour was systematically shut down from first one side, then the other. The fugitive's eyes were in a constant state of motion, taking in perpetual movement to left and right. The time of the programme ticked away, denouement was inevitable, but always to be suspended (Figure 6.1).

I am sure this was a Sunday evening when another time of freedom ticked away, the end of the weekend. These were the days of a new import to Britain, the first of many from the US, the game-show: *Sunday Night at the London Palladium* with its uncannily magnified clock followed by *Double Your Money* and *Take Your Pick*. Each show counted down the seconds on another contestant's hopes of winning an exotic holiday, or a grinning MC counted out the chance of luxuriating in a new three-piece suite.

Was I dreaming that once upon a time and far away, time and space were whole? And that here was a crossroads, where domestic space and travel were to be desired, won, or for the first time bought by those who wished to circumvent the luck of the lucky? Crime and punishment were scheduled to mix with good fortune; escape from the clutches of the law coincided with the chance to win a flight to exotica on an island, or, better still, to take possession of a quality settee and luxuriate in the privacy of one's own home.

THE FUGITIVE

Figure 6.1 David Janssen, *The Fugitive*, 1964

Now on a smaller, flatter screen in another corner, in digital colour, and sometimes on a Sunday, the genres are mixed with the fugitive being pursued by the tele-media – as the surveillance cameras of *Police Camera Action*, *Drivers from Hell* and *Crimewatch* infrared a weaving car or darting figure way below, mimicking the revelation during the O.J. Simpson San Diego freeway dash of 1994, that vast audiences like watching runaways. Winners take all; losers are banged up, deluged by telephone grassers. The domestic and the exotic are all the same now, been there, done that; the hunt and the money are all that's left. The time and space of suspense have come apart with nowhere left to run to and all the time to do it in. Where would the fugitive find refuge now? Justice depended on the time that passed under cover. No hiding place, no justice.

The intensive mapping that has forced the fugitive into the open, which characterises the last three decades in Europe and North America, is fundamentally different from the ordnance of the previous 200. In other words, there has been a paradigm shift since the telegraphic collapsing of space and time, described in Chapter 4. The shift is characterised by the titles of two books at either end of the writing career of Jonathan Raban: *Soft City* (1974) a paen to urban malleability, and *Surveillance* (2006) a prognosis of urban disaffection.

Surveying the street from the air, ordnance has lost control of the delinquent – a satellite shot of the hot-spots of the city is no substitute for 'the beat' where law enforcement began at the time of street lighting by meticulously searching out, at ground level, the location of hidden trapdoors to subterranean cellars, ditches and tunnels, back alleys and connecting passageways. Crowd control has substituted the chase; the city has in Paul Virilio's term been 'over exposed'.[1] From the caves, waiting rooms, palaces, churches, offices and courts that pepper the landscape of the first five chapters of the expanded field of performance mapped in this book, the 'underdeveloped' of Plato's world has been well and truly, now, forced out into the light.

I suspect the fugitive has nowhere to go but 'time to kill'. Homicide is no longer here a matter of dramatic denouement but simply an investment in durational avoidance of the law. The space of the discreet and hidden has been turned inside out by a series of economic, political and legislative assaults, leaving an exhausted landscape as fair game to be worked over by cultural historians, semioticians and geographers. The wastes that are left, the remainder they are working, are a rich one, but nevertheless an increasingly aestheticised one – just on the margins of the sites where a fugitive might properly seek to right wrongs and secure justice. Performance has led us back to that space of justice; it has also, equally often, simply decorated that space to make the fugitive's last hours more comfortable and pleasing to the eye and ear. While decoration would seem to have held sway in the 1990s, a deeper set of alliances with those who know space, who spent little time taking it for granted, has opened the terrain of the site-specific to some new and surprising politics over the first decade of the twenty-first century. This chapter is concerned with how that happened, and examines three examples of where the 'politics of aesthetics', as Jacques Rancière would put it, inherent to seeing, hearing and speaking, were played out at the interface between the social and the sensible.

But looking back, before looking out, it has to be admitted that the discourses of space, built form and urban context *had* become the pre-eminent critical idiom of the late twentieth century. Sensitive to questions of community readdressed in other languages, artists, theoreticians, social scientists and those within and beyond the architectural profession reached out towards the strategies and structure of the populated street to articulate the sense, the relevance perhaps, of their work. To be 'spaced out' was no longer to be depleted, as Terry Eagleton wrote around this time.

These attractions and invigorations would seem to have opened up an arena for affirmative, politicised discourse. But what should be noted from the outset about these languages is how they were predominantly conducted by men (with the eminent exception of Doreen Massey, Saskia Sassen and Jane Rendall), how insensitive to race and the realities of the urban everyday they could be (with the exception of Paul Gilroy, bell hooks and Guillermo Gomez-Pena) and how unacquainted they were with the diverse discourses of the performative and long-term community engagement that had for some time been the bread and butter of theatre studies (with the exception of nobody). Here, what Judith Butler once called the 'merely cultural' relegated the potential relationship between theatre knowledges and experiences below the 'more' significant work of economic and political analysis. This was a curious continuity from a time when the separation of base and superstructure was taken as a somewhat simplistic Marxist 'given' within cultural theory.

This was a particular loss for theory rather than practice. Ironically it was within the performance arena, the 'last human venue' as I call it in *Theatre, Intimacy & Engagement*, with its dissonant terrain of appearance and concealment that the distribution of the sensible was playing itself out, over and over again for some to see and hear. The appeals made by those within the theoretical field 'not to forget space' as a dynamic of social relations, space as gendered territory, space not as stasis but the ground for action and reaction were bountifully answered by the complex operations of performances through space and time of the last two decades in the UK and across Europe.

For instance, the exemplary performance work of groups such as Platform, and the duos Forster and Heighes and Cornford and Cross, exemplifies performance within a spatial moment, precisely resisting the trite classification of the political.

Platform's truly durational research and installation practices re-forged concealed histories of geographical and global markets. In their early work, the 1990s project *Homeland* for instance, Platform mixed social science research, practical experimentation, installation and performance to interrogate the Londoner's conception of home while inviting this capital to consider its part within a wider European homeland. Through the conceptual and physical link of light, its practical manifestation in the light bulb and the search for its source of electric power in Europe, Platform traversed a copper mine in Portugal, a coal mine in South Wales and a sand quarry in Hungary, via three institutional conglomerates who control power to the light switch: General Electric, British Coal and Rio Tinto Zinc. This pan-European and international enquiry was then re-imagined within a mobile installation that caravanned across London, stopping at significant junctions to embrace the perceptions and experiences of an audience reconfigured as participatory research projects. I recall drawing my idea of home on a small piece of paper and seeing it clipped up with hundreds of others on the wall of a mobile home.

The intimate Anglo-Saxon acts of historical recovery that Forster and Heighes conduct in 'principled' buildings, such as Union Chapel, the Mary Ward Centre in London and Ruskin's Brantwood House in the Lake District in NW England, would appear to be as distinct to the global complexities of Platform as one could imagine. Yet, as Gaston Bachelard remarked, the simple is only ever the complex simplified, and it is this resistance to reduction that characterises their work. *Preliminary Hearing*, produced as part of the 1997 London International Festival of Theatre, was an early example of their archaeological excavation of the ethical foundations of architecture and location, the hidden moralities that shaped London's meeting places and congregational centres. In the case of the recovery of the historical narrative of Mary Ward House in Bloomsbury, a series of lectures, demonstrations, installations and site constructions revealed the historical components of modern welfare provision, school meals, nursery education and care for people with disabilities. I recall being inundated by Morris Dancers, white, workingmen, dancing vigorously but gently together in public.

Installations by artists Cornford and Cross, *Camelot* in Stoke-on-Trent and *New Holland* in Norwich for instance, evidence another kind of relational awareness between site and work. In Stoke, in the English Midlands, 100 metres of security fencing 3 metres high was placed around 3 neglected grass verges, drawing out an array of ambivalence and anger from those who thought they knew their town, while in Norwich at England's eastern edge, a steel barn was placed adjacent to the Sainsbury Centre for Visual Arts, simultaneously evoking a Bernard Matthews's turkey breeder unit while playing-off Norman Foster's technocratic architecture and emitting a continuous soundtrack of Garage and House music.

Each of these artists works with a sense of the temporary, the fleeting and the inherent politics of site, avoiding dogmatism at every turn. Their points of departure for each project are ideas driven with no fear of the conceptual responses to place and its echoes. There is no 'apparent' audience in mind for the work and while drawing out dimensions of place that would otherwise go unnoticed they make no claims for unmasking the ideological conditions of a site's construction. Their politics would appear to be about wishing things a bit too far, to let something run unchecked and see what happens. For instance, in the case of Cornford and Cross's *Camelot* the question of space is conducted through an encroachment upon and enclosure of urban wilderness, with the act of privatisation and sectioning of space conducted as an operation of protection. For Cornford and Cross, pedestrianism is not just the hackneyed poetics of the urban flaneur of modernity, often ironically figured at large *in* Hackney; it is a necessity as well as an aesthetic choice. For families in Stoke it is a necessity in the absence of any vehicle, never mind what Paul Virilio once called a 'last vehicle'. Cornford and Cross have worked on these projects without a studio, distrusting the inhibition of scale such spaces induce, valuing the basic relationship between local bodies and spaces, the relations between pacing out and direct physical experience. Each of these works has to be circumvented on foot and might draw out surprising affiliations with the work of formalists such as Carl André and Richard Serra if we had not been warned off such gendered historical continuities by Rosalind Krauss in her essay 'Sculpture in the Expanded Field', which provided the opening frame for this book.

But how far do these relational projects of the last two decades take us with regard to questions of politics and justice now? Is the loss of the oppositional for the 'relational' necessarily a forfeiting of contested ground? The response of this chapter to the politics of site grows from a suspicion that the spatial turn itself, in the contemporary affection for the site-specific, has inadvertently led to an elision of politics in work that believes itself to have serious political freight. My proposition here is that the aestheticisation of space which occluded the transparency of events that once occurred 'on site', that jeopardised the meanings that might be drawn from actions, that covered the sense of what performance in place might be for has more recently given way to a more affirmative embrace and subtle autopoietic looping between aesthetic acts and social efficacy.

This two-decade-long evolution is not surprising given what immediately preceded it in the public realm. The deconstruction and distribution of the Berlin Wall in 1989 as a public art object has become its wider social significance after the tyranny it once embodied; over Baghdad, twice, in the 1990s and then again in the early 2000s, the observation of anti-aircraft flak becomes a pyrotechnician's dream; the valorisation of Swampy and the eco warriors protesting the tarmacing of England's green and pleasant land is predicated on their expertise as subterranean designers; the return of Hong Kong to China sparks a debate about the decibel level of an eve-of-handover concert by Elton John or the aesthetics of post-colonial nautical departure. Berlin, Manchester, Hong Kong, an international club circuit with each location divested of anything but its banal aesthetic associations by the end of the last millennium.

While activism has retreated from the public realm it has regrouped, over the last decade at least, around less localised and more trans-national objectives.

A historic association with protest and place has been superseded by global affiliations and space: Pride in London and Sydney, Carnival in Jamaica and Koln, Feminism in Beijing and New York, Ecology in Rio and Amsterdam, Occupy everywhere. Here the site of action is displaced by the network of affiliation. But these political shifts are simultaneous with a harsher, faster proliferation of networking – a global chain initiated by companies such as Google, Microsoft and Exxon, and entrepreneurs like Rupert Murdoch, Bill Gates and Lakshmi Mittal, moving from production, through distribution and cross-border agreements before they can be regulated.

It is in the asymmetry of these local and global tensions that aesthetic acts, in and on site, can no longer make privileged claim to the specific and particular over the universal and general. Through a hermeneutic sleight of hand it had been implied that access to the everyday and its politics meant that a 'return to the real' was now possible. The truth, as well as being 'out there', was thought to be down the road if you looked closely enough. Local knowledge proliferated in these hopeful conditions in the 1990s in direct reciprocation to the disavowal of the meta-narratives that were said to have once bound district to region to nation. These might always have been illusory ties, but in their stead the heavy duty bonds of corporate finance and international capital were busy reasserting other, less sympathetic relations. And it has been these grander shifts of power that the street sweepers of the everyday, among whom I number myself, have missed as they passed by on the sunny side of a millennial turn. It was this lack of capacity to recognise the vertiginous shifts of capital that precluded any serious cultural consideration of the critical state of the economy until well into the financial crisis of 2007 and beyond.

The degree to which street speak can be critical at any level now would seem to be an apposite question being asked by a significant range of artists and performance makers. Siting their work in the interstices between pedestrianism and panopticism, the work of contemporary artists would appear, if the following examples are anything to go by, neither to have settled with the 'Soft City' of Jonathan Raban's early fictional work nor the 'Surveillance' fears of his later dystopic non-fictions. The retreat into the crevices of the street was a necessary corrective at the end of a century to the overarching ambitions of the colonial imperative of the century before: to map space as a precursor to invading it and appropriating it.

From Brian Friel's play *Translations* (1981) via Gordana Stanisic's three-week walk to Belgrade on a travelator in the Showroom London (1994), the shift from a dramaturgy of observation to a performance of survival paralleled the same two-decade switch from a semiotic poetics of watcher to a phenomenology of the watched. Consider the fulcrum between these parallax modes of work, between the Birling family's imperious view in J.B. Priestley's *An Inspector Calls* (1946) and the solipsistic wanderings of Spalding Gray's monologues across the US (1985–2000), between the beholden estrangement of Vladimir and Estragon (1955) and the aural meanders of Graeme Miller's *Sound Observatory* (1992). It has for over half a century been the axis where the symphonic relations within the human laboratory of theatre have transmuted to become the site of the last human venue. This move is neither surprising nor conclusive, despite the finality of the venue's name. Perhaps it is just the equivalent of architectural eclecticism, comparative spiritualities, Freud-resistant therapies and participant-observer ethnographies documented through this book that have simultaneously unsettled the narratives of the theoretical field.

The following performances where the social and the sensible would appear to interface in a theatrical presence, or appearance, have been chosen for the fundamentally ethical opportunity they would appear to offer us now to move beyond what Ulrich Beck described as the characteristic feature of a 'risk society', that is the move from something good to the urge to prevent the worst. In these works the commonality of anxiety is not perceived as a mask for ignoring the commonality of need. I want here to heighten a tension between the visually driven work in performance studies that I developed in earlier chapters from *Homo Spectator* on, and examine and introduce here the parallax between sight and sound that the recent theatre interest in witnessing, and witnesses, has exposed.

In the following three studies I want to supplement this emphasis with a sequence of 'sensible' histories that provide a pitch of performance, that is a *site* and a sound, the combination, congruence or incongruence of which reveal what Jacques Rancière calls 'the distribution of the sensible'. If the distribution of the sensible reveals who it is who is in a position to 'see', 'hear' and 'speak' back to an aesthetic act, if it can reveal those who have a share in the commonality of community, as Rancière suggests, then the practise of that distribution, tracing an activity which is performed in time and space, is what the rest of this chapter undertakes.

Jacques Rancière, interested as he has always been in theatrical processes, helpfully privileges the 'stage' as a locus for such public activity where what he calls 'fantasies' disturb 'the clear partition of identities, activities and spaces'.[2] But despite the prominence of aesthetics in his projects, Rancière (like the other theatre-wise philosophers of his generation referred to in earlier chapters,

Alain Badiou and Giorgio Agamben) does not make specific play of plays and playing. As with many of these *arondissment* analysts theatre is their thing, and a peculiarly attenuated Parisian version of theatre it is, indeed. The irritations of performance would appear to French theory at least to be a bridge too far. Should any of them be at a Symposium on Hypnotism now, as Freud was a hundred years before them, you would not, from their writings at least, imagine them popping out to catch the latest performance artist at work (as their predecessor Freud made a point of doing).

If the 'political' is to be guarded against for its premature account of the ongoing performative process, as I would suggest it must be if we are not to sink into 'pseudo action', then 'politics' in this chapter becomes the term that best describes that interruption of the sensible that Jacques Rancière describes. There is a good deal being said about the interruptive social force of performance at the moment, but the ambition to expand the collective, to supplement the ordering of the sensible with those who have previously played a weak part, or no part in their arrangements, is to repeat the unusual affirmative nature of this project, these Approaches to Performance for the sake of *Theatre in the Expanded Field*.[3] It is commonly understood that aesthetic acts are unusually well suited to expanding sense perceptions, but Jacques Rancière invites us to think further about the way such acts 'induce novel forms of political subjectivity'.[4] It is that promise I wish to examine here.

Performance theory as I discussed it earlier has aligned itself with a broad front of critical thinking in which baring witness to the un-representable becomes a continuous concern and cause for the nuanced articulation of mourning. This reticence concerning the possibility of representation was a necessary and welcome interruption to those patriarchal projects identified by Rosalind Krauss in 'Sculpture in the Expanded Field' in which the mental and the material, thinking about and acting upon something, were serially mixed up in the patriarchal bravado of hermeneutic strategies that presumed invaded fields were conquered fields. But the attractions of mourning the resistance to representation, should not in my book, become the excuse to ignore some more telling *exclusions* from representation that Jacques Rancière is deeply mindful to. This chapter written as it is 'on the part of those who have no part' at least marks this intention, even if it is fated not to deliver on its promise.

The subjects recovered in this chapter, ignored elsewhere for their banality, sad scale or plain unattractiveness, are the objects of scrutiny not for any intrinsic political merit each might have but rather for the way that each disrupts our expectations as to what might be worthy of attention in the first place. Along with Jacques Rancière, I am less interested in the part of those who already dominate the aesthetic airwaves by flaunting their old *avant garde* credentials and more interested in those who have, until now, never entered the scene. It is in this sense that, critically, the project becomes one of politics as much as the social of this chapter's title. Establishing a debate's conditions of intelligibility is the governing principle of enquiry here, not a retroactive mourning on behalf of those without a part, nor the justification of that mourning by continuing to contribute to those conditions that ensure those 'excluded others' continue to have no part. Equality is considered the founding, pri-mordial, principle of this redistribution of the sensible, not its goal, nor the cause for resigned solipsism when the redistribution of the sensible inevitably fails. The affirmation is, as always, to 'begin again', to maintain the potential of theatre in its expanded field. Starting with Atom Egoyan's work *Steenbeckett*, each and all of the performances and installations discussed as part of this chapter represent some such potential as part of their repetitive mechanisms.

The constitution of this scene of repetitive appearance is what performance does. It is this process of a continuous convening of litigious subjects, at odds with the affrontery of the political constitution of parties, that maintains the efficacy of politics. Within the distribution of the sensible, therefore, performance does not have to seek the political because it is already politics. By being the privileged means of mimetically 'passing' in the arts, in confusing the orders of those with parts and those who have no part, by attracting the racket of the *theatrocracy*, as Plato would have put it, performance is already doing the business of confounding the personal and the common, the private and the public, the immunised and the communal, and most importantly redistributing these various parts within the sensible whole. It is *this* performance, not *that* political theatre, that most effectively and movingly perturbs all prior 'policing' arrangements as Rancière would remind us are critical to the maintenance of any order. This is the mode of acting that Rancière says institutes 'within its perceptual frames the contradictory theatre of its appearances'.[5]

The much talked about notion of *dissensus*, as distinct to the voluntaristic bankruptcy of consensus, then becomes the figure for the coming reflection upon practices. Dissensus is not simply some form of disagreement or division of opinion; it is rather the productive act (always performative) within a sensible world, 'of a given that is heterogeneous to it'.[6] Dissensus allows for making visible something that was at odds with its milieu, against the grain of its surface, which was otherwise obscure in that perceptual field, making audible something that was noise before, making something available to oral responsiveness in the form of critical feedback or plain 'answer'. In other words dissensus becomes an affirmative act wholly, politically, adversarial to one of the founding precepts of performance studies, the ambiguity of the unmarked. This highly visible, 'antagonistic subjectivation' is what Rancière believes politics to be, and for there to be any progress in the audit and countering of inequality, there need to be case studies made of the individual and collective forms of such subjectivisation. While such forcing into view might appear wholly at odds with the nudge and wink susceptibilities of the late twentieth-century critical sophisticates, the urgency of post-neo-liberal collapse requires sterner stuff than playful hybridities and the presumptions of human rights' discourses.

It is in *these* situations that the haunted look of the Fugitive, introduced from the sofa at the outset of this chapter, may return and impose itself once again upon those who would once have aspired to furnish a room or escape to the sun. But this reappearance is a reappearance not just of the fugitive but also of the actor David Janssen, still on the run with no mercy from the schedules, but arriving at a place where as an actor, living 'as if', he might recognise affinities with his art of the suspension of disbelief and the art of making believe. Here he would recognise himself, as others did in the opening years of the twenty-first century, in the spooling turmoil of Atom Egoyan's *Steenbeckett* (2002) in the communitarian cacophony of Janet Cardiff's *Forty Part Motet* (2001) and on the run, on the road, in Graeme Miller's motorway memorial *Linked* (2003–ongoing).

Seeing: When All the Dust Has Settled

The grain, now what I wonder do I mean by that, I mean ... [hesitates] ... I suppose I mean those things worth having when all the dust has – when all *my* dust has settled; I close my eyes and try to imagine them.
  Samuel Beckett, *Krapp's Last Tape*[7]

There is no forgetting Artangel's extraordinary projects that I have witnessed over two decades principally in London, but also across the UK. Different states of remembering maybe a reversed alabaster white fireplace in Rachel Whiteread's *House*, a hospital illuminated by divine performative painting in Neil Bartlett's installation, *The Seven Sacraments of Nicolas Poussin*, at the London Hospital, an impossible billiard table in an architectural anomaly where privacy met publicity in Gabriel Orozco's *Empty Club*, a second un-civil war battle for the soul of

England in Jeremy Deller's *Battle of Orgreave*, the aural seduction of *noir* ethnic streets in Janet Cardiff's *Missing Voice (Case Study B)*, the falling play of seriously grown-up children in William Forsyth's bouncy castle treat *Tight Roaring Circle*, long-playing sound with the time of light in Jem Finer's *Longplayer*, the remorseless logic of a catalogued identity crisis in Michael Landy's *Breakdown*, and for the purposes of this chapter where I want to dwell for a while, John Hurt's hands spooling back the years in *Steenbeckett* (Figure 6.2).

These are the things worth having when all the dust has settled. They do not account for what the name *Artangel* stands for, that is the curatorial production company based in London directed by Michael Morris and James Lingwood, nor do they stand in for the memories of others whose itinerary might have taken them as far as these are wide in a reverse vertigo of spiralling attractions. But they do remind us, as if we had forgotten, how material is the grain of realised imagination. How tactile was the larger than life presence of John Hurt as Krapp on the screen, 'in our face', playing out his last tape while next door, from the projection room there flowed and decomposed the very cinematic tape that had once captured his tears. For here, in Atom Egoyan's *Steenbeckett* the dust is the grain and as the dust hurtles to and through and from the projector gate the film is veiled by the material violence of its exhibition. To watch the technicals splicing this volatile creation is to witness the uncanny, fearfully familiar underside of all

Figure 6.2 John Hurt, *Krapps Last Tape*/Atom Egoyan, *Steenbeckett*, 2002

real artistic illusion. And here in *Steenbeckett*, the dust is my dust, as it is John Hurt's dust, and Krapp's dust and your dust: 'Just been listening to an old year, passages at random. I did not check in the book, but it must be at least ten or twelve years ago'.[8] Can it have only been ten years? Surely twelve or twenty for all this coming and going against the grain, there must have been more than a decade of life before this afterlife.

The recollection of these images, here, now, induces recollections from elsewhere in an epileptic encounter with the excuse for this work. Epileptic in the best sense of the word if the recovery of pathological states to the side of enthusiasm might be said to be one afterlife of cultural creation – in the sense of the origin of the word epilepsy in Greek, 'surprise'. We are all too aware from our own experience of the bouncy-castle the pleasure children take in turnings, spins and the disequilibrium, the sensations of vertigo and the pleasure of toppling over, down and into others. For William Forsythe in *Tight Roaring Circle* in a bouncy castle inflated in a collaboration with Deborah Bull to provide for children, adults and other animals a soft landing for choreographies of social disorientation and limit loss. But here the state of exception induced by this unstable floor to the world, we might say Artangel's 'trapdoor', becomes not the exception but the rule. As though a state of emergency were declared on gravity, bringing into question all that we stand for.

The epileptic knows this state only too well and lives it daily. And for the picno-leptic (from the Greek *picnos*, frequent), the frequently surprised state becomes less the exception and more the equilibrium within the rocky rule. Paul Virilio described the state of the picno-leptic when he says:

> The lapse occurs frequently … the absence lasts a few seconds, its beginning and its end are sudden. The senses function, but are nevertheless closed to external impressions. The return being just as sudden as the departure, the arrested word and action are picked up again where they have been interrupted. Conscious time comes together again automatically, forming a continuous time without apparent breaks … these absences, … can be quite numerous – hundreds every day often pass unnoticed by others around.[9]

A way of presenting ourselves to this work perhaps? For us, through the very nature of the turning pages of a book that catalogues Artangel's illustrious history, we have become like picno-leptics encountering images of past events like a stroboscopic encounter with material we believe we have had some feeling for elsewhere, once before. Perhaps nothing really did happen, the time of these events never really existed, but rather in each critical encounter with the work in its own place, just a little of our life escaped. Where *did* that time go?

We cannot in this continuous state of exception believe that our dust will settle, nor that all of it will be there when we come to it, for the economy of these works is such that we recognise the irregularity of the epileptic, surprising state into which we have entered, the unpredictability of the circulating forces there, not so much of the *attention* of dramatic encounters nor the *tension* of artistic approaches but the charged and alternating *suspension* of faculties we thought were secure from the confusions of culture. This might be because, in a condition articulated by Dostoevski, the inexplicable enthusiasm induced by these experiences 'precedes the accident of the shipwreck of the senses, that of the body'.[10]

I am not so much interested in 'the body' here, as I doubt there is such a stable single thing, if mine is anything to go by, though I *am* interested in the embodiedness of these works over a duration, their grain, and the material presence they manifest through their accumulation of dust. Given that epilepsy and its way of seeing rest at the advent in Hippocratic texts of the absolute dichotomy between the magical and the scientific, and given my own treatment for *petit mal* when I was a child was undertaken at the interface between medicalised electricity and incantations, the *nervous system* might sum up a way of combining these mental and material conditions in which all artistic practice is conceived and received.[11]

Yes, as Jeremy Deller's reconstruction and film of the key battle of the Thatcher years in the UK between the unions and the government, *The Battle of Orgreave,* showed, the system is nervous. But to determine that which is political in these works, while disconnecting those politics from their materiality, would do grave injustice to the politics inherent in all these interventions. To engage with Beckett's invitation to (hesitate) when considering what we might be recollecting when we recollect the grain of something is to (hesitate) to presume the political within these works. This hesitation would require another way of looking to the work, and one which the Artangel archive of photographic encounters exemplifies beautifully in a useful second remove from their origins.

These archival photographs, which I am looking at now, and that can be seen quite readily in the sumptuous plates of the volume *Off Limits: 40 Artangel Projects* (2002), are not so much an afterlife of the work as the granting or giving of another 'lease of life'. This pleasing economic circuitry is itself reminiscent of the nervous system it seeks to mimic. The lustrous works here have made journeys from one destination to another; in another medium, they are cut out and turned over into a montage that has an implicitness with the matter of their creation, far closer perhaps than some would like us to think between the photograph and what it purports to represent. Contrary to what Jean Baudrillard said about mediatised images inviting us to think that 'the Gulf War never took place', these images invite us to consider the ways in which work *did*, precisely and with attention to material detail, take its place.

So an ironic inversion of cause and effect has taken place. While in the original experience of the work on site in its place there has been the suspended disorientation of the epileptic state, the witnessing of the event as a flicker flash of consequential moments (sometimes broken as with the flying loop of *Krapp's Last Tape*, sometimes continuous but contradictory in the endless circuitous belt of Michael Landy's interminable, though did it terminate, *Breakdown*) in stilled archival *images*, these distillations of representation are contiguous with what we recall as the residue of the work's material, archaeological evidence of the work having happened. In this aspect looking at photographs of art can be like looking at the animal next to the actor; while one senses the nemesis of the one in the other, one cannot but help only understand the one *through* the other.

One knows from reading Walter Benjamin that the challenge to perception at critical moments in history is unlikely to be solved by such optical contemplativeness but through the continuous disruption of habit through *tactile* appreciation. As he said, the decisive blows in history were likely to be struck left handed, and in this sense the gestures of the work being considered here are decisively verso over recto. In a contrary formation, the conceptual enthusiasms of the second half of the twentieth century have been overturned here through an artisanal, imagistic and sensual approach to materials that *is* ideational but only in as much as it invites us to contemplate the material sense of the work itself. Even where there would appear to be a punning or ironic contemporaneousness at work, say in Matthew Barney's *Cremaster* film series, it is a peculiar kind of knowledge formation that derives from the work, one that is more seismic than semiotic to borrow a phrase from Bertolt Brecht. It is not so much *what* this or that image means but its affects that would, for Walter Benjamin, have placed this work on the side of the angels with advertising and against criticism. For 'What in the end makes advertisements so superior to criticism? Not what the moving red neon sign says – but the fiery pool reflecting it in the asphalt.'[12]

These urban-specific conditions of reception also apply to much that those 'botanists of the asphalt', Artangel, have engineered, but not in any facile sense of 'pedestrian poetics' or the fetishisation of the foot soldier in the campaign against aerial perspectives beloved of the last twenty years of thinking cultural practice and characterised in the first part of this chapter. Rather what is at work here is the more primordial, truly epileptic state of 'hide and seek', the only children's game worth playing. Janet Cardiff's ubiquitous work *Missing*

Voice (Case Study B) (2001) began with a gap on a shelf, but was the volume ever missing from the Whitechapel library issue desk? Rachel Lichtenstein and Iain Sinclair's *Rodinsky's Whitechapel* (1999) was a stone's throw away from that library but occupied a wholly different generic and domestic realm where archaeology of dwelling (found) met the politics of melancholy and exile (loss). And perhaps most neatly within the realm of the hidden and found, one might situate Tony Oursler's *Influence Machine* (2000) in its chiaroscuro of city-square gothic menace, where building-sized faces appeared and faded across Soho Square shrubbery. Each of these ammendations to a pre-existent site produced space in the best sense of the term, each pulse with the *fort-da* of 'now you see me, now you don't', the peek-a-boo of the picno-leptic, a very different kind of public–private partnership.

As stakeholders, we are waiting to impale the shadowy figure behind or beyond this work, in the spirit of significance wanting meaning where there is merely material, authorship. We are happily doomed. The dominant critical practice of reading works allegorically in which 'the surface phenomenon [...] stands as a cipher for uncovering horizon after horizon of otherwise obscure systems of meanings'[13] cannot operate here. There are no *codes* at work, constructed for the decipherment of the jigsaw addict, but as Johnny Depp knows only too well from his experience as a pirate in the Caribbean, guidelines to an event, staged very precisely for the distracted collective reading of the tactile eye. This, not that, is the typical engagement in an Artangel event that I would like to insist adds up to more than the sum of its parts. I am thinking here of the grazing of *Steenbeckett,* the herding of *The Influence Machine*, the drifting of *Empty Club* (1996), the wandering of *Missing Voice,* the falling of *Tight Roaring Circle* (1997) and the spiralling of the Kabakovs' *The Palace of Projects* reaching up in its Tatlinesque ascension to the umbrellaed canopy of the Roundhouse in North London (1998).

These social pulses of people, dare I say 'communities with something in common' if only an appetite for Artangel and what it cares for in its unique manner of curation, come and go, more or less audience, participant, observer and outsider at any one moment, taking on the bigger epileptic charge we previously conceived as the perceiving of the individual in a distracted, suspended state. What the individual and the group share, and what makes for the coherence of this project, one's ease and pleasurable dis-ease in its company, is a regard for 'the thing itself', not the cultural project of criticism that spends too much of its time dwelling *close* to 'the thing itself' but philosophically and materially seeking the soul of 'the thing itself'. This material recovery of 'these things, themselves', into speech and into the writing of photographic record are acts, against the grain of memory loss: 'To restore the thing itself to its place in language and, at the same time, to restore the difficulty of writing, the place of writing in the poetic task of composition: this is the task of the coming philosophy'.[14]

Speaking: Testimony to Thomas Tallis

The doors of Caruso St John's beautiful Walsall Art Gallery (1995–2000) are silent and strangely prescient. They form a solid, then predicting your arrival, moving mass, that seamlessly continues the mixture of metal, glass, cement and wood that marks out the building from the neighbouring Woolworths and British Home Stores in their middle England. This material combination has already characterised the landscape from the train window, bound from London, since leaving the dough-eyed puppy atop the Birmingham Dog's Home. On the way into town the Royal Automobile Club (RAC) Control Centre in its cantilevered glass overlooks the Tiphook Freight wagons, their cargoes clogging the arteries of Midlands' sidings. Here the automobile and its disrepairs imperiously oversee the industrial weight of a previous British era of haulage with its cement wagons and hoppers. Peppered through this landscape the allotments of the metropolis give up their shattered anatomies, their dilapidated vegetation and sundered glass houses, reduced now to so much white matchwood: Cornelia Parker run Peckinpah riot on a community outreach scheme sponsored by the exterminists Fisons. As though to mimic and parody these exertions through domestic inversion, an absurdly florid hexagonal conservatory, again in wood and glass, hangs off the edge of a modest terraced house, dominating the surrounding field into which it blankly stares.

The New Art Gallery in the English Midlands is a well-oiled building and from the muffled quiet of its atrium entrance to its top-floor restaurant and wine list ('Orobio Rioja: A bouquet of strawberries, raspberries and redcurrants with the exquisite finesse that follows through on the palate') there is a palpable sense of aesthetic security and curatorial care, as though a country house, whose owner had a penchant for sky-high brute cement ceilings had organised a continuous open day to the public.

To taunt this minimalist landlord the vista from the restaurant towards 'Courts Furnishings', 'Blockbuster Video' (currently bankrupting itself), 'Albert Jagger Ltd' and the curiously modest 'Royal Casino' flaunt the harsh realities of a luxuriously over-indulged domesticity coupled with a miasma of financial gamble and risk. Back inside, the toilets, with their sturdy Armitage Shanks sinks and 'ceiling to floor' heavy metal doors, bring to mind a recent lottery-inspired indulgence in aqueous gravitas. These must be the heaviest and most secure lavatory fittings since Haworth Tompkins's work at the Royal Court Theatre in Sloane Square, London, ended that institution's long and inspired celebration of fragile plumbing as an artistic rite. It may be the soundtrack that permeates this galvanised environment, but here Janet Cardiff's work *Tableau*, a stainless steel utility sink, turned functionless by continuously circulating water, comes to mind before Duchamp reinforces a historical perspective to these ready-made fonts. It is wholly appropriate that these stirrings of anti-elitist, gallery-questioning precedents should serve to aestheticise the natural demands of this gallery's visitors.

Every so often a burst of choral music permeates the further reaches of the building. The bookshop assistant on the ground floor, the woman serving tea on the fourth, the information officer and the security man in the foyer look up in an orchestrated bewilderment and smile at the regularity of this aural intrusion. In as much as the space is, to use Didier Anzou's phrase, an 'acoustic envelope', we are the erect, deafened letters that inscribe that domain, and we find sound uneasy.

Janet Cardiff's work, rendered here, understands this ambivalence. *Forty Part Motet* plays off our anticipation of Thomas Tallis harmonies with intimate mundanities and preparatory rites of the choir who sing for us, and us alone. For while this piece works as a bravura display of contrapuntal harmonics, bringing audience and performers together in an arena bordered by 40 B+O speakers on five foot stilts, an aural collectivity of sorts, its real impact lies in the wholly individual hearings one makes in this black country of sound. Janet Cardiff says it like this: 'When you are listening to a concert the only viewpoint normally is from the front, in traditional audience position. With this piece I want the audience to be able to experience a piece of music from the viewpoint of the singers'.[15] The slippage of signifiers here, between the aural and the visual, is characteristic for an artist who confounds the sense of seeing voice and hearing sight.

My own experience begins with a walk through the centre of the space towards a window that looks out and back over the route I have just traversed outside the building. The canal continues beyond the window and away and over the shoulder of five speakers facing down the length of the gallery towards me. Given there are forty speakers for forty voices in groups of five, the speaker to the left of this group might be number 36 and the speaker to the right, the last for now, is number 40. The circularity of the piece, both Tallis's original score and Cardiff's treatment of it, reinforces the continuous and braided nature of these individual outposts to vocal idiosyncrasy. To the left at number 36 a man is ostentatiously clearing his throat. His colleague asks him from somewhere off: 'Have you got a bottom B flat?' A sequence ensues that exhausts the possible punning permutations of this innocent musicologist.

Meanwhile, on second hearing, for the two are not available simultaneously without exertions between the speakers, at number 40 a girl in her teens is exhorting another to 'stand on your spot'. Here the geometry of the choral making is revealed and gives an insight to the strategic overview that ensures that the piece is more than the sum of its parts.

The pragmatics of creation can only rarely have been so laid bare as they are here to the eavesdropping listener. And while free to roam one is caught magnetically by these speakers and the infidelities to genius they reveal. At this point the choral master cuts in and there is a loaded silence broken from behind by the rush of vocal energy that marks the divide between the speaking we have heard to this point and the singing of Tallis's *Spem in Alium Nunquam Habui*.

The work is that much more than *Spem in Alium* not just because of the quotidian revelations that prologue then humanise this most beatific of scores, but because of the intense sense of mortality these preparations bring to heavenly sound, that when it arrives sweeps across the floor with all the reverse energy of the standing waters in the canal outside, tidal waves those gathered within its arc. Two of this marooned number mark a distinctive relationship to the eddying sounds they are experiencing. A woman I will refer to as 'J' is interpreting for students with hearing impairment from the Walsall College of Arts and Technology. Her hands and face are working to mediate this combination of speech and music. The jet-black floor of the gallery is the primary resonating surface for a young woman who listens with a different expectation of return. She is 90% deaf. She places her hands to the speaker gauze and works across numbers 40 to 36 looking for sound. The basses of 36 are just evident but little else apparently registers. But I wonder what registering here might imply; what thresholds are we talking about when we say that this piece cannot be heard? Who here could claim they were in any position to hear the work? *Forty Part Motet* becomes in these hands something else that no amount of 'social exclusion speak' can rationalise nor prepare for: 'Forty One Part Motet'. The piece is conducted again and in new and unfathomable ways by these hands and for all to see, as by its performative inclusivity all such ammendations to the noirish minimalism of the site are registered as luminescent flares on the installation's surface.

A young but confident hand asks on the responses board: 'But where does the MOTEL come in. Puzzled.' A fortuitous confusion, as they all are here, in a 'walk in' that allows you to check in and out of genres with the ease of the passing traveller. As with Cardiff's previous sound-inflected work – *Whispering Room* (1991), *An Inability to make a Sound* (1992), *Dark Pool* (1995), *Playhouse* (1997), *La Tour* (1998) and *Missing Voice (Case Study B)* (1999) – there is an inherent invitation within the work to join the artist in her composition and to participate through renewed and enlivened if disorientated sensing. Here the voyeurism and surveillance modes of the artist Sophie Calle are apparently democratised while at the same time destantiating and unnerving the consenting participant through destabilising narrative ploys. The glorious ephemerality of Tallis is profoundly enhanced by the complex personalities of those who reveal themselves in whispers just prior to his performance. It is impossible to forget who is singing whether one comes upon the *dramatis personae* before, during or after our hearing of *Spem in Alium*.

In Gallery sites like this 'function' is often the overplayed trump and weary cliché of a resistance to decoration. But Tallis, and Cardiff's treatment of Tallis in *Forty Part Motet*, reminds us of another deeper sense of functionalism, an era prior to the Reformation when musicians were employed as clerks.[16] They were to all intents and purposes craftsmen in the service of the church. In the spirit of this artisanal complexity, here in this tower clad with terracotta and hung with works that confound the relations between form and function, there is a reimagining of the relations between signing and singing. Whose signature is on this work? Who is singing and for whom? And where is the innovation here? Not from where you might expect, for the contemporary banalities of what constitutes the progressive in art practice falls apart in the legacy of this composition. As the Tallis scholar Paul Doe says:

> Tallis, by temperament and training, belonged to a late-medieval generation of monastic musicians to whom novelty as such was no more a virtue in music than in any other sphere of religious life … it was apparently not until the second half of Elizabeth's reign that composers became particularly conscious of the concept of 'pioneering'.[17]

Tallis retreats from view behind a polyphony that was in his time under threat from the Puritan legislation that we encountered, in Chapter 3, at the defaced West portico of St Paul's.

From within this contrapuntal forest of sound another way of hearing and seeing emerges. For if Tallis foregrounded the liturgical over the biblical as he does in *Forty Part Motet* and thus retained a curious but compassionate distance from the passions of the sufferer, we, as listeners to Janet Cardiff's work, are reinscribed within the technical challenges and curiously objective craftsman-like concerns of the singers. The fear of the high G's in the piece for instance goes before the girl in speaker 40 who admits to them so readily. Some seventy years earlier Gillies Whittacker had written of his own treatment of *Spem in Alium*:

> A study of the score convinced me that the great danger to be avoided was a meaningless stodging through the vocal lines, an inevitable temptation when so many bewildering and conflicting sounds would be heard by the singer on all sides, and when in the nature of things no member of the choir could realize the effect as a whole … the frequent high G's for the soprano voices would lead to an over-prominence of that note and monotony of colour.[18]

It is this architecture that remains the telling innovation of the work here, Tallis's ability to 'design and control a large structure … a reward of his early training in the rather extravagant edifices of late – Gothic England'.[19] If *Spem in Alium* is quite unlike anything produced in Europe around its time, then Janet Cardiff's humanistic treatment of this Gothic splendour and imagination makes *Forty Part Motet* quite unlike anything her European counterparts have been able to achieve in the aesthetic or performance field more recently. The gallery in which this work is housed shares something coincidental and fortuitous, though meaningful and resonant, with these works and those that surround them and make sense of them, in this context, on this day of aural witnessing.

Hearing: The Arithmetic of Belief

Inverting Katherine Hepburn's immortal words to Humphrey Bogart in *The African Queen*: 'Nature, Mr Allnut, is what we are put in this world to rise above', we might ask ourselves how a return, from above, might be possible? Graeme Miller's compositional works from *The Sound Observatory* in 1992 to *Linked* in 2003, via *Listening Ground, Reconnaissance, Feet of Memory* and *The Roosting Tree*, are a sonic reminder of a remainder to landscape, those sounds which though invisible are on the air if only a way of listening were possible. There is not here just the need for a suitable apparatus of 'high enough' fidelity, though Graeme Miller never underestimates the tactile pleasure we take in the technologies of reception, mini-speakers here, invisible transmitters there, hanging branches of babble, the comfort of headphones, but a *disposition*, an attitude to the charged, human static in the atmosphere.

Charged with narrative, yes, reminiscence maybe, gossip and rumour perhaps, but in *Linked* an invitation to come back down to earth, to walk, to talk, to encourage a pedestrian in the presence of the automobile at the outskirts of London's eastern edge, where cherished housing, including the home of the artist, has been swept way in the interests of 'progress', to engage with two presents: the present that is the first-person narrative of the speaker speaking, now in a present that must have been back then, at least eight years ago if the words are to be taken at face value somewhere in the vicinity of what is now the M11 motorway, and a second present that is the insistent present of the landscape transformed, where is that garden shed being enjoyed right now? And between these two presents a tension, held like a refrain from a faraway room, of the sound of memories comes into being, just long enough for them to fail again in the forgetting of the insistent demands of time. There is of course a third person present, a third person's voice, that is the speech of those who speak on behalf of others, those residents of this parish who, willing to be recorded, are in that recording returned to back then and in so doing become willing to accompany us forward into the storm of history.

In this case the storm is the combustion-engine, barely contained by the motorway wall. It is the rollers that flattened the tarmac to within a centimetre of itself over a three-mile run. It is the weather that like a microclimate fuelled by lead rains downs a reminder to those whose sheets still grace this corridor as though beyond that parapet lies an alpine fjord. But where the protest group *Reclaim the Streets* might dig up and depart, *Linked* insinuates and stays. Graeme Miller as a long-term resident of this neighbourhood is less interested it would seem, though not disconnected from protestation and indignation; rather working with the tactics of rescue and resuscitation he gently breathes a certain life back into that endangered species, the community of those who have nothing in common but their collusion in crisis, a community who in a sense only were brought into being by their premature disappearance at the very moment they found themselves.

Where a ventriloquist would force the dumb to speak, Miller solicits, listens, records, edits and replays. There is a certain tact at work here which Kant would have recognised as being special to the tightrope walker who adjusts their equilibrium, as they proceed, to circumstance. This tact is by no means an excuse to abnegate the artists' agency; Miller after all shapes the outcome from the opening bars by insisting on the audacious presentness of all that is said, but from that clear compositional frame the small mercies of the banal, the trivial, are rightfully given poetic license to flourish. The banal here has of course nothing to do with the stupid and vapid that the word has now become associated with, but, as in its origins describing the shared ovens in a French country village, the common and the adaptable to circumstance. In other words, the pragmatically beautiful, the accessible and the thoroughly convivial. Trivia was once the essential domestic information shared by women at the Roman crossroads – reflections on the domestic and the household that literally guaranteed the rights of the city to flourish. Again wondrous in their small details in this new, monumental, landscape.

But what kind of memorial or monument might *Linked* be? It thankfully dismisses the aesthetics of marble statuesque permanence that Rosalind Krauss did so much to disrupt, and which provides the title for this book, for this work gravitates to us with its tuned impermanence. It does no glory to the hero, nor pays homage to the unknown. It has no truck with sentimental reminiscence nor futuristic illusions. It simply, if somewhat slyly, attunes us to the arithmetic of belief. It manifests witnesses to experience, multiplies them, loops them and situates them until one has quite lost sense of how many were there in the first place. Of course the houses, now lost, marked by these voices were never witness to a first place, a founding, and have to take their place within a litany of other testimonies to lives once lived here. There can be no spurious claims to origin and therefore to ownership which marks these murmurings out as fatally incapacitated when it comes to practically resisting the inevitable progress of the Leviathan carriageway.

In this proliferation, a sleight of sound, one might say to link the composer's undoubted mathematical adequacy to the skill of the cardsharp, the sheer statistical ambition of the work, its multiplication of witnesses, becomes overwhelming and moving in a more poetic and profoundly political sense. This is the best form of dissent conducted through a marvellous use of mathematics. For all the stats' and vectors of spin, the graphics of water drainage and the dynamics of friction that the road could conjure up, all the totalising number-crunching that a motorway demands before ribbons can be cut, here is an equal, opposite and ultimately resistant set of figures. They do not ghost the road so much as host our ultimately guest-like presence. They greet us and warm us, intimate within the ear but eminently able to enter our memories later that day or year. They are insidious in the best sense, inside us.

And perhaps most of all when, on another more pressing occasion, we drive by, on our way to Cambridge, shooting a furtive glance at a neighbourhood once walked. What of those villains of the piece who drive through, middle finger raised to the complaint of history, the retarded, tethered prostration to the past? Those at one with their moulded dashboard enjoying the infinitely subtle realignment of their posture-sensitive seat as they motor here and there and back to here. Well unless I am much mistaken that is me, as Socrates might have said, and you maybe, unless you have worked out a way East that does not require the logistical resources of an eighteenth-century Grand Tour. Is the hum of the radials on the 4 × 4 not the sound of the satisfaction of progress? Are these voices not just the inevitable recalcitrance of yesterday's twilight, wishing it did not have to face up to today's dawn?

The car might promise the ultimate protection, a safer place to sleep than the contemporary home in one well-known and shocking vehicle advertisement, but it is not always the best place to hear the winds of change. When the philosopher Martin Heidegger, who knew a thing or two about motoring, made one of his most telling observations on the intelligence of feeling, 'We hear the Mercedes in immediate distinction from the Volkswagen. Much closer to us than to all sensations are the things themselves', he was writing *on* the Freiburg side street, not *in* his car. The logic of the automobile is now an acoustic envelope so secure as to prohibit any disturbance to one's sonic equilibrium. But it is the very static of our senses, the porousness of our listening and our inherent tonal faculties, our potential to form narratives that are the things that distinguish our natural history as a sensible species. It is in this sense that Graeme Miller is, in these late days of humankind in the face of autogeddon, reminding us not so much of who we are, or indeed who we were, but who we can no longer be and what might become of us.

When Katherine Hepburn says those words to Humphrey Bogart the landscape that surrounds them simply reminds us that Nature is never just 'out there' but always in the process of being made by us and others. Suspended between the way landscape is determined by us and simultaneously makes us possible, *Linked* is a coda to one ecology, the appeal of roots in auto-habitus, and an overture to another, the appeal to transience in auto-biography. The time-signature on this work, 2003, Graeme Miller, and ongoing, might one day remind others of a botanist of the asphalt who revealed the sonic undergrowth of modernity as surely as Gilbert White cared for the life of pre-modern Sherborne. Both share a pleasure in pedestrianism, in observation over ordering, in collection over classification, in all that is best about an enthusiasm for living and therefore a truly felt relationship with that life, no less than when that life is lost for good.

Seventh Approach
Tactical & Critical

My final approach to performance will take its starting point from Bill Readings's eloquent work that echoes still in its insights for the university today: 'We have to recognize that the University is a *ruined institution*, while thinking what it means to dwell in those ruins without recourse to romantic nostalgia'.[1] The university as a 'ruined institution' does not seem so far from the theatre as an abandoned practice as I figured it from the outset of this book. But the university's reason for 'being' is quite different to that of theatre when one moves on to Readings's rationale of its *past* raison d'etre. Indeed, you might say it is precisely a fetishisation of 'performance' amongst university managements that has squandered its hard fought for Enlightenment gains in the public eye.

For Readings the university has had three divergent and non-contemporaneous discourses on which it has founded its credibility over three centuries of Post-Enlightenment survival: the Kantian concept of 'reason', the Humboldtian idea of 'culture' and the techno-bureaucratic notion of 'excellence'. I would like to propose, by way of conclusion to this book, that we have now entered a fourth, especially charged and potentially *terminal* era for the university, that of the phantom of the 'Public'. I would briefly add, though this chapter is not an obituary for the university, I say terminal simply because should the twenty-first-century university really seek its public, I mean *really*, it might find that public, from Delhi to Lagos, has already registered with another, much more fluid operation, widely known by its acronym, A2K, the *Access to Knowledge* movement, which is a truly international 'University of the Commons' without walls.[2] The walls that we began by imagining ourselves within before the advent of theatre and the address of an audience.

But back to Europe, and North America, where Readings laid his ground. Here Reason lost its specious authority, Culture lost its nation status and

Excellence had, by definition and slightly problematically, when we looked more closely at what managers were extolling when they extolled its virtue, *no content*. Now I would suggest, this upper-case *Public*, evoked by performance measures for the calibration of academic research such as 'impact' and 'engagement' – the inevitable symptom of an increasingly privatised domain – has no form.

I once knew a commons, a people, a multitude, maybe even a Public. It *had* form for me, at least I think it did. It certainly resisted me for years and I felt its push and pull through the means of performance – performances of all kinds, night and day, in schools, streets, launderettes, factories, on the river, in homes. Directing a neighbourhood theatre in the Docklands area of South East London, for a decade in the 1980s, working with my colleague David Slater amidst countless groups and individuals, what I called in the book *Theatre & Everyday Life,* a 'Lay Theatre', somehow beyond the constraints of the profession but always cognisant of the way that profession shapes the distribution of theatre's sensibility and its potential publics: a counter-public constituted, largely, here, by economic necessity and *needs*.[3]

And then becoming aware of *other* publics, working on Folk traditions and ceremonies of Catalan urbanised rural culture in the 1990s in Barcelona, exploring the relationship between folklore and fakelore, that twice restored behaviour of performance, for these *Corre Foc* (fire run) Human/Dragon hybrids, who appeared for centuries in the pastoral domain from within a folk tradition, and then reappeared on the streets of Barcelona from the mid-1960s, recovered and orchestrated by the urbanised Adjuntamente, to resist centralist Fascist influence from Franco's Madrid. Here was a Public constituted by *demands*.

And, for the next four years, directing something in the region of 500 talks at the Institute of Contemporary Arts in London, with curator Helena Reckitt, for a multifarious form of fashionable counter-publics, of heterogeneous desires and polymorphous identities, before I sloped off into academic life, where I might have expected to be able to forget the Public, but I had timed it wrong.

A Public was insistent, in mind, if not quite so apparent in presence. At Roehampton University at the west end of London a five-year project in the first half decade of the twenty-first century on *Performance, Architecture and Location* was conducted mainly in the neighbouring Alton East and West Estates, estates in which a post-war idea of the public was invented and subsequently betrayed, in which the possibility of rethinking what a 'Civic Centre' might be resisted the inevitable marginalisation of the radical particularities that performance people might prefer to the possibility of becoming more generally accessible, universally available, to a disenfranchised Public even?

And latterly at King's College London, as explored already in Chapter 3, dwelling in its privatised ruins, working with others in hard hats, with cost ledgers, with planning constraints, to resist *that* University's institutional amnesia, to defend against the dementia of disciplines that forget their recent separation in Modernity from multiple publics, a separation that happens to coincide with the commodification of the 'University' with an avowedly upper case U – a temporary separation, not a divorce. I like to think we have never been Modern in performance; paraphrasing Bruno Latour, we have never recognised such silos and schisms, for we were first baked at the moment in the 1960s when Roland Barthes described our inter-disciplinarity as the 'cream puff of the new university'.

So, some hardening up on a Public, if not *the* Public, might be in order from the very discipline that has long harboured a special desire *for* a Public. As I made clear in the previous chapter I took this on foursquare over 250 pages of *Theatre, Intimacy & Engagement*, insisting intemperately that the political presumptions of performance were wildly overrated and that some slower, more careful thinking of theatre's social relations was necessary, in order to avoid what Slavoj Žižek has called the threat of 'pseudo action', which would presumably have a phantom public as its favoured subject.

I am not alone, and never have been, my interests and practices are others'; communities came before me, that's for sure. *Performance Studies international* in Toronto in 2010 dedicated itself to the theme of publics, and just last year I was with Theron Schmidt, Nicholas Ridout, Una Bauer and others in Zagreb exploring these questions in the light of the writings of Michal Warner and Judith Butler on publics and counter-publics. So the Public is everywhere, but still, *happily*, not quite within reach.

But enough set up to this chapter, here's the substance, or whatever substance I can recover from the ruins. Within this final chapter I would like to ask quite how an understanding of performance, a genetic responsiveness as I have figured it in this book, which calibrates shifting degrees of community, a commitment *to* others, and immunity, a distinction and separation *from* others, might interrupt the phantasmic discourse of the Public I have been experiencing all these years, tactically and critically.

In this chapter I will try to take Bill Readings's example literally and explore how we might examine something that he describes as the 'tactical use of the space of the University, while recognising that space as an historical anachronism'.[4] Such a *tactical* project, as my chapter title suggests, recognises the critical nature of accountability to those with little or no access to knowledge, while resisting any accounting for a Public who remain, happily, beyond our best efforts.

Let's start by making tactical use, in other words, *reuse*, of the strategic use of the 'people'. How might we redeploy the energies of such a public, theatrical or otherwise, back towards a project which Bill Readings would suggest is the one purpose left for the university, perhaps the *only* one following the loss of Reason, Culture and Excellence. That purpose is defined by Readings as a process of *re-meaning* for an institutional system.

While the university of this century has put 'Thought' under threat (as Readings indeed suggested), it has over the last decade done the opposite of what he said it would do. Where *his* prognosis indicated a *decline* in the ideological function of the university, if he was around now he would notice *an increase in ideological* function through the accelerated *referentiality* of the Research Excellence Framework in the UK, the publish or perish ethos of the US tenure track system, at whose human beating heart one might find if one opened up that bounteous chest a Public waiting to be tested for the *impact* it has felt from our research.

This is what the university in an age of nation states used to do, for Readings at least:

> Within modernity, the University held a central place in the formation of subjects for the nation-state, along with the production of the ideology that handled the issue of their belonging to that nation-state, or culture. Its internal organisation as a community was meant to reflect that structure of belonging to community in which a general culture of conversation held together diverse specialities in a unity that was either organic, societal or transactional.[5]

But post nation state, in a globalised world, the university is no longer central to the question of a common life. The clue for Readings lies in that word *conversation*. His, and in performance I could say, *our*, preference for dissensus over consensus is paramount as it guarantees that the process cannot be institutionalised, or at least resists easy institutionalisation. What I do know is there can be no further use of the Public *as alibi*, now that the Public is about to be hunted down by what are known as 'REF' panels across the length and breadth of the UK, and asked for its opinion as to our degree of referentiality. No hiding place indeed. Don't misunderstand me; I would argue here that institutional practices cannot be their own reward. I certainly do not, and clearly from how I have spent my life never thought that the university is unaccountable, pursuing knowledge for knowledge's sake. Having grown up in a working-class family in Essex with a widowed mother for whom knowledge was not a hereditary right but a daily battle of wits, that would be unlikely.

I am also, I hope, not naive. I take the freedom to spend my life contesting performance, making performance, enjoying the cream puff of inter-disciplinarity, must have been secured at a heavy cost. And that cost is of course the utter irrelevance of what I do to anyone other than a very modest constituency, a vast reduction over a century of the social significance of agency within a university and our expectations of our relevance *outside* the university. Universities have bought these freedoms at a price, a cost that is in direct reciprocal proportion to their Public relevance. And that is where we join Readings in his aspiration to *dwell in the ruins*, without recourse to romantic nostalgia, by which I think he means nostalgic heritage projects such as the Globe on London's south bank and its various worldwide progeny of shining reified irrelevance.

Of course the Romantic sensibility has always valued ruins *as ruins* and in this narrative it is precisely Art (or perhaps therapy) that redeems a fractured life. As we saw in Chapter 5 Freud kept images of Roman ruins in sight in Vienna, at Bergasse 19, and latterly in London, at Maresfield Gardens, where you can still see them, to remind himself that in the Unconscious, as in ruins, two buildings of memory from heterogeneous historical periods are impossibly co-present. The past is not erased but *haunts* the present. The threat of the repressed memory is a constant and one that reminds us that any inhabitation of the ruins we might like to take up will, inevitably, unleash such telling remainders.

Unleashing such energies, negative or otherwise, from defaced things is surely performance's appropriate rôle, which is why I have assumed as a professor of theatre at King's College London, it was my rôle. It is what we are charged to do, and it is what the theatre makers Forster and Heighes (discussed in Chapter 6) are doing as in part of the performance project that owes its own debt to Richard Southern, *The Seven Generations of Performance*; they surface the long history of the East Wing of Somerset House in London, recently acquired by King's College, as the first 'purpose built' Public Offices in the UK and perhaps even Europe. It was in these offices that taxation to sustain warfare was first localised, where the Public record office attempted to name and catalogue a Public for the purposes of their better administration, where the Probate Office provided, literally, what it says on the door, an office for probate, probate being the will, the will of the people, the public presumably. But what of that will? Where has that will gone now we have occupied these spaces? The *Performance Foundation* which took up residence in that very set of offices in 2013 sets that question as its first task, if only to ward off the return of the repressed that all recovered ruins threaten.

So let's treat the university for what it is, as I am trying to do here, *as an institution* rather than a sacred mystery. In the spirit of the research that Liz Austin has been working on at Roehampton University in the UK, taking that institutional history seriously and its future sceptically.[6] I would only add here that we might simultaneously want to ask what it is that is being 'instituted' by this institution, performatively that is. We are not looking on, from the suburbs at these ruins; *they are ours.* And if they are not yours, it might be our responsibility to ask why?

Amongst these university-shaped ruins, 'Thought' belongs to an economy of *waste*, ruins proper, not to a restricted economy of calculation, the Research Excellence Framework and the refaced ruin. Thought is non-productive labour, as Bill Readings describes it, and hence does not show up on balance sheets except as *waste*. The point is not to create a restored university as a ghost town, a sanctuary to thought; I have little patience for university departments who bleat their way through the threatened austerity-driven economic cuts process while forgetting to come to the union protests, to witness student support of our actions.

'To dwell in the ruins of the university' is, therefore for Bill Readings, 'to try to do what we can, while leaving space for what we cannot envisage to emerge'. I took this call very much to heart with the creation of a landscape of spaces on the Strand, in central London, within breathing distance of Inigo Jones's centre of operations, the *Anatomy Theatre & Museum* and the *Inigo Rooms*, where a certain rhythm of disciplinary attachment and *detachment* might operate through a simple invitation: to imagine what kinds of performance they are made possible by, and in turn they make possible? This of course is only possible if we defend a core curriculum, protected from market conditions, from which our students can make an informed choice about such matters. Here disciplinarity becomes a permanent and founding question, which is why I insist on the *Performance Foundation,* for performance describes for me a *dissenting discipline* not an anti-discipline as some of my colleagues would have it.

None of this is an alibi for copping out, and while voluntarism, cosy concensus and pseudo-action have all been castigated as this book proceeded, the continuous provocation of the irritiant of performance insists on the critical articulation of the relations between community and immunity, publicity and privacy at every turn. The referentialising of the university of the twenty-first century I am describing, with the return and invasion of the Public to its concerns and commitments, is precisely an opportunity for those of us who chose performance because it, somewhere, implied there was something other than an ego lit on a stage unable to see their audience out there. An awareness that it was especially in the theatre that some people might have gathered to gain immunity from the invitation to 'dramatic engagement', what happens to be going down on the stage, and that this desire might well be as urgent for their well being as any fleeting pursuit of community amongst this temporary public that has found itself in an auditorium together yet alone. And in so doing that very act of seeking separation reveals the continuous existence of some sort of community from which a leave-taking takes place. It is this apparent contradiction that begins to articulate, gesture towards or even measure what Timothy Campbell has called (with reference to Roberto Esposito's work) a 'political semantics that can lead to a non-immunized (or radically communitized) life'.[7]

It is patently obvious that a university can no longer fulfil a rôle it might have played once, but certainly no longer plays, as some kind of ideal community in a socialised disinterested pursuit of the Idea. I am not about to propose in these final pages of this book that the coming community I have been 'approaching' is to be found anywhere near the university precinct today. I work in a friendly and supportive English Department, but Rousseau, if no one else, might worry I don't spend nearly as much time dancing there as I do elsewhere, and that strikes me as being peculiar given a university might be well suited to a community of interest such as dancing.

The problem is of course, or the freedom, perhaps, that unlike in Inigo Jones's time, community does not come to us anymore because of obligations of subjects to a monarch or a land. Community is the outcome of the autonomous decisions of individuals to communicate with each other as subjects of state. This universalising tendency based on a shared human capacity for communication is precisely what performance study revels as a *chimera*, wholly dependent on the contradiction that we are in some kind of ideal speech situation in which we mean what we say. For Bill Readings, at least, the university has built itself on such a rôle within this state, *to pretend to be the institution that is not an institution* but simply the structure you get if transparent communication is possible.

Here performance enters the scene one penultimate time to expose the fact that there are no pure instances of communication, there are *rhetorics* to each and all forms of communication, and that such communication when it comes to the university and its practices is closer to brute domination than reason, justice and fairness for those outside its immediate closed, autopoietic system. It is not a question of a better truth being protected, to be set free, as some colleagues would believe in the university, but rather a revelation that does justice to the secret, the *public secret,* that is that the university is currently ill-equipped to account for the continuous failure of the representing of a Public, of *any* public.

Rather than presume the community to be the condition of the university, one might think with Bill Readings of community *without identity*, and again it is here from Jean-Luc Nancy's 'Inoperative Community', Giorgio Agamben's 'Whatever Community', to Alphonso Lingis's 'Community of those who have nothing in common', that performance with its demanding interest in the complexity of audience, a Public even, might have something to offer. Those of you picking up this book may have nothing in common, but we are *aggregated* together by this precisely modern 'state of things'. Our obligation as a community of sorts is to the current, pressing, *condition* of such things, and it would be a community wholly lacking in consensus as to its limits. In my work I have called this *radical inclusion*; we are obligated to those beyond us precisely because we can't quite say why, and in that group I would include a public. That public can neither become an *alibi* for the university remaining as it is nor can it become a compensation to free the university from its social bond.

I am not being religious here, though this commitment to some sort of unpayable debt might sound like it. I have shown in *Theatre, Intimacy & Engagement* exactly how such debts are played out with animals, children, props, landscapes, buildings as well as those human others who we fetishise through performance and live arts for their differences of class, race and gender. But we are of course not alone, if the walls we work within are university walls, because by definition we are with students. I would have thought *that* was the foundation of any university, and those students present to us the pedagogic possibility that compels a continuous obligation to the existence and complications of otherness. And students, or pupils as Walter Benjamin liked to call them, are people and publics too.

This model is one that, I have argued elsewhere, is to be recognised as one of two-way dependency rather than autonomy and emancipation. We are after all, faculty and students alike, dependent rational animals, as Alistair McIntrye called humans, and, as Shannon Jackson has made clear in her book *Social Works* (2012), it is *support* that characterises us, and necessarily reciprocates this dependency. This is not the immaturity of the human, it is our defining quality and it is one that performance study dedicates itself to observing, understanding and articulating as best it can.

I have said quite enough about the university for the moment, and would, in the spirit of this book, like to move further afield with my concluding analysis.

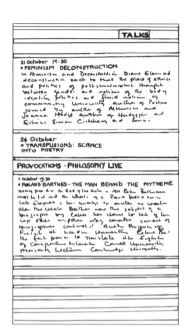

Figure 7.1 'Feminism, Deconstruction', ICA Programme, October 1994

But before moving on I would like to acknowledge a passing member of the *public* who started me thinking about these things (Figure 7.1).

'Feminism, Deconstruction' was the title of one of those many public talks that Helena Reckitt and I worked on and staged together at the Institute of Contemporary Arts in London in the 1990s. It comes to mind in the context of this chapter, not for a public, but for a person, a very private individual, who might wish, should they have been able to read this and the way I have taken their words in vain, to have remained anonymous. Diane Elam had been talking about her new book as part of the ICA programme of talks, with Joanna Hodge, who was scheduled to appear, and Jane Moore who replaced Alison Assiter, for a reason I no longer recall.

It was 21 October 1994 and I was relatively new at the ICA and still had a budget to work with at the bar. After the event, from amongst the crowd, dare I say 'the public' given how complicated were the attendees at this venue, we were joined by a quiet, critical presence whose work I had not read, but who captivated me over that late evening with his prognosis for the crisis in the University. I knew nothing *about* the University, never having worked in one in two decades of theatre involvement, but he made me feel like it might be worth it, it might be worth taking a look. And he took the trouble to encourage me to think of the University as a 'coming community'. I asked him to come back the next day, when we (or more specifically, I) were more sober, to discuss how we might progress an event that could respond to his invocation of 'dwelling in the University's ruins'. I wanted to introduce him to Midas Dekkers, the brilliant author of *Dearest Pet*, much more than a book on bestiality, and *The Way of All Flesh: The Romance of Ruins*, and other 'ruinous' souls who hung around the ICA bar in those days. But he could not stay, because he had a flight to catch early the next morning. He smiled and said: 'next time'.

I was later to discover this person was Bill Readings, the author of *The University in Ruins*, which was published posthumously. As Diane Elam says in the Foreword to that work: 'Bill Readings was in the process of making final revisions to this book when he died in the crash of American Eagle flight 4184 on October 31, 1994'. Any work which I do, in respect of the University now, whether it be written or wrought, academic or architectural, I consider a form of *marginalia* to the work of someone whose writing I deeply respect. Such an acknowledgement can barely begin to do justice to the fluency of that work, the point might here rather be to continue to occupy that *tactical* space in the University identified by Readings by sharpening one's *critical* resources at every turn. I will have one, and for this book, last, go at that here.

The Emaciation of the Spectator

In this spirit of tactical critique in *Theatre, Intimacy & Engagement* previously, I proposed some sternly expressed, yet comically touched, empirical enquiries into what I called 'a science of appearance'. The book was intended as a reminder that claims for the special status of theatre as a pre-eminently social, communitarian act have long been exaggerated as a convenient means to defer, yet again, some more pressing questions as to why there is 'never enough immersion', 'never enough equality', however welcoming the theatre act in its expanded form now seems to be.[8] Why, to put it too bluntly, the theatre always, by definition, *fails* in its political aspirations at the same time as perpetuating, refashioning and ornamenting the social imaginary. Or, as a student put it to me the other day in the very University I have been discussing with regard to its pursuit of a phantom Public, combining my problem and my potential of theatre much more poignantly than I could achieve, how they felt *shamed* by their incapacity to relate to the participatory invitation of the work of certain, quite distinct yet avowedly 'interactive' theatre companies with anything but 'suspicion', despite the performers' generous offers of inclusivity. Just for the record, if it does not seem too indiscreet a revelation, the companies they felt shamed by included Punchdrunk and Shunt Theatre Cooperative (UK), Fuerza Bruta (Argentina), Rimini Protokol (Germany) and Toneelgroep Amsterdam's *Roman Tragedies* (the Netherlands). This was not an impoverished repertoire by any standard of contemporary European theatre-going.

Given what I have just said about 'being with students', I am quite prepared to dedicate the final part of this book to diagnosing a student's sense of shame in the theatre, for it occurs to me that that very expression of shame may touch a nerve among some of those reading these words, and that it would be such shame that could act as a sober reality principle in our undoubted, well-deserved century-long celebration of a certain dissembling of theatre's impervious borders in the expanded field. It is not that the companies and productions referred to are in any way homogenous, there is more than an aesthetic mile between Shunt and Toneelgroep, rather that a participant-observer, an audience member and a student of theatre have chosen one of the oldest words in the English language to characterise their resistance to engaging with them. And in that long history of the feeling of pain that arises from the consciousness of a dishonouring of one's own conduct in such an invitational situation, I wish to propose in the coming concluding words that it is the *theatre* that has acted as the calibrating machine for this degree of offence felt. It is the performance gene that has heightened an emotion, and an awareness, that this precarious situation might offend one's sense of modesty or decency, and it is the student's gauging of this peculiar phenomenology of threat to decorum that I presume amounts to what they mean by being shamed within such operations.

I am inclined to accept the student's diagnosis at face value not just because they have chosen their words carefully, but specifically because they have precisely that 'face value'. That is the face, which presumably is the pre-eminent presence of appearance as an audience member, while not necessarily seen by others, is *felt* by its beholder to have registered this degree of shame. But beyond the face, I would also wish to recall shame and its longer history, more than just embarrassment for instance, because while I enjoy those flushed discomforts, what Nicholas Ridout describes in his work as the 'after affects' of theatre, I am not sure they can tell me more about the theatre than an enclosed, circulating libidinal economy, *autopoiesis* as Niklas Luhmann might put it. I wish to retain shame for its second most common usage, that is the way it invites us to think about an offence against propriety in the very place where impropriety would always appear to be its commanding other. Such proprieties I presume operate to a set of cultural codes that are felt, administered and activated in the wider social sphere, and it is theatre's historic tension with such proprieties that has made it worthy of human interest for so long, and worth recovering again, now.

In this respect I need not, I am sure, rehearse here why the theatrical invitation to participate, to 'join in', has very little to say about or do with emancipation proper, and hence my immediate reversal of the philosopher Jacques Rancière's now well-known figure, at the time of writing six years under intense discussion among a certain community of critics, of the 'emancipated spectator'.[9] Here, Rancière, in what appears a tongue in cheek mode of *live* address, summarises the self-defeating trajectory of a century-long attempt to transcend the separation of stage and auditorium:

> The precise aim of the performance is to abolish this exteriority in various ways: by placing the spectators on the stage and the performers in the auditorium; by abolishing the difference between the two; by transferring the performance to other sites; by identifying it with taking possession of the street, the town or life.

Of course Rancière is having nothing of this and he concludes:

> this attempt dramatically to change the distribution of places has unquestionably produced many enrichments of theatrical performance. But the redistribution of places is one thing; the requirement that theatre assign itself the goal of assembling a community which ends the separation of the spectacle is quite another. The first involves the invention of new intellectual adventures, the second a new form of allocating bodies to their rightful place, which, in the event, is their place of communion.[10]

Leaving aside what on earth Rancière might mean in such a congregational-liturgical term as 'communion', what prognoses does he offer this Brechtian/Artaudian, we might say following Hollywood's appetite for economic conflation, Brartaudian, stasis? Significantly for Rancière it is a question of community, again. He sides with the individual being of the *singular* in the plural, he has to for the sake of the rest of his philosophical legacy. He says:

> What our performances – be they teaching or playing, speaking, writing, making art or looking at it – verify is not our participation in a power embodied in the community. It is the *capacity* of *anonymous* people, the capacity that makes everyone *equal* to everyone else. This capacity is exercised through irreducible differences; it is exercised by an unpredictable interplay of associations and dissociations.[11]

Notoriously for us, if 'us' means theatre people, and among other performance specialists who might be expected to be reading this work, he concludes with the only act possible in the circumstances. He proposes, following in a tradition of 2000 years of anti-theatrical rhetoric, to

> revoke the privilege of vitality and communitarian power accorded the theatrical stage, so as to restore it to an equal footing with the telling of a story, the reading of a book, or the gaze focused on an image. In sum, it proposes to conceive it as a new scene of equality where heterogeneous performances are translated into one another. For in all these performances what is involved is linking what one knows with what one does not know.[12]

Jacques Rancière is of course not innocent as to the potential impact of these words, given that he is saying them among performance specialists at the *Sommerakademie* in Frankfurt, Germany. I was a fellow keynote speaker at the same *Sommerakademie*, in 2004, at which Rancière unveiled these ideas, in what has become such a well-circulated text. My name is there in the programme somewhat to the right of Rancière and just above the performance-maker Franco B, which is an uneasy place to be in any programme. Thinking back now to the event as distinct to the subsequently well-travelled text, from *Art Forum* to the publisher Verso, I recollect little *of* Rancière's talk as I was exhausted, having been up throughout the night before Rancière spoke.

What I *cannot recall,* to adapt Rebecca Schneider's marvellous testimony to theatrical memory loss, of Rancière's live performance then, of course gives us the hint of the elision, the sacrifice of the intelligence of feeling that has somehow been conflagrated in Rancière's egalitarian economy committed to a certain kind of knowledge.[13] Rancière's knowledges seem peculiarly distanced from the affects of performance that I, and I think readers of this book, might be interested in. These feelings that I was having during his talk on the *Emancipated Spectator* for me went something like this in my distributed sensibility: a thick head after too many drinks with members of the performance company Forced Entertainment in a private members' Frankfurt bathing club, a sore throat from drinking the fetid lake water when I inadvisably dived in to try to swim to the shore and a stiff back from sleeping on a park bench because I could not return to my hotel. I did begin to feel better when Rancière started speaking; he is very caring, avuncular in his words and performances as well as the measured and accessible tonalities of his writing, but I *was* sore.

My taciturn side would wish to turn that *emancipated* spectator, that saturated figure of potential for democratic alliance, somehow in excess of the stage spectacle, always somehow more independent than reception theory would have us believe, into an *emaciated* figure.

I choose the word with some caution as its proximity to hunger and starvation, in the wasted leanness of those who lack flesh, is a stark reminder of the 'really real' worlds the reals of performance might not always reach. But I did come to the term, I have to admit, through the peculiar, prosaic phrase that in the English theatre suggests a disappointing event, a 'thin audience'. While this has no direct translation in other European languages, it retains its force for another, historical reason.

Emaciation, I suggest, derives another, supplementary leverage as a term in the modern period from a specific theological-monarchical genealogy that is the very condition within which shame is enabled and thrives. The spectator can hardly be *emancipated* when the spectator is part of a public and a people whose very construction has been brought about by the processes described in detail in Chapter 3, what Eric Santner has called the 'royal remains'. In case you are reading this book in reverse, Santner's thesis is that with the coming of European democracy, the concept of the nation replaced the monarch and *sovereignty* was dispersed from the king's bodies to *all* bodies.[14] With the previous behavioural, social and sartorial codes gone, bodies were perceived, in Santner's account, as 'less legible', a person's place in the nation had become markedly less clear. It is this quality I am prescribing in the form of emaciation. It is this lack of clarity that sets conditions for the precarity, the vulnerability, the dependency of the human that I have previously written about at length in *Theatre & Everyday Life*, and *Theatre, Intimacy & Engagement*, but has also more recently become the focus of work by Judith Butler on 'precarity' and Shannon Jackson on the significance of social 'support'.

It is, I have suggested earlier in this book, the human's attempt to *immunise* themselves from such vulnerability, such emaciation I want to say, which partly accounts for the shifting dynamics of arrangement between audience and performer in twentieth-century theatre, dynamics which when understood by performers can serve to intensify such feelings in the form of theatrical affect among audiences. And such feelings presumably might be understood to include that sense of shame expressed earlier. This in my view might account for the *repetition compulsion* of attendance at the true 'theatre of the poor', *Les Misérables*, which has been witnessed by 60 million people in forty-two countries in this late age of Monarchy. Here it is the *sovereign public* who look down on the destitute communards from the Royal Circle now.

But what do the royal remains in the form of popular sovereignty have to do with emaciation as I am proposing it as a figure in this chapter? I would like to suggest, in an inversion of Santner's claim that a Public is somehow inflated by the surfeit of sovereign power that distributes among the people, that we are all, in our retarded relationship to sovereignty, prone as a public to atrophied or enfeebled, *emaciated* versions of those sovereign powers. Our power, as a public, has become glorified to the point of absurdity as we feel the thrill of voting for the 'unemployed' poor, Susan Boyle, on *Britain's Got Talent,* in order that she might 'dream her dream'. The ubiquity of *The X Factor* in diverse national and international settings is testament to the mobility of this 'emaciated' force masquerading as democratic power.

You may think with this emaciated excursion I have lost my bearings given the title of this book and the foregoing chapters within it. I would doubt my own equilibrium having spent some years writing and working in theatres towards what Claire MacDonald has described as *radical inclusion*: not just the inclusion of minorities in the theatre, those beyond the professions that I call the 'lay theatre', but more recently objects, things, animals and children previously denied any sensible relationship to the work that we do in the theatre.[15] But I have to admit, none of this writing, not a page, made any claims for the audience; I have never thought an audience *as such* existed on the grounds that all my efforts were working towards exploring the ingenious ruses of erupted 'post-audiences', or to take a term from the quixotic recording artist Prince the retooling of the *artist formerly known as audience*. So, when I come to that spectral figure and its potential for participation I want to start with *less* not more than Rancière dares to imagine. Hence my figuring of the emaciated in distinction to the emancipated spectator.

I want to do this just in case I mistake what is happening in the theatre as readable across much more complex and fragile practices such as social change, justice and ethics in the expanded field. A mistake that leads so many conversations in and around theatre into thinking there is action and progress when in fact there is, following Slavoj Žižek's provocation proposed in *The Parallax View*, 'pseudo action' and return. For instance, the model of the theatre audience in its close proximity to the stage and the action has often been taken for some sort of change despite the fact that there is still, so many years on, almost no touching allowed. As a perhaps trite, yet telling example nonetheless, this was the text from Kevin West, the sales manager of the Royal Court Theatre in London, notifying me as the tutor of a visiting class of students why one of those students would be asked to move from their seat on arrival at the theatre. It is not so much the courtesy of the treatment that is in question (the care is outstanding given the tickets were cheap) as the refined sense of immunity that is expected in this apparently public place:

> Thanks for booking to see Bola Agbaje's *Off the Endz* at the Royal Court Theatre on 9 March. You originally booked seats that included Stalls A5, but the director has requested that this seat be kept reserved for one of the actors, who jumps off-stage at one point in the play and would otherwise land dangerously close to you! We have therefore moved one of your party to the other end of the row, Stalls A18, which offers an excellent view of the stage and joins up with the rest of your party (you already had Stalls A17), and I hope you will not be too disappointed with the change. Please accept our sincerest apologies for the last minute alteration.

When the aforementioned 'jumping off' took place I was sitting in A6, so was up close and dirty to the action. The threat though was hard to imagine given the actor lugubriously descended into the auditorium from the raised playing space and sashayed past us to the exit. As a former member of the rap group *So Solid Crew* his every word was met with whoops and critical interjections from an unusually culturally mixed audience and one that, at times in this dynamic play, threatened to transform this often staid auditorium into a genuine chamber of, well what, a community of care? Perhaps I imagined far too much given what I have said so far regarding the reinforcing habits of the immunised theatre. I could not help noticing that the young man behind me who had had the temerity to shoot a mobile phone picture of the performer's groin at the moment of a particularly well-received disrobing was being interrogated by an usher in the aisle under an illuminated green sign that said EXIT.

I suspect some reading this might agree about my reservations regarding pseudo action when they compare the continuing injustices of the world set off against the warm glow of a participatory theatre event and its modest freedoms and curtailments. So sordid is this yawning gap that a young student of mine should express his frustration at this continuing separation as a *shame*. This *is* a shame, but I do have to admit not the most pressing shame when considering such questions, especially when a word like *emaciated* is in the frame. Given this chapter will conclude with a text by Primo Levi, my responsibility here is to secure the broadly, almost metaphoric deployment of the term 'emaciated' as I have situated it as the after-effect of the distribution of sovereign power, through an art object that reverses Theodor Adorno's fears as to the aestheticisation of politics. Here we will see that the much-vaunted, and circulated 'relational aesthetics', is as much about the brute politics of separation and isolation as it is about the intimacies of engagement, of community of any kind.

How It Is

Historically one might wish to trace the dissembling of the audience–performer relationship as being in tension with the ubiquitous idea of the late nineteenth- and twentieth-centuries' ideal of the 'black box', that is the volume that replaces the illuminated theatre of another age. If that figure is significant in this narrative I wanted to go to find it. I went to look for a black box where shame might be at work, and I found one at Tate Modern in London in March 2010. By definition, being a black box, this shame would not be *visible,* but it might be *felt.*

Mirosław Bałka's monumental work, installed in the Turbine Hall from late 2009 to early 2010, is named after Samuel Beckett's incarcerated, muddy, prose work *How It Is.*

This is how it is described in the Tate Modern programme, a printed free-sheet handed to all visitors, which while prominently promoting the sponsor of the Unilever Series, of which Bałka's work is the latest incarnation, does not credit the author at any stage. It is unlikely to be a text of the artist referring to Bałka in the third person (Figure 7.2):

Figure 7.2 Mirosław Bałka, *How It Is,* Tate Modern, London, 2009–2010

The latest commission by Mirosław Bałka in The Unilever Series is a giant grey steel structure with a vast dark chamber, which in construction reflects the surrounding architecture – almost as if the interior space of the Turbine Hall has been turned inside out. Hovering somewhere between sculpture and architecture, on 2 metre stilts, it stands 13 metres high and 30 metres long. Visitors can walk underneath it, listening to the echoing sound of footsteps on steel, or enter via a ramp into a pitch-black interior, creating a sense of unease.

The Tate, through an author who wishes to remain anonymous, perhaps for security reasons, chooses to position this troubling work in the following, deeply suspect way:

> Underlying this chamber is a number of allusions to recent Polish history – the ramp at the entrance to the Ghetto in Warsaw, or the trucks which took Jews away to the camps of Treblinka or Auschwitz, for example. By entering the dark space, visitors place considerable trust in the organisation, something that could also be seen in relation to the recent risks often taken by immigrants travelling. Bałka intends to provide an experience for visitors which is both personal and collective, creating a range of sensory and emotional experiences through sound, contrasting light and shade, individual experience and awareness of others, perhaps provoking feelings of apprehension, excitement or intrigue.

'Auschwitz, for example' seemed a brutal comparator. I am always suspicious of cultural organisations, especially ones as risk averse as Tate, who stage associations of this kind within the audible range of an espresso machine, delivering coffees, lattes, cappuccinos to those like me who need a 'double skinny' with an 'extra shot' to take on what the curators of such *relational spaces* would wish me to take on in the line of duty. From their description of *How It Is* I take this to be a kind of living proof that Nicolas Bourriaud was always right and that relationality is what this work *is* about. But my question is: relational to what? In relation to the movements of a refugee, or in relation to the death camps? Surely this could only be a relation of *shame*?

This is what *I feel* when I move and look into the obscurity, the darkness at the back of *How It Is*, in its deepest recesses. This is what I brought back into the light, having been alone and on leaving this chamber remaining alone. Contrary to the claims of increasing relationality what we seem to have here is that very interesting state that I would like to return to for a final time, after the Italian philosopher Roberto Esposito: *immunity*. One would have to be blind not to notice an increasing degree of distinction, difference and distance between the participants, what I want to call here against proximate relationality, what theatre people used to call perhaps quite naively but nicely, community, an *immune* condition.

As claims for community within relational art works and participatory performance grow, the unavowable evidence of rapacious immunity is on show. What is startling in *How It Is*, which may be not so different from Beckett's first rendering of *How It Is* with its singular voice, isolated deep in mud, with only a sack for company, is *How Separate it is, How Distinct it is, How Singular it is, How never WE it is, How 'I' it is*. And maybe that singular force, that anti-communitarian ethic is exactly how it is for Mirosław Bałka; he is, after all, an artist who has given considerable thought and labour to the material demands of the labour camp, in which singularity was not an aesthetic nicety: not least in his film installations *Bambi (Winterreise), Carousel* and *Pond (Winterreise)* that were made in Auschwitz and Breslau from 2003 to 2007 (Figure 7.3).

In identifying the singularity of Bałka's vision I am not just mimicking Rancière's own ideas on this singular theme, what we have already seen him describe in *The Emancipated Spectator* as 'the *capacity* of *anonymous* people, the capacity that makes everyone *equal* to everyone else'. For Rancière, we already know, believes: 'This capacity is exercised through irreducible differences…'. I am proposing something quite different to mend the fundamental break he

Figure 7.3 *Bambi (Winterreise)*, Miroslaw Bałka, video installation, 2010

has to make with theatre's communitarian logic, the way he has to propose some form of equality through anonymity.

Immunity is the opposite of anonymity though it may seek anonymity as part of its defences. Contrary to anonymity it has to know everything about community, and then seek *a part* of it, to immunise itself from it. My proposition here is that theatre, as distinct to the performance gene I have been putting it into circulation with so far, is an extraordinarily rich, complex and misunderstood place where such relations between immunity and community are played out. To make this special claim for theatre will require a brief semantic excursion via a bourgeois theatre of the past that still (for Edmund Husserl and Joe Kelleher at least) sets the scene for the staged audience–performer relations of the present.

'Immunity', as we saw in Chapters 5 and 6, is a term that the Italian philosopher Roberto Esposito has explored in its close relation and semantic proximity to its other, *community*.[16] Briefly to recap, Im*muni*tas is built around the word *Munos*, the Latin word for *gift*; it shares a relation to the gift that is embedded at the heart of both words, the gift that defines com*muni*ty, a word that is built around *Munos*, as well. The gift is what community presumes and what immunity cannot bear the promise of.

When Søren Kierkegaard in his work *Repetition* has his character Constantius go to the Konigstadter Theatre in Berlin, he has him always go alone; he always seeks out the same discrete box seat that is separated out from others by a row, and he is irritated on the one occasion that he has to move among the theatre audience proper when he is forced to take a seat among others.[17] Kierkegaard describes a moment in the play Constantius is watching, a piece of stage action which Joe Kelleher glosses in the following way: 'A smile is given but it is not necessarily in anyone's gift'. This means that while the smile is offered from the stage, no one in the audience can presume it is *theirs*. This is the special quality of theatre. An audience is troubled by the obvious reality that the smile cannot be for them, or at least not for them *alone*. For Constantius this troubles him so much that he spends days irritated by its paradox and in this irritation expresses his frustration at not being able to immunise himself from the gift that was shared among the community of which he does not wish to be a part, what we call audience.

Immunity sounds complicated but is readily understood, Esposito suggests, when you think not so much of its *biomedical* meaning, a certain resistance of an organism faced with disease, and more to the *political-juridical* meaning of the term that we began to lay out in Chapter 5. This is how Esposito defines that politico-juridical meaning: 'a temporary or definitive exemption is offered, or taken, on the part of a subject with regard to concrete obligations or responsibilities that under normal circumstances would bind *one* to *others*'.[18]

In my view this very nicely describes the 'real reals' that make theatre reals, such as the irritation of Constantius, seem rather trivial: for instance, General Pinochet's immunity from prosecution for the torture and murder of countless Chileans; Tony Blair and George Bush's immunity for their involvement in an illegal war prosecuted in Iraq. But it does help us with those theatre reals: the capacity of the modern audience, and I think it is a modern audience, to immunise itself from whatever is put before them, round them, amongst them is the story of the modern theatre. This is the *emaciated* narrative I am proposing in the light of Rancière's emancipated narrative. This emaciation is indeed our defining quality because it describes a state from within, wherein our willingness to enter the contract of performance stems from a genetic preference for immunity *from involvement*. That is what going to the theatre is all about. It is not a pathology, it is not a disease of outmoded theatre; it *is* the theatre, it is the norm of theatre.

Where the condition for entry to a meeting might be an assumption of *engagement* at a certain level of listening, voting or indeed action, irrespective of the expansion of the spectatorial role, there remains in performance in general, and theatre in particular, the immunisatory paradigm to protect us. This is why Plato did not have to worry so much about the power of the poets in the Republic – that immunisatory principle has been at work between life and politics throughout our recent history and most especially in our theatres.

Immunisation is a negative form of *the preservation of life*, nicely summed up by an audience member's, let's say Constantius at the Konigstadter Theatre, avoidance of the one free seat in the front row at the spectacle, however apparently distanced and safe, with the peculiarly morbid English phrase 'over my dead body'. Immunity saves, insures and preserves the organism, either individual or collective. The important thing to remember here is how Esposito suggests immunity does this, the mechanisms it operates through. Immunity does this by introducing a minute foreign element to the body, whether that be an individual such as a patient, a community or political body, introducing a fragment of the same pathogen from which it wants to protect itself, and it is *this* that blocks natural development, and with it the risk of further infection. But how might such a process operate in the theatre? I would suggest the *pathogen of performance* is the contract *we make* at each staging of the theatre, the dissembling of that stage, to reassert the very protocols we thought we were paying to see dispelled.

My proposal here is that this repertoire of affects of *adjustment to immunity* is what makes sitting in the dark watching the traffic of illuminated stages so interesting. This is the immunisatory logic of theatre, something that performance in all its consumptive character has done little, finally, to contaminate or curtail. And, in my view, this is the inherent power of theatre that uses all its theatricality to unpick its own communitarian stupidity. Examples are myriad for they *are* modern theatre's history: Pirandello's *Six Characters in Search of an Author* (1921) to Meyerhold's production of *Earth Rampant* in 1923. Or indeed consider those auditoria that knowingly and judiciously unpicked their own distances of spectatorial arrangement: the Werkbund Theatre Cologne (1914), Walter Gropius's theatre for Erwin Piscator (1927) and of course Lissitsky's space for Meyerhold's production of *I Want a Child* (1934). These are Erika Fischer-Lichte's telling examples of what she signifies as *the* theatrical revolution of the twentieth century.

And what this list leads to is, perhaps inevitably for that theatre trying to immunise itself against the charge of distance, the discovery that it has only arrived back from whence it came, but somehow, in peculiar but symptomatic sites, more conservative than it ever was. If you doubt my analysis of the return of the repressed go to St Martin's Lane Theatre in London and have a good look at the rhetorical strategies of a play there called *The Mousetrap*. This 60-year-old (at the time of writing and counting) enduring spectacle makes Tehching Hsieh's year-long durational performances look positively glancing, temporally challenged. We are indeed living in the century of *The Mousetrap* and *Les Misérables* and I think most neo-liberal cities have their own version of long runs that reassure at the same time as appalling for their sheer, Artaudian cruelty.

Our whole last century in this industrial West, recognised as such since Nietzsche commented on this at least, has been a play of protective containment, self-protection and immunity, an ethos of virulent vaccination. It is this, what I want to call after Esposito, *immunisatory logic*, that ushers in a century of the negative: that which contradicts norms, order, values becomes history's productive impulse. It is only this negative that allows individuals to free themselves in order to realise their 'greater performance' as Nietzsche might have put it. I suspect this is where the shame of that theatre event was coming from for that student, or partly the shame of an experience of sudden and inexplicable entropy in the face of an apparently generous invitation to greater involvement. Indeed this comes as a double disappointment if one attends to the earlier constitution of the Public, from among which I would expect spectators to make themselves available to theatre, as one predicated on the transmission, distribution and atrophy of a sovereignty which really did have the power to decide on the state of exception.

It is this alienation that represents the indispensible condition of our own, essentially modern identity as alienated humans; we would not be a witnessing human audience if we were not feeling that shame. Shame here, like other embarrassments in theatre witness, immunises us from the excess of subjectivity that simultaneously liberates us and yet of course deprives us of experience. This modern sense of self-representation is partly predicated on the urgent social need to constrain what are perceived as *excessive* forms of expression, such as violence, within the individual psyche. Where 'theatre manifestations' of violence such as the Covent Garden theatre riots of 1762 in London or more recently the *Playboy* of *the Western World* riots at the Abbey Theatre in the early years of the twentieth century in Dublin were latent eruptions of the audience *as violent*, these have been sublimated, I would like to say 'supined', into more socially manageable valences such as blushing, coughing (something Harold Pinter took to be inherently violating of his plays) and that peculiar form of judgemental clapping that acknowledges the performance but somehow simultaneously evokes disregard for a particular performer.

Immunisation does not of course just register at the level of internal, psychic states. It is manifested outside for all to see. The whole *machinery* of the theatre has been a history of regulated assumption of *conflict within order*. I have shown in my book *Theatre & Everyday Life* how the London council authorities effected this shift in nineteenth-century fire regulations and the invention of the 'safety theatre' in 1888 to ensure that everyone was safe from burning, from risk, to ensure that the sibling of the hotel in this regime of public safety, the theatre, should be treated as *a safe place to sleep*. There is no point in appealing to Antonin Artaud's romantically singed figure 'signaling through the flames', galvanising us to close the gap between audience and act, when we know just how powerful the fire chief is in our immunised environments.

Such immunisation protects us though through negation from something I suspect we should not underestimate given where I am heading with this chapter: the anihalation inherent to the performance gene. I was not asking for anihalation by burning when I wrote about combustion, indeed, as conservative a director as Peter Brook once said that the one quality he valued in a theatre space was its combustibility. Rather I was suggesting that this negotiation between safety and less safety, risk and more risk, was in a neo-liberal context wholly subsumed to a set of market and entrepreneurial machinations way beyond our control and rarely truly available to the rest of us subjected to the seriously fatal consequences of those neo-liberal risk takers who drive the capital markets within which our entertainments entertain.

Having been invited to set my gaze upon two of Romeo Castellucci's performers in the second act of *Giulio Cesare* (Queen Elizabeth Hall, London, 1999), who were played by two anorexic women, one of whom has since died, demands here that we pause to note that we are always and everywhere talking about a material reality when the word anihalation is in the frame, not just a metaphoric figure (such as Giorgio Agamben's 'bare life', which as a figurative condition may be responsible for the deaths of many but can never be held responsible for the death of *any-one*). The emaciation of the system did not start with *The Hunger Artist* by Kafka, but he did put his finger on something thin and getting thinner, about artists and audiences, when he said:

> Over the last few decades, the interest in hunger artists has suffered a marked decline. While it may once have been profitable to put on great public spectacles under one's own production, this is completely impossible today. Times really have changed. Then, the whole town got involved with the hunger artist; from day to day of his starving people's participation grew.[19]

One might contest that the real leverage the immunisatory paradigm offers is in its tension with that great shibboleth of theatre, the term 'community' as it has run through this book. As I have described it immunity has a contrastive symmetry with community. Etymologically, *immunitas* is the negative, or lacking form of *communitas*. This is how Roberto Esposito puts it: 'One can generally say that immunitas, to the degree it protects the one who bears it from risky contact with those who lack it, restores its own borders that were jeopardized by the common'.[20] In this process Esposito wants to characterise our modern age as an age of immunisation. Immunisation implies a substitution or an opposition of private or individualistic models with a form of communitary organisation. Immunity is the 'non-being' or the 'not having' of anything in common. This might sound like Jean-Luc Nancy's 'inoperable community' or indeed Alphonso Lingis's 'community of those who have nothing in common'. But of course immunity is inherently inhabited by its opposite, it cannot do without it; there is no immunity without the community from which it gains its force of exclusion.

Immunity is the fold that in some way protects community from itself, sheltering it from an 'unbearable excess'. To survive, the community, every community, is forced to introject the negative modality of its opposite. It is the theatre's place I would suggest, quite literally, to provide the peculiar conditions that make immunity from the prosecutions of performance possible. It would be this perverse dynamic that I would assign as theatre's greatest social measure, indeed perhaps its only measure, as it enters the twenty-first-century proper. Theatre is there to resist performance at all costs. In its very resistance to performance theatre reveals itself for what it is, exclusive, untouchable and, as the author of Azdak might once have said, alienating. Following this counter-argument it would be just such a knowing introversion of theatre's once proud communitarian logic that would be its intelligence, an intelligence way beyond the now slightly exposed and quite dumbly literal relationalities, performative or otherwise, of the 'artists' with their one-trick pony installations. They have no purchase, no tension as we have become wholly immune to their special pleading to be considered *sui generis*. I would suggest, ironically, that is precisely *theatre* that has that purchase once again, for unlikely as that seems for something not so long ago called an abandoned practice, it is theatre that would appear in the twenty-first century to have begun to get to grips with itself, as the problem it so obviously is. And the possibility it was and might be.

In this 'problematic' theatre one might wish to shorten the history of immunisation being spoken of here to the beginning of theatre's secularisation, with the end of sovereignty, what I have been characterising as the devolution of sovereignty from monarch to people. That is the moment when the monarch with the perfect seat with the only true perspective, the theatrical expression of the divine right of kings as discussed in Chapter 3, gives up that seat and retreats to the royal box above the action with the worst view in the house, better to be seen than to see. But that would be to underestimate much longer histories of exclusion that have shaped theatre in the expanded field. For that would be a wilful misreading of the *continuous* part biopolitics, that is the relationship between power and biological life, crucial mechanisms shaping what performance can and cannot do, community can and cannot be, has played since the most ancient times, since pre-history in fact, where this book began.

Very briefly let us track that relation between power and life back through the contents of this book, starting with the humans figuring themselves at the edge of the animality of the hunt 20,000 years ago on the walls of the caves of Lascaux, laughing in shame at their own use and abuse of the animal; they record for us that the 'I' of the human subject is of course dependent for survival on the not-I of the animal.

Or, the biopolitical logic that continues, 6000 years ago, at the outset of what I have called the Ceramic Age, with the advent of a suspended narrative in a glazed tile, understanding that those veneered, 2D representations floating in glaze were distinct from the *live action* that they were in the presence of, which they provided the backdrop for. Suspended life, still lives were now available for scrutiny and administration within a medium from which historical traces could be erased.[21]

Or the biological, zoological and pastoral perspective, in which an animal economy begins to be separated out from the human for profit, where the shape of relations at a distance begins to predict the shape of human–animal performances in relation to those other animals, where forms of assembly and structures of feeling are ones experienced through the multiple and the multitude before they are realised alone.

Or the indeterminate point at which the theological belief in a 'divine right of kings' becomes, through acts of defacement and the distribution from the flesh of the monarch to the 'body politic', a historical and political sensibility that is now immanent to a people and their democratic will. Where the verticality of the petrified life of the monarch in stone is brought to the horizontal to be broken down and shared amongst the poor, who in turn can be raised up, on barricades, and commiserated with for their enduring lack of power.

Or the telegraphic transition from the proximity of speech, in its social setting, to the extended voice and distance of international communications, in which the digital touch of the hand has been replaced by the promise of ultimate connectivity in the continuously oscillating long wave. Where such a history can be retrieved through three 'lives' dedicated to technology, weaving and fables, that share a dwelling whose memorial signs reverse the historical logic of these practices, a site that confounds the powers one might associate with each.

Or the social and psychic conditions within which law and psychoanalysis operate through performative, autopoietic systems in which the office of the practitioner becomes the investiture of offices of state and psychology. Where the totalitarian exclusion of the juridical person becomes the pre-condition for the white-collar crime, the desk-fascism that bureaucratically accounts for the consequences that follow the effects of self-perpetuating systems that lose all relation to the affects of those systems.

Or the razing of the ground by those authorities in search of the hiding place for the fugitive, whose life at large has been further exposed by the rendering of that social terrain by aestheticians and artists for whom the occupation of landscape has become an imperative without limit. Where sites for the sensible engagements of seeing, speaking and hearing have become so specific as to be off-limits to those whose habitats represent more than a 'distressed' lifestyle choice.

Or, to conclude that biopolitical record as we are here, with the tactical occupation of the ruins of the university in pursuit of a critical means to engage with the shame of a disappointed promise, of interaction with, and the recognition of, a Public. Where a life that was once referred to, by Victor Hugo and others, as a 'student's life' has become a 'client's brief', a legal contract of commitment to care while a government privatises the very means of support such lives once might have presumed were publicly owned and owed.

Following these approaches to performance, from the archaeological to the critical via the biopolitical, that have become by way of this book a partial geography of theatre in the expanded field, it is the immunisatory principle that might, of course, most adequately elucidate our understanding of the shame that comes with 'not enough immersion' in the theatrical act. But by way of conclusion here, and in keeping with an argument which in this chapter was initiated by a student, I wonder to what extent this shame is also our awareness of *too much immersion* now, a saturation in an image field that we know to be all too real and yet have few tools to comprehend? The kind of images indeed I have noted here made for us by the artist Mirosław Bałka. By this I mean that we, those of us who might consider themselves in support of students, are a generation who uniquely have incontrovertible evidence of a barbarity brought to us by witnesses to inhumanity. This is the shame that links that laughing figure in the cave, in shame at their own awfulness, to the shame of recognition that this is *our* story – it is the performance of a *human* history.

The Truce

In Primo Levi's coruscating encounter with the Nazi death camps there is just one chapter dedicated to the *theatre*, one might say that it is one chapter too many given the irradiation of the Real at the heart of the rest of the work.[22] But this encounter with theatre occurs on a journey away from the camps that has already been figured as treacherous but somehow *towards home*, or what might be left of home for a chemist who has endured what he has in order to be a witness to that endurance through writing. In the chapter titled 'The Theatre', surely a place if we are interested in the theatre we would wish to go, the following episode is described.

I will not abbreviate this passage for obvious reasons, and will let it speak for itself with two emphases brought to the fore that appear to me to deepen and complicate any arguments I have been making in this book. All I want to acknowledge is that there is a profound and disturbing relationship established here between theatre, performance and the witness of those acts. On the one hand a figure, who appears to have an excess of flesh, is revealed to be a cook with nothing but an excess of clothes, a test of strength is revealed as a theatrical artifice. But in that revelation there is perhaps the performed relief that the weight of production on this stage has been equalled out on behalf of the weak, to allow for a denouement that the world off stage would never allow.

The act is in the end achieved, after all, if 'only' theatrically. To be weak here, as Gianni Vattimo makes clear, does not deny the potential of these people to be strong; it is to recognise their *lack of power*. It is in this vertiginous rending of *images* that a distance between the reader, the perceived event and the performer is opened up. But beyond all such considerations is an emaciated audience that is not described, which is left to be imagined by Primo Levi, whose bare existence demands the scene be one not of their but of our shame, as witnesses to their witnessing: a distance that is as measurable as another magnitude of the shame I have been trying to discuss in this chapter:

> A large fat person came on to the stage, with hesitant steps, and legs wide apart, masked, muffled and bundled up, like the famous Michelin man. He greeted the public like an athlete, with his hands clasped above his head; meantime, two assistants, with great effort, rolled alongside him an enormous piece of equipment consisting of a bar and two wheels, like those used by weight lifters.
>
> He bent down, gripped the bar, tensed all his muscles; nothing happened, the bar did not move. Then he took off his cloak, folded it meticulously, placed it on the ground and prepared for another attempt. When the weight again did not move from the ground, he took off his second cloak, placing it next to the first; and so on with various cloaks, civilian and military cloaks, raincoats, cassocks, greatcoats. The athlete diminished in volume visibly, the stage filled up with garments and the weight seemed to have grown roots into the ground.
>
> When he had finished with the cloaks, he began to take off jackets of all kinds (among them a Haftling striped jacket, in honour of our minority), then shirts in abundance, always trying to lift the instrument with punctilious solemnity after each piece of clothing had been removed, and renouncing the attempt without the least sign of impatience or surprise.
>
> However, when he took off his fourth or fifth shirt, he suddenly stopped. He looked at the shirt with attention, first at arm's length, then close up; he searched the collar and seams with agile monkey-like movements, and then with his thumb and forefinger pulled out an imaginary louse. He examined it, his eyes dilated with horror, placed it delicately on the ground, drew a circle around it with chalk, turned back, with a single hand snatched the bar from the ground, which for the occasion had become as light as a feather, and crushed the louse with one clean blow.

After this rapid parenthesis, he continued taking off his shorts, trousers, socks and body belts with gravity and composure, trying in vain to lift the weight. In the end, he stood in his pants in the middle of a mountain of clothing; he took off his mask and the public recognized in him the sympathetic and popular cook Gridacucco, small, dry, hopping and bustling, aptly nicknamed 'Scannagrillo' (Cricket Butcher) by Cesare. Applause burst out: Scannagrillo looked around *bewildered*, then, as if seized by sudden stage fright, picked up his weight, which was probably made of cardboard, put it under his arm and scampered off.

Shortly after this episode Primo Levi and his fellow survivors hear of their imminent release, and of course where else should such a redemptive scene be staged than in the spectatorial chamber of the modest hut that is operating as a makeshift theatre:

> finally the announcement came: the announcement of our return, of our salvation, of the conclusion of our lengthy wanderings. It came in two novel unusual ways, from two different sides, and was convincing and open and dissipated all anxiety. It came in the theatre and through the theatre, and it came along the muddy road, carried by a strange and illustrious messenger.[23]

The trust this witness puts in the theatre here is startling but perhaps should not be surprising given the gravity of the really real from which that theatre cannot in these circumstances take its leave. This is not a metaphorical figure, perhaps like that of Giorgio Agamben's troubling association of bare life with these scenes and realities of the Musselman, the one in the death camps who has to bear witness. And it is not the metaphoric precarity of the imaginary louse that, at the very same moment as another more fortunate occupant of a chalk circle, is snuffed out, pushed back into oblivion with a cardboard prop. Indeed this is so much not a figure because it is a material, thin person, an emaciated spectator of a history that demands to be told. Indeed the imperative to witness this for history is the precise imperative to survive, here the separation I have been sustaining between an audience and their object of attention collapses into the community of witness; it repels forgetting in the immunity of a feigned ignorance. This is not 'The Truce' that Primo Levi is referring to in his title, but it is a small truce between the theatre and performance, and between both and the world, a crossroads where performance and its politics might meet, theatre and its thought might return, a direction from which salvation eventually comes. It is, as Primo Levi says, 'in the theatre and through the theatre' that anxiety is relieved, but this 'in' and 'through' would mean nothing without the muddy road, the path that messages come along. It is the mud of that road, a teeming community of its own kind that determines how it is.

Notes

To My Readers

1. Rodolphe Gasché, 'Something Like an Archaeology' in *The Honor of Thinking: Critique, Theory, Philosophy*. Stanford: Stanford University Press, 2007, pp. 276–290.
2. Hal Foster, *The Return of the Real: The Avant Garde at the End of the Century*. Cambridge: MIT Press, 1996, p. x. Also quoted by Adrian Kear in 'Preface', *Psychoanalysis and Performance*. Ed. Patrick Campbell and Adrian Kear, London: Routledge, 2001.
3. Richard Yates, *Revolutionary Road*, London: Methuen, 2000, Chapter 1, pp. 3–11, and the specific quotations here from pp. 5, 7 and 11.

Preliminary

1. Richard Southern, *The Seven Ages of the Theatre*. London: Faber and Faber, 1962, p. 21.
2. Southern, *The Seven Ages of the Theatre*, p. 22.
3. Southern, *The Seven Ages of the Theatre*, p. 23.
4. Peggy Phelan, *Unmarked: The Politics of Performance*. London: Routledge, 1993.
5. See Shannon Jackson, *Professing Performance*. Cambridge: Cambridge University Press, 2004.
6. See Jon McKenzie, *Perform or Else*. London: Routledge, 2001.
7. See Jean Starobinski, *Action and Reaction*. Trans. Sophie Hawkes. New York: Zone, 2003, p. 87, for a detailed history of these movements.
8. Starobinski, *Action and Reaction*, p. 87.
9. Beth Hoffman, 'Radicalism and the Theatre in Genealogies of Live Art', *Performance Research*, Vol. 14, No. 1 (2009), pp. 95–105, and Dominic Johnson (ed), 'Live Art in the UK', *Contemporary Theatre Review*, Vol. 22, No. 1 (2012).
10. Hoffman, 'Radicalism and the Theatre'.
11. See Alain Badiou, 'Theses on Theatre' in *Handbook of Inaesthetics*, Stanford: Stanford University Press, 2005, pp. 72–77.
12. McKenzie, *Perform or Else*, p. 270.
13. For recent developments in the study of action and reaction and specifically the work of the European Bioinformatics Institute, see 'Shakespeare and Martin

Luther King demonstrate potential of DNA Storage', Ian Sample, *The Guardian*, Thursday 24 January 2013.

14. See Georgina Guy, *Displayed & Performed*. Thesis submitted for the award of PhD at King's College London, 2012. Guy's research traces an emerging field of arts practice, including *theanyspacewhatever*, *Double Agent* and *The World as a Stage*, which, as both displayed and performed, is distinct from but related to an increasing curatorial provision for 'live' performance. Guy's project assesses how contemporary exhibition practices display performance and how object-based representations expand prevalent ontologies.

15. Shannon Jackson, *Social Works*. London: Routledge, 2012, and Claire Bishop, *Artificial Hells*. London: Verso, 2012.

16. While this work might appear as a reflection on past projects, at the time of writing Oleg Kulik was showing *Deep into Russia* and other works at the Regina Gallery in London (2012) with widespread responses from the press and critics.

17. Jacques Derrida, *Without Alibi*. Ed. and trans. Peggy Kamuf. Stanford: Stanford University Press, 2002.

18. The condition of working 'without alibi' is nothing new in the juridical sphere. The Guildford 4, the Birmingham 6 (to mention just two numerical signs given to miscarriages of justice in the UK judicial system), know what it is like to live without recourse to excuse, but it is a relatively new conceit in the economy of signs beyond the daily, in the consciously cultural sphere associated with spectacle and show, where alibi is all.

19. As developed in 'How to do Things with Words' as part of the *William James Lectures* of 1955.

20. Jacques Derrida, *Without Alibi*, p. 234.

21. See Peter Sloterdijk, Hans-Jurgen Heinrichs, 'In Praise of Exaggeration', *Neither Sun Nor Death*. Trans. Steven Corcoran. Los Angeles: Semiotexte, 2011, pp. 26–31.

22. An expansion attested to in works such as Jon McKenzie's *Perform or Else,* and a movement recognised with the creation of the *Performance Foundation* at King's College London, accessible online: www.performancefoundation.org.uk

23. I am grateful to Stephen Bottoms for furnishing me with the precise quotation I am referring to here, a quotation that he has written about at some length himself: 'The fact is that theatre as we have known and practiced it – the staging of written dramas – will be the string quartet of the 21st century: a beloved but extremely limited genre, a subdivision of performance.' Richard Schechner, 'A New Paradigm for Theatre in the Academy', *TDR: The Drama Review*, Vol. 36, No. 4 (1992), pp. 7–10.

24. By way of example, references here are drawn from Isabelle Stengers, 'Diderot's Egg: Divorcing Materialism from Eliminativism', *Radical Philosophy*, Vol. 144 (2007) pp. 7–16, and Giorgio Agamben, 'In Praise of Profanation' in *Profanations*. Trans. Jeff Fort. New York: Zone Books, 2006, pp. 73–92, two short works which

summarise long-held interests and ideas developed by both individuals over two decades. Also of interest in relation to these themes would be an annual series of summer schools devoted to the exploration of Abandoned Practices, following a curated 'Shift' at *Performance Studies international* Zagreb (24–28 June 2009), which have taken place under the guidance of Mark Jeffery, Matthew Goulish and Lin Hixson in Chicago and Prague, see www.abandonedpractices.org

25. Stengers, 'Diderot's Egg', p. 7.
26. Agamben, 'In Praise of Profanation', p. 73.
27. Agamben, 'In Praise of Profanation', p. 75.
28. Agamben, 'In Praise of Profanation', p. 76.
29. Rosalind Krauss, 'Sculpture in the Expanded Field', *October*, Vol. 8 (1979), pp. 30–44. I am grateful to Beryl Robinson for her reading, interpretation and introduction to this work.
30. Krauss, 'Sculpture in the Expanded Field', p. 30.
31. Beth Hoffman, 'Radicalism and the Theatre'.

Chapter 1

1. See Vilém Flusser, 'Bare Walls' in *The Shape of Things, A Philosophy of Design*. London: Reaktion Books, 1999, pp. 78–80.
2. Marie José Mondzain, *Homo Spectator*. Paris: Bayard, 2007, pp. 11–58.
3. Plato, *The Republic*. Trans. H.D.P Lee. Harmondsworth: Penguin, 1955, pp. 278–279, with interruptions from the author.
4. See Samuel Weber, *Theatricality as Medium*. New York: Fordham University Press, 2004, pp. 3–12.
5. And in the 'falling man' from reality to fiction in Don De Lillo, we share a stock image of the opening of the twenty-first century whose singularity became the defining moment for a collective of grief, if not a community that became unable to operate.
6. Jean Luc Nancy, 'Introduction', *The Birth to Presence*, Trans. Brian Holmes, Stanford: Stanford University Press, 1993, p. 1. I am grateful to Mark Taylor-Batty for his scrupulous editing thoughtout this volume, but no more so than in respect to this passage whose sense he rendered from my nonsense.
7. Nancy, 'Introduction', p. 1.
8. See Alan Read, *Theatre, Intimacy & Engagement: The Last Human Venue*. Houndmills: Palgrave, 2008, especially 'On The Social Life of Theatre'.
9. Jean-Luc Nancy, *The Inoperative Community*. Trans. Peter Connor. Minneapolis: University of Minnesota Press, 1991, p. xxxvii.
10. Nancy, *The Inoperative Community*, p. 3.

11. Nancy, *The Inoperative Community*, p. 19.

12. Jean-Luc Nancy, *The Muses*. Trans. Peggy Kamuf. Stanford: Stanford University Press, 1996, p. 69.

13. Georges Bataille, *The Cradle of Humanity*. Ed. Stuart Kendall, trans. Michelle Kendall and Stuart Kendall. New York: Zone, 2005, p. 16.

14. Bataille, *The Cradle of Humanity*, pp. 31–46.

15. Georges Bataille, *Theory of Religion*. Trans. Robert Hurley. New York: Zone Books, 1989, p. 19.

16. Nicolas Bourriaud, *Relational Aesthetics*. Paris: Les Presse du Reel, 1998, pp. 26–32.

17. Georges Bataille, *The Cradle of Humanity*. Ed. Stuart Kendall, trans. Michelle Kendall and Stuart Kendall. New York: Zone, 2005, p. 145.

Chapter 2

1. The following chapter is partly drawn from material presented at five spoken events over the last five years (2007–2012). I have retained the colloquial quality of the original events where it serves the purpose of informality. The first, *Performing Literatures*, through the invitation of Stephen Bottoms at Leeds University, UK, established the possibility of moving between a founding work of western dramaturgy and the unheralded part some workers had in that drama (Poetics – Practices). The second, an event ostensibly committed to the work of Alain Badiou curated by Adrian Kear for *PSi New York*, gave rise to the idea that a sheep may 'suffer' an appearance and a wolf generate an 'intensity of appearance' despite being to all contents and purposes invisible. A research seminar in the French Department at King's College London from an invitation by Nicholas Harrison exposed the Rancièrian propositions of democracy to too expert a scrutiny than I deserved and gave rise to the weak version of politics written here. The fourth at the invitation of Bojana Kunst and the Ljubljana *Maska* seminar proposed a further shift from these propositions towards some questions of waiting and works that might be initiated through such an interpretation (Politics). The fifth at the invitation of Patrick ffrench and Carl Lavery for a conference on ritual at Aberystwyth University (2012) for which I began to consider the possibilities of 'weak ritual'. I am grateful to the curators and their audiences for any clarity which might have arisen as a consequence of these public conversations though of course absolve others from any responsibility for the capital I make from some other animals.

2. Sophocles, 'Oedipus the King' in *The Three Theban Plays: Antigone, Oedipus the King, Oedipus at Colonus*. Trans. Robert Fagles. London: Penguin, 1982 (pp. 155–252), p. 172.

3. Sophocles, 'Oedipus the King', p. 174.

4. See Alan Read, *Theatre, Intimacy & Engagement: The Last Human Venue.* Houndmills: Palgrave, 2008, especially Chapter 1, 'The anthropological machine'.

5. Norberto Bobbio, *In Praise of Meekness.* Trans. Teresa Chataway. Cambridge: Polity Press, 2000, pp. 19–36.

6. Plato, *The Laws.* Trans. Trevor J. Saunders. Harmondsworth: Penguin, 1970, p. 75.

7. Jacques Rancière, *Hatred of Democracy.* Trans. Steve Corcoran. London: Verso, 2006, p. 34.

8. See Peter Hallward, 'Staging Equality', *New Left Review*, Vol. 37 (2006), pp. 109–129, for an incisive essay that has informed this reading.

9. See Joe Kelleher, 'The Suffering of Images' in Adrian Heathfield (ed.), *Live: Art and Performance.* London: Tate Publishing, 2004/2012, pp. 190–195.

10. The following section owes a debt to the exhibition and subsequent publication: *Making Things Public* Ed. Bruno Latour and Peter Weibel. Karlsruhe: ZKM/ Cambridge: MIT Press, 2005.

11. Vinciane Despret, 'Sheep Do Have Opinions' in Bruno Latour and Peter Weibel (eds), *Making Things Public*, Karlsruhe: ZKM/Cambridge: MIT Press, 2005, pp. 360–368.

12. See Isabelle Mauz and Julien Gravelle, 'Wolves in the Valley: On Making a Controversy Public', *Making Things Public*, Karlsruhe: ZKM/Cambridge: MIT Press, 2005, pp. 370–380.

13. Mauz and Gravelle, 'Wolves in the Valley', p. 374.

14. Despret, 'Sheep Do Have Opinions', p. 361.

15. Despret, 'Sheep Do Have Opinions', p. 367.

16. Latour and Weibel, *Making Things Public*, p. 5.

17. Sophocles, 'Oedipus the King', p. 240.

Chapter 3

1. See Kenneth Olwig, *Landscape, Nature and the Body Politic.* Madison: The University of Wisconsin Press, 2002, especially '"Masquing" The Body Politic of Britain', pp. 62–79, and 'Performance, aetherial space and the practice of landscape/architecture: the case of the missing mask', *Social & Cultural Geography*, Vol 12, No 3, May 2007, pp. 305–318, upon which the opening of this chapter is based, and Clare McManus, *Women on the Renaissance Stage: Anna of Denmark and Female Masquing in the Stuart Court (1590–1619).* Manchester: Manchester University Press, 2002, within which chapters on dance (pp. 1–17) and spectacle (pp. 97–135) were particularly insightful for any progress this writing makes.

2. Stephen Orgel and Roy Strong, *Inigo Jones: The Theatre of the Stuart Court*. Berkeley: Sotheby Parke Bernet, 1973, pp. 383–385. The three masques detailed in the chapter are excerpts from the archive as comprehensively recorded by Orgel and Strong.

3. Walter Benjamin, 'Elective Affinities' in Marcus Bullock and Michael W. Jennings (eds), *Selected Writings: 1938–1940*, Cambridge: Harvard University Press, 1996, p. 47.

4. Hans-Thies Lehmann, *Postdramatic Theatre*. Trans. Karen Jurs-Munby. London: Routledge, 2006. I have more than lent on Hans-Thies Lehmann's lucid work to prop up my own rather fragile thesis, and in so doing wholly relied upon Karen Jurs-Munby's excellent translation of that work in the Routledge edition to get me over the starting line, even with no apparent coherent conclusion in sight. I am particularly grateful to both for their conviviality and contributions to events over the last half decade at which I have learnt much.

5. See Matthew Goulish, *39 Microlectures*. London: Routledge, 2000; Nicholas Ridout, *Stage Fright, Animals and Other Theatrical Problems*. Cambridge: Cambridge University Press, 2006; and Sara Jane Bailes, *Performance Theatre and the Poetics of Failure*. London: Routledge, 2011.

6. Lehmann, *Postdramatic Theatre*, p. 32.

7. Gertrude Stein, Closing Time, quoted in Lehmann, *Postdramatic Theatre*, p. 81.

8. See Alan Read, 'Romeo Castellucci: The Director on this Earth' in Maria Delgado and Dan Rebellato (eds), *Contemporary European Theatre Directors*. London: Routledge, 2010, pp. 249–262.

9. Giorgio Agamben, *The Kingdom and the Glory*. Trans. Lorenzo Chiesa. Stanford: Stanford University Press, 2011, p. 204.

10. Michael Taussig, *Defacement*. Stanford: Stanford University Press, 1999. See especially 'Prologue', pp. 1–8, for the basis of the following discussion.

11. Walter Benjamin, 'The Origin of the German Tragic Drama', quoted as an epigraph to *Defacement*. Stanford: Stanford University Press, 1999.

12. Orgel and Strong, *Inigo Jones*, pp. 122–123.

13. Orgel and Strong, *Inigo Jones*, pp. 277–278.

14. See Vaughan Hart, *Inigo Jones: The Architect of Kings*. New Haven: Yale University Press, 2011, for the comprehensive history upon which this account is based, particularly Chapters 2, 4 and 8 where his history of Paules and its defacement by the Puritan forces provided the touchstone for this chapter.

15. Eric Santner. *The Royal Remains*. Chicago: University of Chicago Press, 2010.

16. For details of the *Performance Foundation*: www.performancefoundation.org.uk.

17. See Ernst H. Kantorowicz, *The King's Two Bodies: A Study in Medieval Political Theology*. Princeton: Princeton University Press, 1981.

18. See Walter Benjamin, 'Gloves' in 'One Way Street', in Marcus Bullock and Michael W. Jennings (eds), *Selected Writings Vol. 1. 1913–1926*. Cambridge: Harvard University Press, 1996.

Chapter 4

1. I am grateful to David Bradby whose New Testament reading, with a keen eye to the olfactory, was far more alert than my own.

2. See the exemplary essay by Jody Enders, 'Performing Miracles: Mimesis of Valenciennes' in Tracy C. Davis (ed.), *Theatricality*. Cambridge: Cambridge University Press, 2003, pp. 40–64.

3. Translation as in Phillipe Lacoue-Labarthe, *Typography*. Ed. Christopher Fynsk. Stanford: Stanford University Press, 1989, p. 249.

4. See Lacoue-Labarthe, *Typography*, p. 250.

5. See Slavoj Žižek's review of Kojin Karatani's *Transcritique*, 'The Parallax View', *New Left Review*, Vol. 25 (2004), pp. 121–134, and the book that developed from that piece namely, *The Parallax View*. Cambridge: MIT Press, 2006.

6. Lacoue-Labarthe, *Typography*, p. 251.

7. Lacoue-Labarthe, *Typography*, p. 259. Nature has given man nothing but the 'aptitude' for presenting.

8. Tom Tyler, *Ciferae*. Minneapolis: University of Minnesota Press, 2012, p. 19.

9. Judith Butler, *Precarious Life*. London: Verso, 2006, pp. 128–151.

10. *King Lear*, Act III, Sc IV, William Shakespeare Ed. Kenneth Muir, London: Methuen, 1973, pp. 114–115.

11. See Francis Galton, *A Descriptive List of Anthropometric Apparatus*. Cambridge: Cambridge Scientific Instrument Company, 1887 and Michael Bulmer, *Francis Galton: Pioneer of Heredity and Biometry*. Baltimore: Johns Hopkins University Press, 2003.

12. Anthony Kubiak, 'Animism', *Performance Research* 'On Ecology', Vol. 17, No. 4 (2012), pp. 52–60.

13. Judith Butler, *Precarious Life*. London: Verso, 2006, p. 130.

14. See various works over the last decade by David Williams, Lourdes Orozco, Steven Baker, Jennifer Parker-Starbuck, Garry Marvin, Michael Peterson, Sally Banes and Laura Cull.

15. Credit for original source for all drawings in this chapter to Hammersmith and Fulham Archives and The William Morris Gallery Walthamstow, London.

16. William Morris, *News from Nowhere and Other Writings*. Ed. Clive Wilmer. London: Penguin, 1993. I have drawn on the introduction and notes to this volume for points of context included here, p. 31.

17. Morris, *News From Nowhere and Other Writings*, pp. 331–332.

18. Francis Ronalds quoted in Rollo Appleyard, *Pioneers of Electrical Communication*. London: Macmillan and Co, 1930, pp. 303–304.

19. Prof. D.A. Turner, University of Kent, 'Letters', *Guardian* (Newspaper, London edition), 10 November 1998, p. 21.

20. See Scott McQuire, 'Pure Speed – From Transport to Teleport' in Jeremy Millar
    and Michiel Schwarz (eds), *Speed-Visions of an Accelerated Age*. London:
    Photographers Gallery et al, 1998, p. 26.
21. Walter Benjamin, *Illuminations*. Ed. Hannah Arendt. Trans. Harry Zohn.
    New York: Schocken Books, 1969.
22. See Alan Read, *Theatre & Everyday Life: An Ethics of Performance*. London:
    Routledge, 1993, pp. 62–67, and Walter Benjamin, *Illuminations*, p. 90.
23. Michel de Certeau, *The Practice of Everyday Life*. Trans. Steven Rendall. Berkeley:
    University of California Press, 1988, p. 77.
24. Fiona McCarthy, *William Morris: A Life for Our Time*. London: Faber, 1994, p. 397.
25. McCarthy, *William Morris*, p. 392.
26. Francis Ronalds quoted in Appleyard, *Pioneers of Electrical Communication*,
    pp. 303–304.

Chapter 5

1. See Peter Gilgen, 'Introduction' to Niklas Luhmann, *Introduction to Systems Theory*,
   trans. Peter Gilgen. Cambridge: Polity Press, p. xiv.
2. Luhmann, *Introduction to Systems Theory* 'General Systems Theory', p. 77.
3. Luhmann, *Introduction to Systems Theory*, p. 78.
4. Roberto Eposito, *Communitas: The Origin and Destiny of Community*. Trans.
   Timothy Campbell, Stanford: Stanford University Press, 2010, p. 6.
5. Eposito, *Communitas*, p. 6.
6. See *The Oxford English Dictionary*, Second Edition. Oxford: Clarendon Press, 1989,
   p. 942. I am indebted to Mikkel Borch-Jacobsen, John Forrester, Sonu Shamdasani,
   Joel Sanders and Diana Fuss who gave talks related to these themes at the Institute
   of Contemporary Arts in London while I was Director of Talks there between 1994
   and 1997 and to Patrick Campbell and Adrian Kear for their scrupulous editorial
   assistance with an earlier version of this chapter for their collection of essays:
   Psychoanalysis and Performance. London: Routledge, 2001.
7. The 'theatre' of Freud from Oedipus to Hamlet is already well known and poetically
   underpins both the authenticity of his operations and the field of practices these
   works have generated. The pre-eminent place afforded Shakespeare in Freud's study
   attests to his position in a canonical pantheon alongside the complete works of
   Goethe. Yet the prominence of Shakespeare here and in Freud's only titled writing
   on the theatre, 'Psychopathic Characters on the Stage', should not obscure a more
   engaging and multifarious dialogue between psychoanalysis and performance in
   his work and work place.
8. Adrian Dannatt, 'Psychoanalysis?', *lacanian ink*, No. 12 (1997), p. 43.

9. *Appointment*, Sophie Calle at the Freud Museum, London, curated by James Putnam, 12 February–28 March 1999.

10. See Peggy Phelan, 'The Ontology of Performance: Representation without Reproduction' in *Unmarked: The Politics of Performance*. London: Routledge, 1993, pp. 146–147.

11. See Bruno Latour, *We Have Never Been Modern*. Cambridge: Harvard University Press, 1993.

12. See Anthony Vidler, *The Architectural Uncanny*. Cambridge: MIT Press, 1992, p. 42.

13. See Mikkel Borch-Jacobsen, *Remembering Anna O*. Trans. Kirby Olson. London: Routledge, 1996, p. 89.

14. See Michel de Certeau, 'The Fiction of History: The Writing of Moses and Monotheism' in *The Writing of History*. Trans. Tom Conley. New York: Columbia University Press, 1988, p. 322.

15. Adrian Dannatt, 'Psychoanalysis?', p. 42.

16. Freud, *The Diary of Sigmund Freud 1929–1939*. Trans. annotated by Michael Molnar, Freud Museum, London. London: Hogarth Press, 1997, p. 239.

17. Diana Fuss and Joel Sanders, 'Bergasse 19' in Joel Sanders (ed), *Stud: Architectures of Masculinity*. Princeton: Princeton University Press, 1996, pp. 112–139. I am interested in such places as part of a wider project on the locations of locution, the speech sites of the metropolis that have shaped modes of communication at certain historical moments. See Alan Read, 'Speech Sites' in *Architecturally Speaking: Practices of Art, Architecture and the Everyday*. Ed. Alan Read. London: Routledge, 2000.

18. Ernest Jones, *Sigmund Freud, The Life and Work, vol. 1: The Young Freud, 1856–1900*, London: Hogarth Press, 1953. Also see 'Combustion' in Alan Read, *Theatre & Everyday Life*. London: Routledge, 1993, for an account of the historiographical significance of theatre fires.

19. Sigmund Freud, 'An Autobiographical Study' in James Strachey (ed). *The Standard Edition of the Complete Works of Sigmund Freud*, vol. XX, London: Hogarth Press, 1959, p. 16.

20. Freud, 'An Autobiographical Study', p. 17.

21. Sigmund Freud, 'Psychical Treatment' in *The Standard Edition VII* (1890), London: Hogarth Press, 1959, p. 298, quoted in John Forrester, *Dispatches from the Freud Wars*. Cambridge: Harvard University Press, 1997, pp. 75–76.

22. John Forrester, *Truth Games*. Cambridge: Harvard University Press, 1997, p. 67.

23. Forrester, *Truth Games*, p. 68.

24. Forrester, *Truth Games*, p. 69.

25. Forrester, *Truth Games*, p. 74.

26. Mikkel Borch-Jacobsen, *Remembering Anna O*, p. 89. It is not surprising that Jacobsen places Bertha in an overtly theatrical setting of her day, with its panoply of stage, wings and spectation. As George Taylor has shown in *Players and*

Performances in the Victorian Theatre the theatre of 'feeling' and 'passions' of the early Victorian period with its techniques of sudden perception such as 'the start' and 'the recoil' of surprise were, from Garrick onwards, well-known theatrical motifs. Diderot's *Paradox of the Actor* maintained that 'sensibility was not necessary for an actor imitating emotion – the secret was to maintain a cool head in order to be able to give the impression of a warm heart'. But there was a continuing fascination with the dialogue between truth and artifice. Edmund Kean's technique of 'making points', the striking of distinct attitudes to signal new passions, was resented by figures such as Leigh Hunt who described them as 'trickery'. As George Taylor says in summing up the mid-Victorian period, the actors of the period '…relied on an artificial vocabulary of grimaces, gestures and tones of voice which playgoers had learnt to recognise'. While theatre, through the work of the Kembles in Britain, developed the beginnings of a notion of a psychological through-line to characterisation, the latter part of the century still saw handbooks of acting producing detailed instructions of how the passions might best be portrayed. But the 'staging' of the hysteric harked back to an earlier period such as Edward Mayhew's manual of 1840, *Stage Effect*, where he wrote: 'To theatrical minds the word "situation" suggests some starting point in a play likely to command applause, where the action is wrought to a climax, where the actors strike "attitudes" and form what they all a "picture" during the exhibition of which a pause takes place.'

27. Fouveau de Courmelles, *Hypnotism*. London: Routledge, 1891, p. 151.
28. Dr J Gerard, quoted by Courmelles, *Hypnotism*, p. 152.
29. Courmelles, *Hypnotism*, p. 157.
30. Freud, *An Autobiographical Study*, p. 18.
31. Axel Munthe, *The Story of San Michele*. London: John Murray, 1936, p. 224.
32. Munthe, *The Story of San Michele*, p. 228.
33. Munthe, *The Story of San Michele*, p. 229.
34. Sigmund Freud, 'Psychopathic Characters on the Stage' in *The Standard Edition*. Vol VII, p. 305.
35. Freud, 'Psychopathic Characters on the Stage', p. 306.
36. 'The familiarity of estrangement in modern art, Adorno concluded, as opposed to the distance of the apparently familiar "classic" artwork, was a result of the very "repression" of modern art's effects …'. See Anthony Vidler, *The Architectural Uncanny*, for an extended discussion of this question.
37. Bettina Knapp, *That Was Yvette*. New York: Holt, Rinehart, 1964, pp. 313–314.
38. Freud, *An Autobiographical Study*, p. 28.
39. Ernest Jones, *The Life and Work of Sigmund Freud: Volume 1*. New York: Basic Books, 1963, p. 301.
40. Freud, *An Autobiographical Study*, p. 30.
41. The remainder of hypnosis returns one more time, for all time and conclusively for Jacques Derrida in 'Telepathic', writing in the first person as Freud, in Freud's

writing: 'I've never given up hypnosis. I've simply transferred one mode of injunction to another: one might say that I've become a writer and have poured all my powers and hypnogogic desires into the writing, into the rhetoric, into the staging and into the composition of texts.' *Cahiers Confrontation,* Vol. 10 (1983), p. 219.

42. I am indebted in the analysis of the Charcot image to an unpublished paper presented by Forbes Morlock to an MFA seminar at Sheffield Hallam University, England, on 10 May 1994 'The Very Picture of the Primal Scene: Un Léçon de Charcot a la Salpétrière' and provided for me from the archive of the Freud Museum London.

43. Ernest Jones, *The Life and Work,* pp. 230–231, quoted by Morlock to an MFA seminar at Sheffield Hallam University, England.

44. Helène Cixous, 'Fiction and Its Phantoms: A Reading of Freud's Das Unheimliche (The "Uncanny")', *New Literary History,* Vol. 7, No. 3 (1976), p. 548.

45. For a reading of this see Michel de Certeau, *The Writing of History,* p. 312.

46. Certeau, *The Writing of History,* p. 27.

47. Freud, *The Diary of Sigmund Freud,* p. 255.

48. See Anthony Vidler, *The Architectural Uncanny,* p. 13.

49. Vidler, *The Architectural Uncanny,* p. 27.

50. Freud, *The Diary of Sigmund Freud,* p. 255.

51. See Sigmund Freud, *The Standard Edition* XII (1911–1913), pp. 9–82.

52. Daniel Paul Schreber, *Memoirs of My Nervous Illness.* New York: New York Review Books, 2000, p. 313.

53. See Niklas Luhmann, *Law as a Social System.* Oxford: Oxford University Press, 2004.

54. See Schreber, *Memoirs of My Nervous Illness.*

55. Eric Santner, *My Own Private Germany.* Princeton: Princeton University Press, 1996.

56. Santner, *My Own Private Germany,* p. 4, but also see Introduction for a development of these themes.

57. See Alain Supiot, *Homo Juridicus: On the Anthropological Function of the Law.* Trans. Saskia Brown. London: Verso, 2007, especially 'Prologue' and Chapters 1 and 2 on which this section is based.

58. See Hannah Arendt, *The Origins of Totalitarianism.* New York: Harcourt, Brace & World, 1966, p. 447.

59. Roberto Esposito, *Bios: Biopolitics and Philosophy.* Trans. Timothy Campbell. Minneapolis: University of Minnesota Press, 2008, p. 45.

60. Esposito, *Bios: Biopolitics and Philosophy,* p. 43.

61. Santner, *My Own Private Germany,* p. 12, for a full discussion of this idea from Pierre Bourdieu.

62. This and the following quotations from *The Caucasian Chalk Circle* are from, Bertolt Brecht, 'The Caucasian Chalk Circle', Trans. Eric Bentley, in Bertolt Brecht, *Parables for the Theatre.* Harmondsworth: Penguin, 1971, pp. 206–207.

Chapter 6

1. See Paul Virilio, 'The Overexposed City' in J. Crary et al. (eds), *Zone 1, 2*. New York: Urzone, 1986.
2. Jacques Rancière, *The Politics of Aesthetics*. Trans. and Intro. Gabriel Rockhill. London: Continuum, 2006, p. 13.
3. See Adrian Kear, *Theatre and Event: Staging the European Century*. Houndmills: Palgrave, 2013.
4. From Gabriel Rockhill's Introduction to Rancière, *The Politics of Aesthetics*, p. 9.
5. Rancière, *The Politics of Aesthetics*, p. 226.
6. Rancière, *The Politics of Aesthetics*, p. 226.
7. Samuel Beckett, *The Theatrical Notebooks of Samuel Beckett*, Vol. 3, 'Krapp's Last Tape'. James Knowlson (ed). London: Faber, 1992, p. 5.
8. Beckett, *The Theatrical Notebooks*, p. 5.
9. Paul Virilio, *The Aesthetics of Disappearance*. New York: Semiotext[e], 1990, p. 9.
10. Quoted in Virilio, *The Aesthetics of Disappearance*, p. 33.
11. Thoughts here are drawn from Michael Taussig's, *The Nervous System*. London: Routledge, 1992.
12. Walter Benjamin, 'This Space for Rent' in 'One Way Street', in Marcus Bullock and Michael W. Jennings (eds), *Selected Writings Vol. 1. 1913–1926*. Cambridge: Harvard University Press, 1996, p. 145.
13. Taussig, *The Nervous System*, p. 147.
14. Giorgio Agamben, *Potentialities*. Trans. Daniel Heller-Roazen. Stanford: Stanford University Press, 1999, p. 38.
15. Janet Cardiff, *Forty Part Motet*, Castle Keep, Newcastle 20 June–8 July 2001.
16. I rely on Paul Doe, *Tallis*. London: Oxford University Press, 1968, pp. 37–63, for my analysis of Tallis here.
17. Doe, *Tallis*, p. 63.
18. Gillies Whittacker, 'An Adventure' in *Collected Essays*. London: Oxford University Press, 1940, p. 7.
19. Whittacker, 'An Adventure', pp. 46–47.

Chapter 7

1. See Bill Readings, *The University in Ruins*. Cambridge: Harvard University Press, 1996, p. 169.
2. See *Access to Knowledge*. Gaelle Krikorian and Amy Kapczynski (eds). New York: Zone Books, 2010.
3. See 'Lay Theatre' in Alan Read, *Theatre & Everyday Life: An Ethics of Performance*. London: Routledge, 1993.

4. See Readings, *The University in Ruins*, p. 167.

5. See Readings, *The University in Ruins*, pp. 166–179.

6. See Liz Austin's forthcoming work on institutional histories, structures and politics.

7. Timothy Campbell, 'Translator's Introduction' in Roberto Esposito (eds), *Bios: Biopolitics and Philosophy*, Minneapolis: University of Minnesota Press, 2008, p. xiii.

8. Alan Read, *Theatre, Intimacy & Engagement*. Houndmills: Palgrave, 2008.

9. Jacques Rancière, *The Emancipated Spectator*, first presented as a talk at SommerAkademie Frankfurt, 2004, and latterly published in *Art Forum* and then as *The Emancipated Spectator* in Verso, 2010, from which these translations are taken.

10. Rancière, *The Emancipated Spectator*, p. 15.

11. Rancière, *The Emancipated Spectator*, p. 17.

12. Rancière, *The Emancipated Spectator*, p. 22.

13. See Rebecca Schneider, 'What I Can't Recall' in Judie Christie et al. (eds), *A Performance Cosmology*. London: Routledge, 2006.

14. See Eric Santner, *The Royal Remains*. Chicago: University of Chicago Press, 2010.

15. See Claire MacDonald, 'Congregation', *Performance Research*, Vol. 11, No. 1 (2006) pp. 114–115.

16. Esposito, *Bios: Biopolitics and Philosophy*. I am grateful to Annelisa Sachi, whose own work on Esposito is currently widely discussed in the seminars that she shares it, for introducing me so generously to these themes and work.

17. I am indebted to Joe Kelleher for a detailed and artful development of this context as part of a paper given to the *Traces of …* seminar series at King's College London, March 2010, curated by Karen Quigley and Georgina Guy.

18. Esposito, *Bios: Biopolitics and Philosophy*, p. 27.

19. Franz Kafka, *The Hunger Artist*. Harmondsworth: Penguin, 1996, p. 252.

20. Esposito, *Bios: Biopolitics and Philosophy*, p. 24.

21. See Alan Read, 'The Ceramic Age: Things Hidden Since the Foundation of Performance Studies' *Performance Research*, 'Performatics', Vol. 13, No. 2 (2009) pp. 47–58.

22. Primo Levi, *If this is a Man / The Truce*. Trans. Stuart Woolf. London, Abacus, 1987, pp. 342–351.

23. Levi, *If this is a Man / The Truce*, p. 350.

Bibliography

Agamben, Giorgio, *The Coming Community*. Trans. Michael Hardt. Minneapolis: University of Minnesota Press, 1993.

———, *Means Without Ends*. Trans. Vincenzo Binetti and Cesare Casarino. Minneapolis: University of Minnesota Press, 1996.

———, *Homo Sacer*. Trans. Daniel Heller-Roazen. Stanford: Stanford University Press, 1998.

———, *Potentialities*. Trans. Daniel Heller-Roazen. Stanford: Stanford University Press, 1999a.

———, *Remnants of Auschwitz*. Trans. Daniel Heller-Roazen. New York: Zone Books, 1999b.

———, *The Open*. Trans. Kevin Attell. Stanford: Stanford University Press, 2004.

———, *Profanations*. Trans. Jeff Fort. New York: Zone Books, 2006.

———, *The Kingdom and the Glory*. Trans. Lorenzo Chiesa. Stanford: Stanford University Press, 2011.

Appleyard, Rollo, *Pioneers of Electrical Communication*. London: Macmillan and Co, 1930.

Arendt, Hannah, *The Origins of Totalitarianism*. New York: Harcourt, Brace & World, 1966.

———, *The Human Condition*. Chicago: University of Chicago Press, 1998.

Aristotle, *The Topics*. Trans. W.A. Pickard-Cambridge. Montana: Kessinger Publishing, 2004.

Artangel, *Off Limits: 40 Artangel Projects*. London: Merrell, 2002.

Auslander, Philip, *Liveness*. London: Routledge, 1999.

Austin, J. L., *How to Do Things With Words*. Harvard: Harvard University Press, 1962.

Badiou, Alain, *Ethics: An Essay on the Understanding of Evil*. Trans. Peter Hallward. London: Verso, 2002.

———, *Handbook of Inaesthetics*. Trans. Alberto Toscano. Stanford: Stanford University Press, 2005.

Bailes, Sarah Jane, *Performance Theatre and the Poetics of Failure*. London: Routledge, 2011.

Bataille, Georges, *Theory of Religion*. Trans. Robert Hurley. New York: Zone Books, 1989.

———, *Visions of Excess: Selected Writings, 1927–1939*. Trans. Allan Stoekl. Minneapolis: University of Minnesota Press, 1999.

——, *The Cradle of Humanity*. Stuart Kendall (ed). Trans. Michelle Kendall and Stuart Kendall. New York: Zone, 2005.

Beckett, Samuel, *The Theatrical Notebooks of Samuel Beckett*, Vol. 3, 'Krapp's Last Tape'. James Knowlson (ed). London: Faber, 1992.

Benjamin, Walter, *Illuminations*. Hannah Arendt (ed). Trans. Harry Zohn. New York: Schocken Books, 1969.

——, *Selected Writings Vols. 1–4*. Marcus Bullock and Michael W. Jennings (eds). Cambridge: Harvard University Press, 1996.

Bishop, Claire, *Artificial Hells*. London: Verso, 2012.

Bloch, Ernst, *Traces*. Trans. Anthony Nassar. Stanford: Stanford University Press, 2006.

Boal, Augusto, *Theatre of the Oppressed*. Trans. Charles A. and Maria-Odilia Leal McBride. London: Pluto Press, 1979.

Bobbio, Norberto, *In Praise of Meekness*. Trans. Teresa Chataway. Cambridge: Polity Press, 2000.

Borch-Jacobsen, Mikkel, *Remembering Anna O*. Trans. Kirby Olson. London: Routledge, 1996.

Bourriaud, Nicolas, *Relational Aesthetics*. Paris: Les Presse du Reel, 1998.

Bratton, Jackie, *New Readings in Theatre History*. Cambridge: Cambridge University Press, 2003.

Brecht, Bertolt, *Poems 1913–1956*. Trans. Edith Anderson et al. London: Methuen, 1976.

Brook, Peter, *The Empty Space*. London: Macgibbon and Kee, 1969.

Bulmer, Michael, *Francis Galton: Pioneer of Heredity and Biometry*. Baltimore: The Johns Hopkins University Press, 2003.

Butler, Judith, *Excitable Speech*. London: Routledge, 1997.

——, *Precarious Life*. London: Verso, 2006.

Caillois, Roger, *Man and the Sacred*. Trans. Meyer Barash. Chicago: University of Illinois Press, 2001a.

——, *Man, Play and Games*. Trans. Meyer Barash. Chicago: University of Illinois Press, 2001b.

——, *The Edge of Surrealism*. Claudine Frank (ed). Trans. Claudine Frank and Camille Naish. Durham: Duke University Press, 2003.

Carlson, Marvin, *Performance: A Critical Introduction*. London: Routledge, 1996.

——, *The Haunted Stage*. Michigan: University of Michigan Press, 2003.

Castellucci, Romeo, *Epitaph*. Milan: Ubulibri, 2003.

Cixous, Helene, 'Fiction and Its Phantoms: A Reading of Freud's Das Unheimliche (The "Uncanny")', *New Literary History*, Vol. 7, No. 3 (1976), pp. 525–548.

Dannatt, Adrian, 'Psychoanalysis?', *lacanian ink*, No. 12 (1997), pp. 30–44.

Daston, Lorraine (ed), *Things That Talk*. New York: Zone Books, 2004.

Davis, Tracy C. (ed), *Theatricality*. Cambridge: Cambridge University Press, 2003.

De Certeau, Michel, 'The Fiction of History: The Writing of Moses and Monotheism' in Trans. Tom Conley, *The Writing of History*. New York: Columbia University Press, 1988a, pp. 308–354.

——, *The Practice of Everyday Life, Volume 2*. Trans. Timothy Tomasik. Minneapolis: University of Minnesota Press, 1998b.

——, *The Practice of Everyday Life*. Trans. Steven Rendall. Berkeley: University of California Press, 1988c.

De Courmelles, Fouveau, *Hypnotism*. London: Routledge, 1891.

Dekkers, Midas, *Dearest Pet: On Bestiality*. Trans. Paul Vincent. London: Verso, 1994.

——, *The Way of All Flesh: The Romance of Ruins*. New York: Farrar Straus & Giroux, 2000.

Deleuze, Gilles, *Essays Critical and Clinical*. London: Verso, 1998.

——, *Pure Immanence: Essays on a Life*. Trans. Anne Boyman. New York: Zone, 2002.

Deleuze, Gilles and Guattari, Félix, *Anti-Oedipus*. London: Continuum, 2004.

——, *A Thousand Plateaus*. Trans. Brian Massumi. London: Athlone Press, 1987.

Derrida, Jacques, 'Telepathic', *Cahiers Confrontation* Vol. 10 (1983), pp. 201–230.

——, *Archive Fever*. Trans. Eric Prenowitz. Chicago: University of Chicago Press, 1998.

——, *Adieu to Emmanuel Levinas*. Trans. Pascale-Anne Brault and Michael Naas. Stanford: Stanford University Press, 1999.

——, *Without Alibi*. Trans. Peggy Kamuf (ed). Stanford: Stanford University Press, 2002.

——, *The Animal That Therefore I Am*. Marie-Louise Mallet (ed). Trans. David Wills. New York: Fordham University Press, 2008.

Descartes, René, *Discourse on Method and the Meditations*. Trans. F.E. Sutcliffe. London: Penguin, 1968 [1637].

Despret, Vinciane, 'Sheep Do Have Opinions' in Bruno Latour and Peter Weibel (eds), *Making Things Public*, Karlsruhe: ZKM / Cambridge: MIT Press, 2005, pp. 360–368.

Diderot, Denis, *The Paradox of Acting*. New York: Hill and Wang, 1957.

Dickens, Charles, *Our Mutual Friend*. Harmondsworth: Penguin, 1995 [1864–5].

——, *David Copperfield*. Harmondsworth: Penguin, 2004 [1850].

——, *Bleak House*. Harmondsworth: Penguin, 2012 [1852–1853].

Doe, Paul, *Tallis*. London: Oxford University Press, 1968.

Dolan, Jill, *Geographies of Learning*. Middletown: Wesleyan University Press, 2001.

du Bouchet, André, *The Uninhabited: Selected Poems of André du Bouchet*. Trans. Paul Auster. New York: Living Hand, 1976.

Empson, William, *Some Versions of Pastoral*. New York: New Directions, 1974.

Enders, Jody, 'Performing Miracles: Mimesis of Valenciennes' in Tracy C. Davis (ed), *Theatricality*. Cambridge: Cambridge University Press, 2003, pp. 40–64.

Esposito, Roberto, *Bios: Biopolitics and Philosophy*. Trans. Timothy Campbell. Minneapolis: University of Minnesota Press, 2008.

——, *Communitas: The Origin and Destiny of Community*. Trans. Timothy Campbell. Stanford: Stanford University Press, 2010.

——, *Immunitas: The Protection and Negation of Life*. Trans. Zakiya Hanafi. Cambridge: Polity Press, 2011.

Etchells, Tim, *Certain Fragments*. London: Routledge, 2001.

Flusser, Vilém, 'Bare Walls' in *The Shape of Things, A Philosophy of Design*. London: Reaktion Books, 1999, pp. 78–80.

Forrester, John, *Dispatches from the Freud Wars*. Cambridge: Harvard University Press, 1997a.

——, *Truth Games*. Cambridge: Harvard University Press, 1997b.

Foucault, Michel, *Discipline and Punish*. Trans. Alan Sheridan. Harmondsworth: Penguin, 1979.

——, *Society Must Be Defended*. Trans. David Macey. London: Penguin, 2003.

Freud, Sigmund, *The Diary of Sigmund Freud 1929–1939*. Trans. annotated by Michael Molnar. London: Hogarth Press, 1997.

——, 'An Autobiographical Study' in James Strachey (ed), *The Standard Edition of the Complete Psychological Works of Sigmund Freud*. London: Vintage Books, 2001a, Vol. 20, pp. 3–76.

——, 'Psychopathic Characters on the Stage' in Freud, James Strachey (ed), *The Standard Edition of the Complete Psychological Works of Sigmund*. London: Vintage Books, 2001b, Vol. 7, pp. 305–310.

——, *Studies in Hysteria*. Harmondsworth, Penguin, 2004 [1895].

——, *Civilization and its Discontents*. James Strachey (ed). London: Norton, 2005 [1930].

Friel, Brian, *Translations*. London: Faber, 1981.

Frost, A. J., *F. Ronalds Biographical Memoir*. London: Ronalds Catalogue, Society of Telegraphic Engineers, 1880.

Fuss, Diana and Sanders, Joel, 'Bergasse 19' in Joel Sanders (ed), *Stud: Architectures of Masculinity*. Princeton: Princeton University Press, 1996, pp. 112–139.

Galton, Francis, *A Descriptive List of Anthropometric Apparatus*. Cambridge: The Cambridge Scientific Company, 1887.

Gell, Alfred, *The Art of Anthropology*. London: Athlone Press, 1999.

Giannachi, Gabriella and Stewart, Nigel (eds), *Performing Nature*. Bern: Peter Lang, 2005.

Gilroy, Paul, *The Black Atlantic: Modernity and Double Consciousness*. London: Verso 1993.

Girard, René, *To Double Business Bound*. London: Routledge, 1978.

——, *Things Hidden Since the Foundation of the World*. Trans. Stephen Bann and Michael Metteer. Stanford: Stanford University Press, 1987.

——, *Violence and the Sacred*. Trans. Patrick Gregory. London: Athlone Press, 1995.

Glisson, Francis, Bate, George and Regemorter, Assuerus, *De rachitide sive Morbo puerili, qui vulgò The Rickets dicitur, tractatus*. London: Typis Guil. Du-gardi; Impensis Laurentii Sadler, & Roberti Beaumont, 1650. Original from Complutense University of Madrid, Digitized 2008.

Goat Island, *School Book 2*. Chicago: School of the Art Institute, 2002.

Goffman, Erving, *The Presentation of Self in Everyday Life*. Harmondsworth, Penguin, 1990.

Gough, Richard and Kear, Adrian (eds), 'On Appearance', *Performance Research*, Vol. 3, No. 4 (2008).

Goulish, Matthew, *39 Microlectures*. London: Routledge, 2000.

Grenier, Roger, *The Difficulty of Being a Dog*. Trans. Alice Kaplan. Chicago: University of Chicago Press, 2000.

Guattari, Félix, *The Three Ecologies*. Trans. Ian Pindar and Paul Sutton. London: Athlone Press, 2000.

Guy, Georgina, *Displayed & Performed: Visitation, Exhibition and Arrested Attention*. PhD Thesis: King's College London, 2012.

Hallward, Peter, 'Staging Equality', *New Left Review*, Vol. 37 (2006), pp. 109–129.

Hart, Vaughan, *Inigo Jones: The Architect of Kings*. New Haven: Yale University Press, 2011.

Heathfield, Adrian, *Live: Art and Performance*. London: Tate Publishing, 2004/2012.

Heidegger, Martin, *The Question Concerning Technology*. New York: Harper and Row, 1977.

Heller-Roazen, Daniel, *Echolalias*. New York: Zone Books, 2005.

Hitchens, Christopher, *God is Not Great*. London: Allen & Unwin, 2008.

Hoffman, Beth, 'Radicalism and the Theatre in Genealogies of Live Art', *Performance Research*, Vol. 14, No. 1 (2009), pp. 95–105.

Houellebecq, Michel, *Atomised*. Trans. Frank Wynne. London: Vintage, 2001.

———, *Platform*. Trans. Frank Wynne. London: William Heinemann, 2002.

———, *The Possibility of an Island*. Trans. Gavin Bowd. London: Weidenfeld and Nicolson, 2005.

Hughes, Robert, *The Shock of the New*. London: BBC, 1980.

Hugo, Victor, *Les Misérables*. Harmondsworth: Penguin, 2007 [1862].

Jackson, Shannon, *Lines of Activity*. Michigan: University of Michigan Press, 2001.

———, *Professing Performance*. Cambridge: Cambridge University Press, 2004.

———, *Social Works*. London: Routledge, 2012.

Johnson, Dominic (ed.), 'Live Art in the UK', *Contemporary Theatre Review*, Vol. 22, No. 1 (2012).

Jones, Ernest, *The Life and Work of Sigmund Freud: Volume 1*. New York: Basic Books, 1963.

Kafka, Franz, *The Hunger Artist*. Harmondsworth: Penguin, 1996.

Kear, Adrian, *Theatre and Event: Staging the European Century*. Houndmills: Palgrave, 2013.

Kelleher, Joe, 'The Suffering of Images' in Adrian Heathfield (ed), *Live: Art and Performance*, London: Tate Publishing, 2004/2012, pp. 190–195.

Kelleher, Joe and Ridout, Nicholas, *Contemporary Theatres in Europe*. London: Routledge, 2006.

Kierkegaard, Søren, *Repetition and Philosophical Crumbs*. Trans. M.G. Piety. Oxford: Oxford University Press, 2009.

Kleinberg-Levin, David Michael, *Gestures of Ethical Life*. Stanford: Stanford University Press, 2005.

Knapp, Bettina and Chipman, Myra, *That Was Yvette: The Biography of a Great Diseuse*. New York: Holt, Rinehart & Winston, 1964.

Kojève, Alexandre, *Introduction to the Reading of Hegel*. Ithaca: Cornell University Press, 1969.

Krauss, Rosalind, 'Sculpture in the Expanded Field', *October*, Vol. 8 (1979), pp. 30–44.

Krikorian, Gaelle and Kapczynski, Amy (eds), *Access to Knowledge*. New York: Zone Books, 2010.

Kubiak, Anthony, 'Animism', *Performance Research* 'On Ecology', Vol. 17, No. 4 (2012), pp. 52–60.

Lacan, Jacques, *The Four Fundamental Concepts of Psycho-Analysis*. Trans. Alan Sheridan. Harmondsworth: Peregrine, 1986.

Laclau, Ernesto, *On Populist Reason*. London: Verso, 2005.

Lacoue-Labarthe, Philippe, *Typography*. Christopher Fynsk (ed). Stanford: Stanford University Press, 1989.

———, *The Subject of Philosophy*. Minneapolis: University of Minnesota Press, 1995.

Latour, Bruno, *We Have Never Been Modern*. Cambridge: Harvard University Press, 1993.

———, *Aramis or the Love of Technology*. Trans. Catherine Porter. Cambridge: Harvard University Press, 1996.

———, *Politics of Nature*. Trans. Catherine Porter. Cambridge: Harvard University Press, 2004.

———, *Reassembling the Social*. Oxford: Oxford University Press, 2005.

Latour, Bruno and Weibel, Peter (eds), *Making Things Public*. Karlsruhe: ZKM/ Cambridge: MIT Press, 2005.

Lefort, Claude, *Writing The Political Test*. Trans. David Ames Curtis. Durham: Duke University Press, 2000.

Lehmann, Hans Thies, *Post Dramatic Theatre*. Trans. Karen Jurs-Munby. London: Routledge, 2006.

Levi, Primo, *If this is a Man/The Truce*. Trans. Stuart Woolf. London, Abacus, 1987.

Lichtenberg, Geord Christoph, *The Waste Books*. Trans. R. J. Hollingdale. New York: New York Review of Books, 2000.

Lingis, Alphonso, *Foreign Bodies*. London: Routledge, 1994.

———, *The Imperative*. Bloomington: Indiana University Press, 1998.

———, *Dangerous Emotions*. Berkeley: University of California Press, 2000.

———, *Trust*. Minneapolis: University of Minesota Press, 2004.

Luhmann, Niklas, *Introduction to Systems Theory*. Trans. Peter Gilgen. Ed. Dirk Baecker. Cambridge: Polity Press, 2013.

———, *Law as a Social System*. Oxford: Oxford University Press, 2004.

Lyotard, Jean-Francois, *Libidinal Economy*. Trans. Iain Hamilton Grant. London: Athlone Press, 1993.

MacDonald, Claire, 'Congregation', *Performance Research*, Vol. 11, No. 1 (2006) pp. 114–115.

MacIntyre, Alasdair, *Dependent Rational Animals*. London: Duckworth, 1999.

Marion, Jean-Luc, *Being Given: Toward a Phenomenology of Givenness*. Trans. Jeffrey L. Kosky. Stanford: Stanford University Press, 2002.

———, *In Excess: Studies of Saturated Phenomena*. Trans. Robyn Horner and Vincent Berrraud. New York: Fordham University Press, 2002.

———, *The Crossing of the Visible*. Trans. James K.A. Smith. Stanford: Stanford University Press, 2004.

Marranca, Bonnie, *Ecologies of Theatre*. Baltimore: Johns Hopkins University Press, 1996.

Marx, Karl, *Capital Volume 1*. Trans. Ben Fowkes. London: Penguin, 1990.

Mauz, Isabelle and Gravelle, Julien, 'Wolves in the Valley: On Making a Controversy Public' in Bruno Latour and Peter Weibel (eds), *Making Things Public*. Karlsruhe: ZKM/Cambridge: MIT Press, 2005, pp. 370–380.

Mayhew, Edward, *Stage Effect*. London, 1840.

McCarthy, Fiona, *William Morris: A Life for Our Time*. London: Faber, 1994.

McKenzie, John, *Perform or Else*. London: Routledge, 2001.

McManus, Clare, *Women on the Renaissance Stage: Anna of Denmark and Female Masquing in the Stuart Court (1590-1619)*. Manchester: Manchester University Press, 2002.

McQuire, Scott, 'Pure Speed – From Transport to Teleport' in Jeremy Millar and Michiel Schwarz (eds), *Speed-Visions of an Accelerated Age*. London: Photographers Gallery et al., 1998, pp. 26–33.

Mondzain, Marie-José, *Homo Spectator*. Paris: Bayard, 2007.

Morris, William, *News from Nowhere and Other Writings*. Clive Wilmer (ed). London: Penguin, 1993.

Munthe, Axel, *The Story of San Michele*. London: John Murray, 1936.

Musil, Robert, *The Man Without Qualities*. Trans. Eithne Wilkins and Ernst Kaisner. London: Picador, 1982.

Nancy, Jean-Luc, *The Inoperative Community*. Trans. Peter Connor. Minneapolis: University of Minnesota Press, 1991.

———, *The Birth To Presence*. Trans. Brian Holmes. Stanford: Stanford University Press, 1993.

———, *The Muses*. Trans. Peggy Kamuf. Stanford: Stanford University Press, 1996.

———, *Being Singular Plural*. Stanford: Stanford University Press, 2000.

Nietzsche, Friedrich, *The Genealogy of Morals*. Trans. Francis Golffing. New York: Doubleday, 1956.

———, *Human, All Too Human*. Trans. R.J. Hollingdale. Cambridge: Cambridge University Press, 1996.

———, *The Anti Christ, Ecce Homo, Twilight of the Idols*. Trans. Judith Norman. Cambridge: Cambridge University Press, 2005.

Olwig, Kenneth, *Landscape, Nature and the Body Politic*. Madison: The University of Wisconsin Press, 2002.

———, 'Performance, Aetherial Space and the Practice of Landscape/Architecture: The Case of the Missing Mask', *Social & Cultural Geography*, Vol. 12, No. 3 (May 2007), pp. 305–318.

Orgel, Stephen and Strong, Roy, *Inigo Jones: The Theatre of the Stuart Court*. London: Sotheby Parke Bernet, 1973.

Orwell, George, *Animal Farm*. Harmondsworth: Penguin, 1999 [1945].

Peacham, Henry, *The Garden of Eloquence*. London: 1593.

———, *Minerva Britannia*. London: 1612.

Pearson, Mike, 'Marking Time' in Judie Christie et al. (eds), *A Performance Cosmology*. London: Routledge, 2006, pp. 120–123.

———, *In Comes I: Performance, Memory and Landscape*. Exeter: University of Exeter Press, 2006.

Pearson, Mike and Shanks, Michael, *Theatre/ Archaeology*. London: Routledge, 2001.

Perniola, Mario, *The Sex Appeal of the Inorganic: Philosophies of Desire in the Modern World*. London: Athlone Press, 2004.

Phelan, Peggy, *Unmarked: The Politics of Performance*. London: Routledge, 1993.

———, 'Playing Dead In Stone' in Elin Diamond (ed), *Performance and Cultural Politics*. London: Routledge, 1996, pp. 65–88.

———, *Mourning Sex*. London: Routledge, 1997.

Pirandello, Luigi, *Six Characters in Search of an Author and Other Plays*. Trans. Mark Musa. London, Penguin, 1995 [1921].

Plato, *The Republic*. Trans. H.D.P. Lee. Harmondsworth: Penguin, 1955.

———, *The Laws*. Trans. Trevor J. Saunders. Harmondsworth: Penguin, 1970.

Priestley, J. B., *An Inspector Calls*. London: Penguin, 1947.

Raban, Jonathan, *Soft City*. London: Harvill, 1974.

———, *Surveillance*. New York: Vintage, 2006.

Rancière, Jacques, *On the Shores of Politics*. Trans. Liz Heron. London: Verso, 1995.

———, *Short Voyages to the Land of the People*. Trans. James Swenson. Stanford: Stanford University Press, 2003a.

———, *The Philosopher and his Poor*. Durham: Duke University Press, 2003b.

———, *The Flesh of Words*. Trans. Charlotte Mandell. Stanford: Stanford University Press, 2004.

———, *Hatred of Democracy*. Trans. Steve Corcoran. London: Verso, 2006a.

———, *The Politics of Aesthetics*. Trans. and Intro. Gabriel Rockhill. London: Continuum, 2006b.

———, *The Emancipated Spectator*. London: Verso, 2010.

Read, Alan, *Theatre & Everyday Life: An Ethics of Performance*. London: Routledge, 1993.

———, (ed), 'On Animals', *Performance Research*, Vol. 5, No. 2 (2000a), pp. 61–69.

———, (ed), *Architecturally Speaking: Practices of Art, Architecture and the Everyday*. London: Routledge, 2000b.

——,'The Placebo of Performance' in Patrick Campbell and Adrian Kear (eds), *Psychoanalysis and Performance*, London: Routledge, 2001, pp. 147–165.

——, (ed), 'On Civility', *Performance Research*, Vol. 9, No. 4 (2004), pp. 71–85.

——, 'Return to Sender' in Gabriela Vaz-Pinheiro (ed), *Curating the Local*, Torres Vedras: Transforma, 2005, pp. 15–33.

——, *Theatre, Intimacy & Engagement: The Last Human Venue*. Houndmills: Palgrave, 2008.

——, 'The Ceramic Age: Things Hidden Since the Foundation of Performance Studies' *Performance Research*, 'Performatics', Vol. 13, No. 2 (2009) pp. 47–58.

——, 'Romeo Castellucci: The Director on this Earth' in Maria Delgado and Dan Rebellato (eds), *Contemporary European Theatre Directors*. London: Routledge, 2010, pp. 249–262.

Readings, Bill, *The University in Ruins*. Cambridge: Harvard University Press, 1996.

Ridout, Nicholas, *Stage Fright, Animals and Other Theatrical Problems*. Cambridge: Cambridge University Press, 2006.

Roach, Joseph, *Cities of the Dead*. New York: Columbia University Press, 1996.

Rokem, Freddie, 'Witnessing the Witness' in Judie Christie et al. (eds), *A Performance Cosmology*. London: Routledge, 2006, pp. 168–172.

Ronalds, Francis, *Descriptions of an Electrical Telegraph*. London: R Hunter Ronalds, 1823.

Rosolato, Guy, 'The Voice: Between Body and Language' in *Voices*. Rotterdam: Edition Tirage, 2000, p. 106.

Rousseau, Jean-Jacques, *Reveries of the Solitary Walker*. Trans. Peter France. Harmondsworth: Penguin, 1979.

Santner, Eric, *My Own Private Germany*. Princeton: Princeton University Press, 1996.

——, *The Royal Remains*. Chicago: University of Chicago Press, 2010.

Schechner, Richard, 'A New Paradigm for Theatre in the Academy', *TDR: The Drama Review*, Vol. 36, No. 4 (1992), pp. 7–10.

——, 'Towards Tomorrow? Restoring Disciplinary Limits and Rehearsals in Time?' in Judie Christie et al. (eds), *A Performance Cosmology*. London: Routledge, 2006, pp. 229–242.

——, *Public Domain*. New York: Avon Books, 1969.

——, *The Future of Ritual*. London: Routledge, 1993.

——, *Performance Studies: An Introduction*. London: Routledge, 2002.

Schmitt, Carl, *The Concept of the Political*. Chicago: Chicago University Press, 1996.

Schneider, Rebecca, 'What I Can't Recall' in Judie Christie et al. (eds), *A Performance Cosmology*. London: Routledge, 2006, pp. 113–116.

Schreber, Daniel Paul, *Memoirs of My Nervous Illness*. New York: New York Review Books, 2000.

Seel, Martin, *Aesthetics of Appearing*. Trans. John Farrell. Stanford: Stanford University Press, 2005.

Sennett, Richard, *The Fall of Public Man*. London: Penguin, 2002.

Sloterdijk, Peter, *Neither Sun Nor Death*. Trans. Steven Corcoran. Los Angeles: Semiotext[e], 2011.

Sofer, Andrew, *The Stage Life of Props*. Michigan: University of Michigan Press, 2003.

Sophocles, 'Oedipus the King' in Trans. Robert Fagles, *The Three Theban Plays: Antigone, Oedipus the King, Oedipus at Colonus*. London: Penguin, 1982, pp. 155–252.

Southern, Richard, *The Seven Ages of the Theatre*. London: Faber and Faber, 1962.

Starobinski, Jean, *Action and Reaction*. Trans. Sophie Hawkes. New York: Zone, 2003.

Stengers, Isabelle, 'Diderot's Egg: Divorcing Materialism from Eliminativism', *Radical Philosophy*, Vol. 144 (2007), pp. 7–16.

Supiot, Alain, *Homo Juridicus: On the Anthropological Function of the Law*. Trans. Saskia Brown. London: Verso, 2007.

Szondi, Peter, *Theory of the Modern Drama*. Minneapolis: University of Minnesota Press, 1987.

Taussig, Michael, *The Nervous System*. London: Routledge, 1992.

——, *Mimesis and Alterity*. London: Routledge, 1993.

——, *Defacement: Public Secrecy and the Labour of the Negative*. Stanford: Stanford University Press, 1999.

Taylor, George, *Players and Performances in the Victorian Theatre*. Manchester: Manchester University Press, 1993.

Turner, D. A., 'Letters', *Guardian* (Newspaper, London edition), 10 November 1998.

Tyler, Tom, *Ciferae*. Minneapolis: University of Minesota Press, 2012.

Vattimo, Gianni, *The End of Modernity*. Baltimore: Johns Hopkins University Press, 1991.

Vidler, Anthony, *The Architectural Uncanny*. Cambridge: MIT Press, 1992.

Virilio, Paul, 'The Overexposed City' in J. Crary et al. (eds), *Zone 1, 2*. New York: Urzone, 1986, pp. 26–38.

——, *The Aesthetics of Disappearance*. New York: Semiotext[e], 1990.

Virno, Paolo, *A Grammar of the Multitude: For an Analysis of Contemporary Forms of Life*. Trans. Isabella Bertoletti, James Cascaito and Andrea Casson. New York: Semiotext[e], 2004.

Weber, Samuel, *Theatricality as Medium*. New York: Fordham University Press, 2004.

Whittacker, Gillies, 'An Adventure' in *Collected Essays*. London: Oxford University Press, 1940, pp. 86–89.

Wickstrom, Maurya, *Performing Consumers*. London: Routledge, 2006.

Williams, David, 'The Right Horse, The Animal Eye', *Performance Research*, Vol. 5, No. 2 'On Animals' (2000), pp. 29–40.

——, 'Writing [After] the Event: Notes on Appearance, Passage and Hope' in Judie Christie et al. (eds), *A Performance Cosmology*. London: Routledge, 2006, pp. 103–107.

Wolfe, Cary (ed.), *Zoontologies*. Minneapolis: University of Minnesota Press, 2003a.

Wolfe, Cary, *Animal Rites*. Chicago: University of Chicago Press, 2003b.

Yates, Richard, *Revolutionary Road*. London: Vintage, 2007 [1961].

Žižek, Slavoj, *On Belief*. London: Routledge, 2001.

——, *The Puppet and the Dwarf: The Perverse Core of Christianity*. Cambridge: MIT Press, 2003.

——, 'The Parallax View', *New Left Review*, Vol. 25 (2004), pp. 121–134.

——, *The Parallax View*. Cambridge: MIT Press, 2006.

Primary and Production Sources

The African Queen, film adapted from 1935 novel by C. S. Forester, dir. John Huston, produced by Sam Spiegel and John Woolf, 1951.

Appointment, Sophie Calle, curated by James Putnam, Freud Museum, London, 12 February–28 March 1999.

Armadillo For Your Show, Oleg Kulik, Tate Modern, London, 2003.

Artenice, Honorat de Bueil, Sieur de Racan, design by Inigo Jones, The Hall of Somerset House (formerly Denmark House), Strand, London, 1626.

Bambi (Winterreise), Mirosław Bałka, video installation, 2010.

The Battle of Orgreave, Jeremy Deller, a live re-enactment, filmed under the direction of Mike Figgis for Artangel Media and Channel 4, proposed via The Times/Artangel Open and selected by Brian Eno, Rachel Whiteread, Richard Cork and Artangel Co-Directors James Lingwood and Michael Morris, Orgreave, South Yorkshire, 17 June 2001. The film *The Battle of Orgreave* is included in The Artangel Collection.

Bingo, Edward Bond, Young Vic Theatre, London, 2012.

Breakdown, Michael Landy, proposed via The Times/Artangel Open and selected by Brian Eno, Rachel Whiteread, Richard Cork and Artangel Co-Directors James Lingwood and Michael Morris (the other selected project in 2001 was *The Battle of Orgreave* by Jeremy Deller), Former C&A store, Oxford Street, London, February 2001.

Britannia Triumphans, St Paul's and Somerset House, London, 1638.

Camelot, Cornford and Cross, for City Limits curated by Godfrey Burke and Terry Shave, Albion Square, Stoke-on-Trent, 1996.

Carousel, Mirosław Bałka, video installation, 2004.

The Caucasian Chalk Circle, Bertolt Brecht, Trans Eric Bentley. Dir. Geoffrey Winslow, Westcliff High School for Boys, Southend on Sea, Essex, 1973.

Cremaster Cycle, Matthew Barney, five films shot and released out of order: *Cremaster 4* (1994); *Cremaster 1* (1995); *Cremaster 5* (1997); *Cremaster 2* (1999) and *Cremaster 3* (2002). http://www.cremaster.net/

Crimewatch (formerly Crimewatch UK), television programme produced by BBC, 1984–ongoing.

Dark Pool, Janet Cardiff and George Bures Miller, installation, 1995.

Deep into Russia, Oleg Kulik, Tverskoy region, Dudrovky, 1993.

Deep into Russia, Oleg Kulik, Regina Gallery, London, 2012.

Dog House, Oleg Kulik, Interpol, Farkfabriken, Stockholm, 1996.

Double Your Money, quiz show originally broadcast on Radio Luxembourg and then ITV, produced by Associated-Rediffusion until 1964 and then Rediffusion London, 1955–1968.

Drivers from Hell, television show, Channel 5 (UK).

Earth Rampant, Meyerhold, 1923.

Empty Club, Gabriel Orozco, 1996 Artangel/Beck's Commission, The Devonshire Club, 50 St James's Street, London, 25 June–28 July 1996.

Entertainment given by Robert Cecil, Earl of Salisbury, Ben Jonson, design by Inigo Jones, the Library of Salisbury House in the Strand, London, 1608.

Feet of Memory, Boots of Nottingham, Graeme Miller, radio map broadcast on BBC Radio Nottingham throughout the Barclays New Stages Festival, Nottingham, 1995.

Forty Part Motet, Janet Cardiff, Castle Keep, Newcastle, 20 June–8 July 2001.

The Fugitive, drama series created by Roy Huggins and produced by QM Productions and United Artists Television, ABC (US), 1963–1967.

The Good Shepherd, dir. Robert de Niro, 2006.

Giulio Cesare, Societas Raffaello Sanzio/Romeo Castellucci, Queen Elizabeth Hall, London, 1999.

Homeland, Platform, 6 week nomadic public dialogue project, London and the London International Festival of Theatre, 1993.

Homo Egg Egg, Baktruppen, Teglverksgata, Oslo, Nordic Scene, Kaaitheater, Brussels, Perfect Performance, Stockholm, BIT Teatergarasjen, Bergen, 2002–2003.

House, Rachel Whiteread, sculpture, Grove Road, London, 25 October 1993–11 January 1994.

How It Is, Mirosław Bałka, The Unilever Series, Tate Modern, London, 13 October 2009–5 April 2010.

I Want a Child, Meyerhold, 1934.

An Inability to Make a Sound, Janet Cardiff, sound work, 1992.

If…, Lindsay Anderson, film, 1968.

The Influence Machine, Tony Oursler, developed with the Public Art Fund, New York, originally installed in Madison Square Park, New York, October 2000, and then Soho Square, London, November 2000. Recently screened as part of Projections: Works from The Artangel Collection, Whitworth Art Gallery, Manchester, 2–16 July 2011.

King Lear, William Shakespeare, dir. Michael Attenborough, Almeida Theatre, London, 2012.

La Tour, Janet Cardiff and George Bures Miller, installation, 1997.

Les Misérables, music by Claude-Michel Schönberg, original French lyrics by Alain Boublil and Jean-Marc Natel, English-language libretto by Herbert Kretzmer, produced by Cameron Mackintosh, Barbican, London, 1985 – Queen's Theatre, London, ongoing (second longest-running musical in the world, second longest-running West End show after *The Mousetrap*, longest-running musical in the West End).

Life (Work in progress), Janez Janša, Museum of Modern and Contemporary Art (MMSU), Rijeka, 2010.

Linked, Graeme Miller, a landmark in sound – an invisible artwork – a walk, part of London's Voices, an Artsadmin project commissioned by Museum of London, M11 Link Road, London July 2003-ongoing, http://www.linkedm11.net/

Listening Ground, *Lost Acres*, Graeme Miller, series of walks commissioned by Salisbury Festival and Artangel, Salisbury, 1994.

Longplayer, Jem Finer, one thousand year long musical composition, originally produced as an Artangel commission and now in the care of the Longplayer Trust, various locations including Trinity Buoy Wharf Lighthouse, London, 1 January 2000–31 December 2999. A live performance of a 1000 minute section of *Longplayer* took place at The Roundhouse, London on 12 September 2009.

Making Things Public, Bruno Latour and Peter Weibel, ZKM Center, Karlsruhe 2005.

The Masque of Blackness, Ben Jonson, sets, costumes and stage effects designed by Inigo Jones, music by Alfonso Ferrabosco, Banqueting Hall, Whitehall Palace, London, 1605.

Middle Temple and Lincoln's Inn Masque, George Chapman, design by Inigo Jones, composed by Robert Johnson, the Hall of Whitehall, London, 1613.

Missing Voice (Case Study B), Janet Cardiff, an audio walk, beginning in Whitechapel, London, 19 June 2001–ongoing. http://www.artangel.org.uk//projects/1999/the_missing_voice_case_study_b/download_listen/part_1

The Mousetrap, Agatha Christie, New Ambassadors Theatre, London 1952–1974, St. Martin's Theatre, London, 1974–ongoing.

New Holland, Cornford and Cross, for East International, selected by Tacita Dean and Nicholas Logsdail, Sainsbury Centre for Visual Arts, Norwich, 1997.

Off the Endz, Bola Agbaje, Royal Court Theatre, London, 11 February–13 March 2010.

On The Concept of the Face: Regarding the Son of God, Socìetas Raffaello Sanzio/Romeo Castellucci, Barbican, London, 2011.

On The Concept of the Face: Regarding the Son of God, Socìetas Raffaello Sanzio/Romeo Castellucci, Théâtre de la Ville, Paris, 2011.

The Palace of Projects, Ilya and Emilia Kabakov, The Roundhouse, London, 24 March–10 May 1998, Market Place, Manchester 1998, Cristal Palace, Reina Sofia Museum, Madrid 1999, NY Armory Building, New York, 2000, Zollverein Coal Mine Industrial Complex in Essen, Germany, ongoing.

Perfect Crime, Warren Manzi, The Courtyard Playhouse, The 47th Street Theater, The Harold Clurman Theater, Theatre Four, The McGinn-Cazale Theater, Intar, Duffy Theater, New York, 1987–2005, The Snapple Theater Center, New York, 2005–ongoing.

Perimeters/Pavilions/Decoys, Mary Miss, Long Island, New York, 1978.

Pirates of the Caribbean, dir. Gore Verbinski (1–3) and Rob Marshall (4), written by Ted Elliott and Terry Rossio, produced by Jerry Bruckheimer, 2003–2011.

Playboy of the Western World, J.M. Synge, Abbey Theatre, Dublin, 26 January 1907.

Playhouse, Janet Cardiff and Georges Bures Miller, installation, 1997.

Police Camera Action, police video programme made by Optomen Television for ITV, 1994–ongoing.

The Power of Theatrical Madness, Jan Fabre, Theatre of Nations Festival, Nancy, 1983.

The Power of Theatrical Madness, Jan Fabre, deSingel, rode zaal, Antwerp, 2012.

Preliminary Hearing, Forster and Heighes, nine-hour durational performance and installation, presented in the form of a public inquiry, London International Festival of Theatre, Mary Ward House, 5 Tavistock Place, London, February–June 1997.

Reconnaissance, Graeme Miller, map and musical score commissioned by Surrey County Council, South East Arts and the Arts Council of England for the Norbury Park Arts Project, Norbury Park, Surrey, 1998.

Rodinsky's Whitechapel, Rachel Lichtenstein and Iain Sinclair, guided walks, an Artangel commission and part of INNERcity, Whitechapel, London, 2–30 June 1999.

The Roman Tragedies, Toneelgroep Amsterdam, Barbican London, 2009.

The Seven Sacraments of Nicolas Poussin, Neil Bartlett, commissioned by Artangel and co-produced with Gloria, Royal London Hospital, Whitechapel, London, 1–7 July 1997.

Shakespeare in Love, Marc Norman and Tom Stoppard, dir. John Madden, 1998.

Showtime, Forced Entertainment, The Institute of Contemporary Arts (ICA), London, 1996.

The Sound Observatory, Graeme Miller, large scale civic sculpture, commissioned by Sounds Like Birmingham, Birmingham, 1992.

Steenbeckett, Atom Egoyan, short film, 35mm edited on a Steenbeck, commissioned and produced by Artangel, originally shown at the Museum of Mankind, London 15 February–17 March 2002 and then as part of Projections: Works from The Artangel Collection, Whitworth Art Gallery, Manchester, 2 July–4 September 2011 and Happy Days: Enniskillen International Beckett Festival, Clinton Centre Higher Bridges Gallery, Enniskillen, 9–29 August 2012.

Sunday Night at the London Palladium, television variety show produced by ATV for the ITV network, originally ran 1955–1967 with a brief revival 1973–1974.

Take Your Pick, game show originally broadcast on Radio Luxembourg and then ITV, 1955–1968 plus revival 1992–1998.

Tight Roaring Circle, Dana Caspersen, William Forsythe and Joel Ryan, The Roundhouse, London, 26 March–27 April 1997.

Tino Sehgal 2007, Tino Sehgal, The Institute of Contemporary Arts (ICA), London, 2007.

Walk to Belgrade from London on a Treadmill, Gordana Stanisic, The Showroom, London, 1994.

Whispering Room, Janet Cardiff, sound work, 1991.

The World in Pictures, Forced Entertainment, Riverside Studios, London, 2006.

You Me Bum Bum Train, Kate Bond and Morgan Lloyd, originally created in 2004, recent performances include: LEB Building, Bethnal Green, London, 2010, and Empire House, Stratford, London, 2012.

Zoophrenia, Oleg Kulik, programme including: *Deep into Russia*, Tverskoy region, Dudrovky, 1993; *Freedom of Choice*, Patriarchy Prudy, Moscow 1994; *Reservoir Dog*, Kunsthaus, Zurich 1995; *In Fact, Kulik is a Bird*, Gallery 21, St Petersburg 1995; *Dog House*, Fargfabriken, Stockholm 1996; *Police Dog*, Rozentol Night Club, Moscow 1996; *Suspended*, Kunstlerhaus Bethanien, Berlin 1996; *Two Kuliks*, Art Center 'Ark', Riga 1998 and Ikon Gallery, Birmingham 2001; *White Man, Black Dog*, Gallery Kapelica, Ljubljana 1998.

Index

Biographical Notes

Alan Read

Alan Read was Director of Rotherhithe Theatre Workshop in the Docklands area of South East London in the 1980s, a freelance writer in Barcelona and then Director of Talks at the Institute of Contemporary Arts in the 1990s, and was appointed Professor of Theatre at Roehampton University in 1997 and King's College London in 2006. As Director of the *Performance Foundation* (www.performancefoundation.org.uk) he has developed the *Anatomy Theatre and Museum* on the Strand and the *Inigo Rooms* in the East Wing of Somerset House. Alan Read is the author of *Theatre & Everyday Life: An Ethics of Performance* (1993/1995) and *Theatre, Intimacy & Engagement: The Last Human Venue* (2008/2009). He is the editor of *The Fact of Blackness* (1996) and *Architecturally Speaking* (2000). As a founding consultant editor of *Performance Research* Alan Read has edited two issues of the journal *On Animals* (2000) and *On Civility* (2004). Further work by Alan Read can be found at: www.alanread.net

Beryl Robinson

Richard Southern's work, *The Seven Ages of the Theatre* (1962), included line drawings by the author embedded throughout the text. Beryl Robinson responded to *Theatre in the Expanded Field* in a series of drawings intended to thread through the writing as a means to look differently at what is represented here. Her work ranges from such line drawings, etchings and linocuts to large paintings built up through layers of pigment and glazes. She has shown in selected exhibitions at Riverside Studios London, The Tretyakov Museum in Moscow and The Kunstlerhaus in Salzburg, and solo exhibitions in Palo Alto in Barcelona, Carlisle City Museum and Gallery and Calouste Gulbenkian Theatre in Newcastle. Her work is held in many private and public collections. Her London studio is at Palace Wharf in Hammersmith and she also works from a studio in the commune of Truinas, Drôme, in the southeast region of France. Her work can be seen at: www.berylrobinson.com